Teaching Visual Literacy in the Primary Classroom

Teaching Visual Literacy in the Primary Classroom shows how everyday Literacy sessions can be made more exciting, dynamic and effective by using a wide range of media and visual texts in the primary classroom. In addition to a wealth of practical teaching ideas, the book outlines the vital importance of visual texts and shows how children can enjoy developing essential literacy skills through studying picture books, film, television and comic books.

Designed to take account of the renewed *Framework for Literacy*, each chapter offers a complete guide to teaching this required area of literacy. Aimed at those who want to deliver high quality and stimulating Literacy sessions, each chapter contains a range of detailed practical activities and resources which can be easily implemented into existing Literacy teaching with minimal preparation. In addition, each chapter gives clear, informative yet accessible insights into the theory behind visual literacy.

Containing a wealth of activities, ideas and resources for teachers of both Key Stage One and Key Stage Two, this book discusses how children's literacy skills can be developed and enhanced through exploring a range of innovative texts. Six chapters provide comprehensive guides to the teaching of the following media and literacy skills:

- Picture books
- Film and television
- Comic books
- Visual literacy skills
- Genre
- Adaptation.

Teaching Visual Literacy in the Primary Classroom is an essential resource for all those who wish to find fresh and contemporary ways to teach Literacy and will be useful not only to novices but also to teachers who already have experience of teaching a range of media.

Students, primary school teachers, Literacy co-ordinators and anyone who is passionate about giving pupils a relevant and up-to-date education will be provided with everything they need to know about teaching this new and ever-expanding area of literacy.

Tim **Stafford** is a ~~ ~~ and teacher. He has taught extensively across Key Stages
O~~ ~~ and Literature to students at secondary and undergraduate
le~

Teaching Visual Literacy in the Primary Classroom

Comic books, film, television and picture narratives

Tim Stafford

Routledge
Taylor & Francis Group

LONDON AND NEW YORK

This first edition published 2011
by Routledge
2 Park Square, Milton Park, Abingdon, Oxon OX14 4RN

Simultaneously published in the USA and Canada
by Routledge
270 Madison Avenue, New York, NY 10016

Routledge is an imprint of the Taylor & Francis Group, an informa business

© 2011 Tim Stafford

Typeset in Bembo by Wearset Ltd, Boldon, Tyne and Wear
Printed and bound in Great Britain by MPG Books Group, UK

British Library Cataloguing in Publication Data
A catalogue record for this book is available from the British Library

Library of Congress Cataloging-in-Publication Data
Stafford, Tim, 1976–
Teaching visual literacy in the primary classroom: comic books, film, television and picture narratives/by Tim Stafford.
p. cm.
Includes bibliographical references.
1. Visual literacy–Study and teaching (Primary) I. Title.
LB1523.S72 2011
372.133'5–dc22   2010003595

ISBN13: 978-0-415-48984-3 (hbk)
ISBN13: 978-0-415-48985-0 (pbk)
ISBN13: 978-0-203-84679-7 (ebk)

This book is dedicated to my parents, Sheila and Terry, my grandparents, my bfs Derek and Marina, my Auntie Ivy, my Auntie Gwen and Ben, Saffy, Tigger and Bart. Thank you all for your love and support, I love you all.

Contents

Acknowledgements

'No author is an island', to paraphrase John Donne, and I would like to thank all those who have helped me on this journey. First, there are three people without whom this book would not exist: Diane Duncan, whose friendship and belief set me on the road and who gave me my first opportunities in lecturing and in writing; Monika Lee, who supported the project from the outset and whose invaluable assistance helped it develop from an idea into a real book and last, but never least, Derek Watson, who has been there every single day from the very start to encourage, discuss, advise, assist, edit, scan and continually offer his time and unflagging support. He didn't have to do any of it, but he has – and he has done it brilliantly. Thank you.

While writing the book I have had the opportunity to interview several authors who not only are great writers and artists but are also great people. Thank you to the lovely Dave Gibbons who is never anything other than ceaselessly kind and generous; Tim Knapman who so enthusiastically supported the book and who I am now lucky enough to call a friend; Adam Stower for kindly agreeing to be interviewed twice (it's a long story!) and Christian Slade for the interview and for generously giving me two pages of beautiful artwork featuring the brave Ivy and the adorable Sprout. All of these people gave up their time so graciously – it is a pleasure to have them in the book.

On the educational side of things, I would like to thank the headteachers of the following schools who allowed me to come and teach the material for the book: West Earlham Infant School, Knebworth Primary and Nursery School, Nascot Wood Junior School and Hartsbourne Primary School. In these schools, I was fortunate enough to work with some amazing teachers and I would like to thank them and the children in their classes for making my time in school so enjoyable: Stephanie Coates, Sally Meredith, Dave Allen, Debra Higginson and Amanda Bliss. Particular thanks are due to Amanda, who helped plan and teach the activities featured in Sections 1.2 and 2.2. Thank you to all the children whose work is featured in the book and to the parents who granted permission for it to appear. Thanks also to Melanie Porter and Julie Bowtell for their help and input at the beginning of this project.

I would like to express my thanks to my wonderful friend, the brilliant Lisa Marks, whose artwork was spot on and who drew exactly what I described (but a million times better than I could ever have done it) – I am so honoured to have her art in my book.

I would also like to thank my parents for supporting me all through this process – I couldn't have done it without you!

Illustration Acknowledgements

Introduction

What is visual literacy? Why should we be teaching it in today's primary schools? The answers to these questions, as with so many that are related to education, are potentially limitless and unfixed. This is not to say, of course, that we should not bother attempting to answer them (we should), or that we are not able to provide any useful answers (we are). They may not be closed questions with easily definable solutions, but this does not mean that we should assume that they are ephemeral, impossible queries which cannot be discussed effectively.

Let us begin with the first question: what is visual literacy? As with many so-called 'buzz words', much debate surrounds the term and every source we refer to will, no doubt, provide us with a slightly different definition. To endlessly cite the definitions of others is initially illuminating but ultimately fruitless; however, we must start somewhere. If we consider that the term literacy in its simplest form means the ability to read and write words, then it follows that visual literacy must refer to the ability to read and create images. This basic assertion is helpful, but we need to take it further. I like very much the clear definition offered by Giorgis *et al.* that visual literacy is 'the ability to construct meanings from visual images' (1999: 146). This more specific explanation acknowledges that being able to *derive meaning* from images is a key part of the process of visual literacy and, while this may seem obvious, it does need to be stated (the act of reading is not, after all, synonymous with understanding what we read).

My own definition, and the one on which this book is based, is that visual literacy is the active process of reading, interpreting and understanding images and visual media. This is not, of course, to say that any given image necessarily contains an essential 'correct' meaning which we need to decode, but rather that developing our visual literacy provides us with the skills to analyse what we see effectively and offer our own informed interpretations of it. Therefore visual literacy is not simply an ability that we possess; it is something that we 'do' and requires us to develop a set of quite specific skills and abilities. I have included the term 'visual media' in my definition purely because my background and interest in English means that my application of visual literacy concepts and knowledge is one which is biased towards English as a subject. The concept of visual literacy and the skill set it requires will, however, be differently nuanced for each subject area. This book does not deal with what it is to be visually literate in Art, for example, or in History, but what it is to be visually literate in regard to the subject of Literacy. The aim of this material is therefore to develop and use visual literacy concepts in two ways: first, as valuable educational and life skills which deserve to be taught in their own right and, second, as an exciting way of enhancing and supporting existing Literacy teaching in primary schools. As regards the latter point, one of the key ideas here is narrative: the activities contained in this book explore the ways in which images function as sophisticated storytelling methods, helping us to better understand narrative and its associated elements such as plot and character.

So, why teach visual literacy? The simplest and most obvious answer is surely that it is an essential part of an education for citizens of a twenty-first-century society in which images consistently assert themselves. This is not a cliché; in our daily lives, we are constantly surrounded – bombarded, even – by information delivered to us through a variety of visual media, a fact which has inevitably changed our definition of what it means to be literate. This reappraisal of the skills required for contemporary literacy is effectively expressed through Makin and Whitehead's claim that 'Now when people speak of literacy, they often include listening, talking, reading, writing, viewing and critical thinking' (2004: 116). Rumours of the death of the printed word may have been greatly exaggerated but the fact remains that the image, whether static or moving, is a fundamental part of our information-gathering process and our understanding of the world. It may have been over thirty years since Dondis identified the development of visual literacy as being 'as vital to our teaching of the modern media as reading and writing was to print' (1973: 18), but this assertion appears to be more true now than ever before. As educators, our task is to prepare children for adult life and citizenship and if we are, therefore, to enable children to function effectively in our society, it is no longer sufficient to teach them to read only the written word. The idea disseminated by Media Studies practitioners towards the end of the last century, that the term 'text' does not solely apply to books but also to a wide range of media products such as films, television programmes and even static images, is no longer deemed radical at any level of education. If our only sources of information and entertainment were books, we could justify spending the majority of literacy time on the printed word, but this is no longer true. Children need to be taught how to read, understand and critically evaluate the range of media which they are regularly exposed to or they will not be able to participate effectively in society on either a personal or professional level.

It is important to reiterate here that teaching visual literacy is not simply a trendy attempt to make the curriculum entertaining. Children, like adults, spend increasing amounts of time watching television, films, DVDs and music videos, reading comics, magazines and websites and playing computer games. As far back as 1994, Robin Peel and Mary Bell argued that

> once outside the school gates, the majority of the children we teach will have significant and regular contact with language not through reading or being read to ... but through a combination of videos [and] television soaps ... That is what it means to be a child growing up in the West.
>
> (1994: 167)

We do not expect children to learn to read and understand traditional books without first being taught how to do so, so why should we assume that they are able to read and understand these other forms of media without help? Are they to teach themselves?

The primary curriculum is beginning, hesitantly, to reflect these ideas and undergo a twenty-first-century makeover. If we examine the 2006 *Framework for Literacy*, we do find evidence of this multimedia approach to literacy. It suggests the use of podcasts, television advertisements and cartoon storyboards as ICT resources for literacy teaching, shows an awareness of the fact that 'many powerful narratives are told using only images' and, crucially, leans towards the aforementioned contemporary definition of a text, incorporating 'magazines and leaflets' and those texts which are 'on screen'. On a more specific level, certain units of study such as Year 4's 'Stories with historical settings' suggest that children 'watch a short extract of a TV drama set in the past' (Department for Children, Schools and Families 2008). Admittedly, the framework is not consistent in its approach to teaching literacy through a range of media. Why, for example, are television programmes suggested as resources to support learning in the aforementioned unit, but neglected in the following unit 'Stories set in imaginary worlds', where they could be used to equal, if not greater, effect? The framework does, however, constitute a step in the right direction, especially when we consider the manner in which the teaching of visual media has traditionally been neglected in British primary schools through the stubborn refusal of previous curricula to acknowledge it as a viable subject deserving of teachers' time. When I first started teaching in the mid-1990s, the idea of educating children about visual literacy in any consistent or thorough way seemed an impossible dream. During this period, English specialists such as Peel, Bell and Peter Dougill championed the teaching of visual texts in an English programme of study which made only cursory reference to the subject's richer and more exciting elements such as drama and media. In addition, the reality of an already overburdened curriculum meant that even important Humanities subjects such as Geography and Religious Education were fighting for space in the primary timetable. Were it not for the teaching of Media Studies in secondary schools, many children educated at this time would not have had any interaction with visual texts at all outside of their own homes. This was only compounded with the arrival of the *National Literacy Strategy* in 1998, which constituted a major stumbling block on the road towards creative and inspiring English teaching and, sadly, meant that opportunities to teach media and visual literacy became almost non-existent. Therefore, under the guidance of the *Framework for Literacy*, which not only acknowledges the existence of texts other than books but actively encourages teachers to incorporate them into their teaching, primary classrooms are more receptive than ever to the teaching of visual literacy and the exploration of media texts.

But there is another, arguably more important reason why we should teach visual literacy as part of the primary curriculum, namely that it is fun! Yes – I said it. 'Fun' is not a swear word in schools and, contrary to some opinions, its place should never be underestimated in the classroom. Studying film, television and comic books is a refreshing change from the more routine elements of the curriculum and their introduction into programmes of study will hopefully provide a shot in the arm to any Literacy teaching. Personal experience has demonstrated that using such material with the majority of children will almost always generate a high level of pupil excitement and engagement. If we can exploit this initial enthusiasm for these various forms of media and use these sessions to deliver some quite sophisticated concepts to even the youngest pupils, then surely we are on to something special.

How this book works

This book is aimed not only at those primary teachers, teaching assistants and educators who are new to teaching this area of Literacy but also at all those who have already begun to teach it and are perhaps looking to gain a deeper knowledge of the subject and broaden their range of teaching ideas even further. There are many teachers who are brilliantly incorporating film, television and comic books into their everyday teaching and have been doing so for some time, and this book is aimed at them as much as it is the novice. As many of the activities in this book revolve around texts which are commonly found in most homes such as picture books, DVDs and television programmes, it is hoped that parents also find the book useful so that they might be able to help their children gain a more sophisticated understanding of the films, programmes and other visual texts which they encounter at home.

Having been a primary teacher, I have attempted to write a book which I myself would have found useful in the classroom. The book explores the teaching of four visual mediums: picture books, comic books, film and television. In addition, three sections focus on specific aspects of the subject: introducing children to the key concepts of visual literacy, using visual media to teach genre and exploring the process of adaptation across a range of media. Each section is split into three chapters: theoretical ideas, teaching ideas and further ideas and resources. The first chapter(.1) of each section aims to provide the reader with a more detailed exploration of each subject and some key texts, incorporating specialist theory. Incorporated into these sections are the 'Look Closer' features, which examine a range of texts in more detail. The 'Teaching Ideas' chapters(.2) provide clear, practical and hopefully enjoyable teaching activities, which have been developed through workshops in a number of primary schools. It is of course impossible to provide teaching activities for every year group in every subject area so the teaching ideas focus instead on one specific age group in each chapter (for example, the film activities are aimed at Year 5 and the picture book activities at Year 1). This is not, however, to say that the material cannot be taught outside of the focus year groups. To this end, the third chapter in each section, 'Further Ideas and Resources'(.3), has been designed for this purpose, providing suggestions for appropriate resources in addition to guidance for making the material simpler or more complex depending on the needs of the class. Therefore most of the material can, with some adjustments, be adapted to fit the entire primary age range.

It is important to state here that this book is not intended to be a companion to the *Literacy Framework* and, as such, is not manacled to its programme of study. The ideas herein celebrate the teaching of visual literacy in its own right and the book makes no apologies for functioning independently of the framework. As the history of education has shown, curricula, frameworks and strategies come and go and hopefully the material in this book will have a relevance and use that goes beyond any particular curriculum policy. Having said this, it would be naive and unhelpful to assume that teachers can simply dispense with or ignore the proscribed curriculum. To maximise the book's usefulness, therefore, the framework was taken into consideration when creating the activities and they have been designed to help teachers meet the required learning objectives. Accordingly, each activity in the Teaching Ideas chapters is preceded by a number of objectives. These objectives show how the activities are designed not only to develop children's specific visual literacy skills but also to develop more general literacy skills, while also helping teachers to meet the objectives of the framework. Ultimately, however, the ideas in this book will hopefully enable both children and adults to develop and enhance their critical reading skills in relation to a range of visual media texts in ways which are both stimulating and enjoyable.

A final note: this book is not intended for a moment to be a dry, dusty or prescriptive tome for teaching. In its pages you will find an eclectic exploration of diverse subjects and texts. On this voyage through visual literacy, *Doctor Who* sits beside Johnny Depp and Tim Burton, *Where the Wild Things Are* shares space with Wolverine, while Prince Caspian and the Snowman are also on board for the ride. The book has been born from a lifelong love of films, comics, picture books, television and novels and from a desire to make English teaching as exciting and as relevant as it can possibly be.

1.1

Reading Visuals

Visual literacy is a fluid term which can change depending on its context. In its natural home, the subject of Art, definition of the term predictably becomes a rather complex affair, purely because of the multitude of concepts and technical ideas that must be taken into consideration. When it comes to applying the term to Literacy, we must necessarily adjust our understanding of it to better fit the subject. In order to make our study of visual literacy both relevant and useful to the English curriculum, it is important to build our definition around existing literary and linguistic concepts. In other words, it must fit comfortably within the landscape of the present curriculum while at the same time adding something new and worthwhile.

As stated in the Introduction, the key term here is narrative. If we keep in mind that any visual literacy work in English should be linked to the act of storytelling and its attendant concepts such as character, plot, theme and tone, then we should not veer too far off course in our planning and teaching. This is not to say that the development of general visual literacy must always be linked to a recognisable narrative, of course, but in terms of Literacy studies, it is important that we anchor our work and skills to a base which will allow students to develop their English skills. A good example of this comes in the form of one of the activities featured in chapter 1.3. Herein, I suggest that a useful painting to study with children is Joseph Wright's 'An Experiment on a Bird in the Air Pump'. When examining this picture, even a cursory glance reveals a multitude of tantalising and enigmatic details: the child observing the fate of the bird, terrified yet fascinated; the young lovers, self-absorbed and uninterested in the demonstration; and the implacable gentleman, lost in thought. In short, the painting is the locus for a potentially limitless amount of stories and with a little imagination we can consider it in the same terms as we would any novel. For example: How could we describe the characters we see standing around the experiment? What are they feeling? What happened before and after this moment? What is the tone of the scene? How does it make us feel, and why? On the other hand, we would not be able to derive a narrative as easily from more abstract pieces of art such as Mark Rothko's famous paintings, many of which are composed wholly of large blocks of colour.[1] Allow me to clarify my point here (which is not in any way intended to be an argument against modern art): art experts would quite rightly argue that Rothko's beautiful works do indeed transmit narratives, after all they undoubtedly have the power to inspire emotion and provoke strong feelings within us, yet these narratives (in the traditional sense) are unarguably more obscure than Wright's. This is not, however, to say that we have to give in to the rather creatively bankrupt (not to mention boring) view that our work in visual literacy must solely be based around images which contain human beings with recognisable facial expressions. While Wright's picture is a good example of a suitable resource, we could just as easily use a painting such as Henri Rousseau's famous 'Tiger in a Tropical Storm (Surprised!)', that depicts a tiger prowling through the jungle illuminated by a flash of lightning. This work, despite lacking any images of people, nevertheless fulfils the criteria of a narrative image by possessing a clear plot (the tiger stalking through the jungle) and at least one character (the tiger himself) who displays emotion (a visible reaction to the tumultuous storm) – all of which are features that Rothko's paintings, by their nature, do not possess. Indeed, analysis of works such as Rothko's would be better served in the primary school by Art as a subject area, not Literacy.

Yet whether or not we consider Rothko's work too abstract to derive a useful narrative from, the question raised is an interesting one: at which point does an image stop being 'just' an image and take on a narrative dimension? Let us consider, for example, the three images in Figure 1.1. The top image is a large black square against a white background. This somewhat abstract image is difficult to reconcile with even a simple story. Admittedly it is not impossible (a close-up of an alien eye for example? A square hole that has suddenly opened in time and space?), but the image is somewhat self-contained in that any imaginative scope is ultimately limited by the sparseness of what we see. The middle image shows the same block but with two very simple additional elements: an object to the right of the square and a horizontal line running across the width of the picture. Immediately the image and our reading of it must readjust radically to incorporate the new information. By placing the square close to something else, we now have a sense of perspective and the square enters into a relationship with another object. For example, if we read the smaller object as a tree (I say 'if' purely because I wish to stress from an early stage that images, like written texts, should not always be limited to a single unequivocal meaning, especially abstract ones) then we have a sense that the square might be rather large. We might also raise questions about the location of the square (is it outside? Is it supposed to be there or has it just appeared?). If we then examine the bottom image, which shows the same image as the one above but with the addition of two other differently sized squares, a new relationship and narrative dimension is introduced into our analysis. Again, this is perhaps best expressed in the form of questions: Are we looking at a group of buildings? Why are the buildings different sizes? Is the bigger one more important than the smaller ones? Is it a family of strange beings? Even this relatively simple arrangement of lines and shapes has therefore prompted a number of potential stories or ideas. While all three of these relatively abstract images could inspire a story, the middle and bottom images are easier to read and attribute narrative qualities to than the top purely because the extra visual information imbues the image with a relational quality and provides a sense of context.

Therefore, while it is perfectly conceivable that we could develop students' visual reading skills in Literacy to the point where they are able to give an insightful and mature reading of

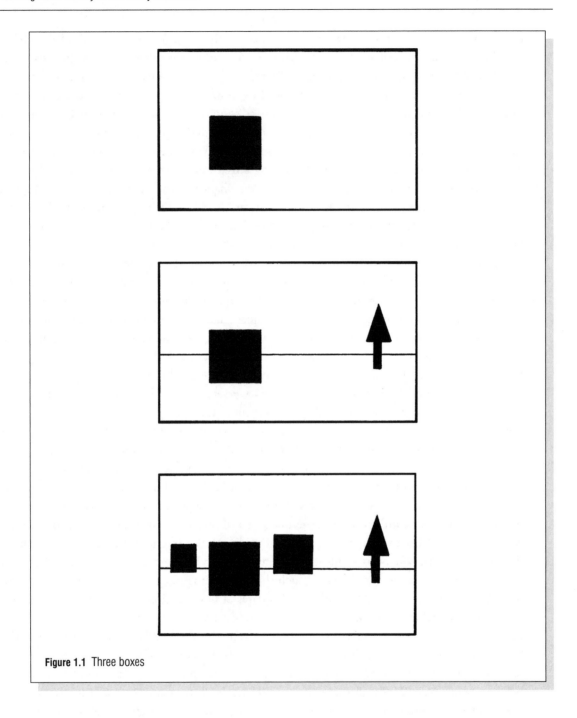

Figure 1.1 Three boxes

highly abstract images such as Figure 1.1, we do in fact need to anchor our work to existing Literacy skills. This does not mean that we are merely re-presenting old teaching material in a new way. Ideally, any exploration of visual literacy should be situated in the context of our existing English work while allowing for the fact that integrating new media and concepts into our teaching will necessarily take us into some previously unexplored educational territory. It should help us to achieve a twofold objective: to explore dynamic new forms of literacy while simultaneously reinforcing and consolidating the skills we have always taught.

Defining visual literacy terms

As with any subject area, a definition of key terms and concepts is necessary to begin with. Admittedly, we are not working towards an unnecessarily complex or overly theoretical study of visual language with children here, but this is no reason not to introduce and clarify some of the more straightforward ideas. As with many of the terms encountered in academia, the more we search and the further we hunt for a definitive meaning, the faster we realise that singular definitions are almost impossible to locate. If we consider the term 'icon', for example, we are offered a plethora of subtly diverse meanings. A traditional definition of an icon is that it is 'an image or statue ... a painting or mosaic of a sacred person', establishing the term firmly in a religious context (*Oxford Reference Dictionary* 1986: 408). However, its meaning has undoubtedly widened beyond these parameters over recent years, as acknowledged by a more recent definition of an icon as an 'abstract or pictorial representation of ideas, objects and actions' (Sassoon and Gaur 1997: 12). Scott McCloud agrees, stating that an icon is 'any image used to represent a person, place, thing or idea', but goes even further, subdividing icons into the more specific categories of symbols ('the images we use to represent concepts, ideas and philosophies'), the icons of language and communication (such as letters, numbers and musical notation) and pictures ('images designed to actually resemble their subjects') (1994: 27). Therefore these concepts vary with each source and while the above definitions are excellent, we need to modify them if we are to understand these terms accurately and in a way which is appropriate to the material covered in this book.

I would offer a slightly different way in which to consider the concepts of image, icon and symbol. It is easier to consider 'image' as an umbrella term, meaning 'the visual material which we are looking at'. In this sense, the number of items depicted is irrelevant, for example we could be looking at a drawing of hundreds of people, yet we would still apply the singular term 'image' to it. The idea of a 'frame' helps to clarify this. Whether an image has a literal frame (such as a traditional painting in a gallery) or a figurative one (such as a photograph, which has no physical frame to speak of but does have boundaries or edges which the image cannot cross), we can usually define an image as anything we see within a given frame. As these examples suggest, image is also a cross-media term. Any two-dimensional photograph, painting, sketch or even mark on a page can be considered an image and in terms of film and television (commonly referred to as the moving image) an image would be what we see when the film or television programme is paused. Therefore 'image' is used here as a general term but certain images (or elements within an image) can be described by the specific terms 'icon' and 'symbol'. An icon is a two-dimensional representation (drawn, painted or printed) of something tangible, such as a dog or a house, or even something intangible such as fear or thoughts. An important point to note here is that icons are indeed *representations* of real life. This is not simply a pedantic semantic point but rather a key idea which we need to establish early on in our study of visual literacy: an icon is, by its very definition, a depiction of something and not the object itself. As McCloud asserts, a drawing of flowers is 'not flowers', just as a drawing of a face is, in actuality, 'not a face' (1994: 26). Of course, the concept of icons can only correctly be used in terms of painted, printed or drawn images – images which are interpretations of reality. You would not, for example, look at a photograph of your friends and say that the people shown in it were icons, because even though the picture is undoubtedly only a representation of reality, the camera has in fact simply exposed light and has not offered an artistic interpretation of the subjects.

The third term to define here is 'symbol'. A symbol is a specific type of icon which represents more than just an object or idea. Here we can turn to literary studies to aid our understanding. In their analysis of poetry and its elements, John Peck and Martin Coyle identify a symbol as 'an object which stands for something else ... [or] signifies something beyond itself' (2002: 77). We can apply this idea to the visual image when we acknowledge that some icons are in fact symbols. Certainly, all icons are not symbols – it is the context of the image which determines this. An example will help here: if we see a painted image of a person holding a skull, the person is an icon (a representation of a human being) as indeed is the skull itself. Yet the skull is also more than just an icon, it could arguably be interpreted or 'read' as a symbol of death and could even provoke the viewer to reflect on the concept of mortality. If, however, we saw an identical skull connected to a human skeleton as part of an annotated illustration in a textbook, the context would demand we view the skull as nothing more than an icon. As with any piece of literature or work of art, we should beware of over-reading and try to avoid looking for a coded, deeper significance in every single aspect of it.

If we return to Figure 1.1, we can analyse it using these terms (but note that the following reading is pitched at an adult's level, not a child's). The bottom panel is an *image* which contains several drawn *icons*: a horizontal line, a large black square, two smaller black squares and another icon which we might view as being an interpretation of a tree (but is not necessarily one). As stated earlier, we should not assume that every icon is necessarily a *symbol*, so we let the context of the image guide us when looking for a deeper meaning than that depicted. The image is relatively abstract and is certainly not an information-based image such as a diagram or a map, so we could potentially interpret some of the icons symbolically. One reading, for example, might be that the 'tree' icon is symbolic of nature, while the blocks (due to their regular, geometric lines) could symbolise industry or civilisation, producing a reading of the image which explores the unnatural effect of human population on the natural environment.

The image–symbol–icon model is only a suggested approach, which will hopefully simplify any reading of images while at the same time showing that there is specific and appropriate terminology that can be used. It is not completely without disadvantages however. It is perhaps a little too complex for much younger children, for instance, and it is not always easy to classify something as a single image using the frame idea (if, for example, we were looking at several paintings on a cave wall, how would we tell if we were looking at one image or many?). Yet it does serve as an introduction to a vast and complex subject area and even if we do not introduce children to these terms immediately it will help to clarify the approach before teaching it. In addition, viewing visual material as icons and symbols reinforces the basic tenets of visual literacy, reminding us that we are in fact looking at representations and interpretations of things, not the things themselves, and that these icons may often possess a deeper, less obvious meaning if we consider them carefully.

Visual literacy and drama

Some of the activities contained in this book are drama exercises and this has been done for two reasons. First, this book intends to offer fresh perspectives on Literacy work and includes differing modes of assessment that, at times, move away from the traditional emphasis on written work. Second, from personal experience as a drama practitioner, I feel that no exploration of visual narrative is complete without establishing strong links with performance and movement and developing children's drama skills. Activities which explore body language and facial expression are not only enjoyable for children, they also help them to gain a practical understanding of how we can read emotions and character through purely visual means. This is particularly useful in relation to the study of comics, picture books and film and television, as we cannot expect children to read a range of often complex emotions through visual cues such as facial expressions if they have not had any experience of doing it themselves. Drama, therefore, offers a safe environment in which students can explore a range of feelings and attitudes and witness how they can be expressed in more subtle, non-verbal and non-written ways. Moving beyond the individual, drama also provides the opportunity to examine how characters interact with one another and to learn how gesture and posture can be decoded to give insight into relationships. As the later chapters show, even very straightforward Drama sessions will enable us to explore theories of stage dynamics (how the positioning and movement of the actors' bodies reflect the social relationships and power hierarchy between the characters). An understanding of dynamics is an essential part of being visually literate and is a way in which we can pick up on the nuances of the relationships between characters. It stems from a realisation that, as Mick Wallis and Simon Shepherd put it, 'a stage group can be organised, not merely mechanically but also into relationships of power and energy' (2002: 105). A nice example of dynamics can be seen in the film adaptation of *Harry Potter and the Order of the Phoenix* (2007). In one of the film's storylines, the malicious Dolores Umbridge (played perfectly by Imelda Staunton) has been sent to Hogwarts School by the Ministry of Magic as an Inspector. She relishes her newfound role and the authority it brings and this naturally creates conflict between her and the existing power base in the school. In one beautifully acted scene, the Deputy Headmistress Minerva McGonagall (Maggie Smith) confronts Umbridge about the cruel punishments she has meted out to students. The scene takes place on a staircase in the castle and begins with McGonagall's polite but firm statement: 'I am merely requesting that when it comes to my students, you conform to the prescribed disciplinary practices.' At this point, the two women have stopped halfway up the staircase on the same step and are facing one another. As Umbridge counters the request and attempts to assert her power, she moves up a step on the staircase but McGonagall swiftly does the same so that they are again equal. When Umbridge cites the Ministry of Magic and the power of the law however, warning McGonagall that 'To question my practices is to question the Ministry and, by extension, the Minister himself', the affronted and shocked Deputy Head takes a step back down the staircase. Her retreat is immediately exploited by the Inspector, who takes another step up the staircase to proclaim to the assembled onlookers that 'Things at Hogwarts are far worse than I feared. Cornelius [Fudge, the Minister for Magic] will want to take immediate action!' What the scene does here is to cleverly articulate in a visual manner a quite complex power struggle between two women. While McGonagall is used to having a position which is almost at the top of the school's hierarchy, she now has to readjust to the intervention of an individual who is imbued with an authority which comes from outside the institution. The women's ascent and descent of the steps works on two levels: first it is, at least initially, a gently humorous sight gag (especially when we consider the difference in height between the two women); second, it is in fact an extremely effective way of transmitting detailed information about the power structure at Hogwarts and the characters of Umbridge and McGonagall. The jostling for position and superiority on the staircase is literal and metaphorical and, in terms of the adaptation process, condenses Umbridge's rise to power (which in the novel J.K. Rowling excellently details over several hundred pages) into a few minutes of screen time. Children can, of course, be taught to look for such things in visual texts, but if we allow them to actually participate in activities which require them to express emotion and narrative through their bodies and faces, they will better understand how to interpret what they see in books, comics and films. Drama work therefore naturally feeds in to the study of visual media to help children read both static and moving images at a more sophisticated level.

Look closer: *Where the Wild Things Are*

Maurice Sendak's *Where the Wild Things Are* is an undisputed classic of the picture book medium. In the forty-five years since its publication, the book has undoubtedly proven to be timeless, remaining consistently popular with generations of children and adults and having recently been adapted for the big screen by acclaimed filmmaker Spike Jonze. Through pictures and minimal written text, the book tells the story of a young boy named Max who, dressed in a wolf outfit, is so naughty that he is sent to bed without any supper. Once confined to his bedroom, we see it transform into a forest, the walls fading away as the bedposts turn into trees and the carpet becomes grass. Max then gets into 'a private boat' and sails to 'the place where the wild things are' (Sendak 2000: 14–17), a jungle inhabited by giant creatures who make him their king. Sendak has made no secret of the fact that the book was heavily criticised by adults upon release and deemed too scary for children (Ludden 2005); however, it ultimately proved to be one of the most beloved books of all time. *Where the*

Wild Things Are is a superb example of a picture book but, beyond that, it is also an excellent text to focus on in relation to the wider context of visual literacy in general. The book, with its complex and multi-layered narrative, is as much a beautiful rendering of a child's psychological state as it is a fantastic adventure and I have selected it for closer examination here because, like the best art, it defies a singular interpretation. Instead, the book skilfully deals in ambiguity; the plot, characters and meaning of the story are all open to debate and we are required, therefore, to read the pictures closely in order to reach our own understanding of Sendak's narrative and themes.

The central area of ambiguity in the text is the plot, which takes one of the popular tropes of children's literature, the journey into the fantasy world, and builds a series of events around it. The protagonist, Max, is not on a quest in any traditional sense; he, like Alice before him, simply has a number of experiences in a strange land before returning to the familiar world. But is Max's journey real, a product of his imagination while conscious or a dream that he has after falling asleep? While an adult may perhaps view the adventure as a product of Max's dreams or imagination and the strange world he visits as being 'a concrete expression of his mental state' (Nodelman 1988: 47), this may not be so obvious to a younger reader. The pictures do, however, offer some tantalising clues. In places, they seem to suggest that Max's adventure is a result of an imaginative daydream which he constructs while awake. One of the first pictures, for example, clearly shows a piece of Max's own artwork hanging on the wall in the background, depicting a drawing of a monster which is an amalgam of several of the Wild Things who appear later (similarly, one of the creatures' tails mimics the long tail on Max's beloved wolf outfit). This small detail implies that Max has previously (and, perhaps, regularly) imagined the Wild Things. In addition, the structure of Max's adventure seems to be closer in form to an imaginative daydream than it is to the random and often unconnected events of a subconscious dream. Once the bedroom has become a jungle, events follows a clear narrative line symptomatic of an organising consciousness: Max meets the creatures, becomes king, uses his authority to indulge in revelry ('the wild rumpus') and then, crucially, comes to the realisation that he misses his mother so much that he wishes to return home. Yet, despite these visual signposts, there is also evidence to suggest that Max has indeed fallen asleep and dreamed the entire episode. The first trees which appear in his room grow symbolically from the bedposts, implying that his bed is the origin of the fantastical story and, as if he has been awakened from a dream by a sensory intrusion from the real world, Max is lured out of his adventure by the smell of his dinner. In addition, the presentation of Max in the last picture with his half-closed eyes, passive smile and hand to his head suggests the demeanour of one who has just woken. Crucially, however, Sendak refuses to didactically state that it was all a dream at the close of the narrative and instead tells us that Max 'sailed back ... into the night of his very own room where he found his supper waiting for him' (2000: 33–5). With this ambiguous ending, the author is in fact sending the empowering message to the reader that they may construct their own interpretation – a message which is consistent with the book's emphasis on the centrality and power of its child protagonist. Sendak clearly understands that many young readers use books

13

to escape from the real world, perhaps as a momentary respite from the authority of parents and school. He therefore refuses to dictate to his readers how they should interpret the events, suggesting instead that if they wish to believe the adventure actually happened, then they may!

A further area of ambiguity in the text is the characterisation. Here, the book requires us to apply one of the basic visual literacy skills: interpreting facial expressions. As Sendak's written text does not reveal a significant amount of information about Max, we must use the visuals to form our opinion of him. When we see images of the young boy causing damage by nailing sheets to the wall and threatening the helpless dog with a fork, we begin to suspect that Max is in fact something of an anti-hero, an *enfant terrible*. Sendak makes little attempt to endear Max to the reader initially. He is a solitary troublemaker who, in the words of Ellen Handler Spitz, '[does] not commune with others and … [does] not try to understand anyone else' (2009: 70). An analysis of Max's expressions reveals that, of the seventeen illustrations of his face, only five show what could be described as a happy or kind expression. He is much more frequently depicted as angry or malicious, especially at the beginning of the book. Like all well-realised characters, Max is capable of change but it is only after the story has reached its turning point – the rumpus – that his face begins to express his loneliness and vulnerability. Here, his body language also alters, moving from rigid poses which suggest that he is angry and in conflict with those around him, to less domineering poses which imply that he is no longer fighting against anything. In the latter part of the book we see Max in a melancholy post-rumpus slump, relaxed as he waves goodbye to the Wild Things and, in the book's final illustration, looking tired but relieved as he finds himself in his bedroom. This last image is particularly significant because it is the first time we see Max looking like a typical child. Gone are the rather aloof and angry facial expressions and body language of the earlier pages and instead we see Max for what he truly is – a young boy who is happy to return to the familiarity and security of home. Here, Jon C. Stott and Christine Doyle Francis note that 'although he still wears his wolf costume, the hood is pushed back off his head' (1993: 226), revealing his hair for the first time. The partial removal of the wolf suit symbolises Max's subconscious desire to abandon his animalistic, egocentric behaviour and integrate with the human world. Through this one simple image, Sendak transmits a quite sophisticated message: Max has returned to his home as a more civilised, mature and socialised individual. What is significant, however, is that Max has chosen to do this himself, reaching his decision independently without submitting to an external authority. This idea is central to Spike Jonze's beautiful and lyrical film adaptation. In his version it is not the rumpus but rather an act of aggression by one of the creatures that is the catalyst for Max's epiphany. It is only after Max (played by Max Records) witnesses an angry and destructive outburst from the Wild Thing known as Carol that he is able to reach a point of objective self-realisation, recognising that Carol's tempestuous behaviour reflects his own and, as a consequence, decides that it is time for him to return home. The film's moving final scene shows Max and his mother (Catherine Keener) reunited as Max eats his dinner, their gazes silently reaffirming their loving bond.

Max, however, is not the only complex character in Sendak's text. The Wild Things themselves are also particularly interesting in terms of their ambiguous characterisation. Initially, the creatures appear fearsome and threatening as they tower over Max baring their sharp teeth, displaying their 'terrible claws' and glaring at him with their yellow eyes (Sendak 2000: 17–18). Sendak accentuates the uncertainty we feel towards the Wild Things through their unique design, ensuring that we are unable to identify the creatures or make visual connections between them and any other familiar, real animals. They are hybrids who variously possess the noses, hairstyles and feet of humans, the faces of lions, bulls and birds and the bodies of bears and the fact that they defy simple categorisation suggests that they may likewise defy any attempt to be tamed. At this point, children are encouraged to use their visual literacy skills to answer a vital question asked by the text: should Max, and therefore we too, be afraid of the Wild Things? Here readers are required to use the same strategies that we would if we were unsure of a person's intentions in the real world: search their face and body language for evidence. Pre-empting this, Sendak answers the question in the following pages by depicting Max's refusal to be intimidated by the creatures, who in fact cower submissively away from him. With each successive image the Wild Things become less threatening and more trustworthy, Sendak tempering their potentially frightening features with smiles and friendly body language (Perry Nodelman also notes that they are made less threatening as a consequence of their 'comfortably round' bodies and the fact that even their claws and horns 'are actually rounded crescent shapes' (1988: 127)).

One of the book's true delights, however, is that the Wild Things never completely lose their ferocious appearance. Even as Max proudly rides on the Bull's back, the creatures' eyes remind us that they are still, unequivocally, *wild* things, an idea which is reinforced by their truly ferocious faces and ambiguous cries of 'Oh please don't go – we'll eat you up – we love you so!' when Max leaves them (Sendak 2000: 27–32). Interestingly, this threatening but thrilling subtext to the story is developed in Jonze's film, in which Max notices that the lair of the Wild Things is littered with bones that look suspiciously human, an observation which the Wild Things attempt to dismiss hurriedly. This unique relationship between Max and the creatures ultimately defies definition and is, perhaps, one of the reasons why the text is so popular, invoking as it does the childhood fantasy of having a wild creature as a pet which can be tamed by no one but the child. Rather than making us concerned for Max, Sendak's gentle reiterations of the creatures' inherent wildness ultimately accentuate the rarity of their bond with the boy they love. Jonze's film goes even further in exploring this relationship. Here, the Wild Things (who are given names and imbued with distinct characters and voices) are presented as physical manifestations of Max's complex inner world. Jonze and co-writer Dave Eggers's screenplay suggests that, just as their bodies are fusions of various animals, their personalities are similarly formed from disparate elements of Max's conscious and subconscious mind. Thus KW, one of the two female creatures, is the embodiment of Max's feelings towards his mother; Alexander represents the part of Max that feels ignored and sidelined; and Carol, the Wild Thing with whom Max forms the closest and most intense friendship, symbolises Max himself, mirroring his capacity for tenderness and love as well as his occasional fits of anger and moments of sadness.

The ambiguity of the text is therefore one of its greatest strengths, ensuring that readers are able to return to it repeatedly. In terms of visual literacy, the text engages both younger readers who are beginning to develop their skills and more experienced readers who are able to appreciate its subtlety and liberating potential for multiple interpretations. The depth, complexity and beauty of *Where the Wild Things Are* have deservedly made it one of the most popular books of all time.

1.2

Reading Visuals

Teaching Ideas

The following sessions aim to help pupils develop general visual literacy skills and help them respond to visual texts appropriately. The sessions can be taught individually or as part of a longer programme of study. The activities in this chapter are aimed at Year 1, but can be adapted for any age group. Extension ideas and resources for other age groups are listed in Chapter 1.3.

Reading and discussing images: *Where the Wild Things Are*

Learning objectives

- To identify and discuss key events and characters in a story
- To encourage children to engage and empathise with a story by using their imagination
- To discover how pictures can convey information in a fiction text
- To use the facial expressions and body language of characters in pictures to ascertain how they are feeling
- To use visual information in a text to support a viewpoint.

Resources

- Book: *Where the Wild Things Are* by Maurice Sendak
- Interactive whiteboard
- Some scanned pictures from the book (either saved as images onto your computer, or use a visualiser).

- Ask the children to sit in pairs (talk partners if appropriate). Introduce the text *Where the Wild Things Are* and ask the children if they are familiar with the book. Some of the children may well have read it before or will have seen the 2009 film. Ask a child who is not familiar with the book to come up and say what they think the book is going to be about, based on the title and the front and back cover pictures.

- Read the first few pages of the book then stop to ask the children what they think Max is like as a character.
  - What do the pictures show him doing?
  - How is he behaving?
- As you continue to read, it is worth stopping to look in detail at the page where Max's room begins to transform into a forest (p. 8 of the Red Fox edition, 2000).
  - What do you think is happening here?
- When you reach the pages where the Wild Things first appear (pp. 17–18), ask the children what they think about the creatures.
  - How would you describe the Wild Things?
  - Do they look friendly or unfriendly?
  - How do you think Max feels?
  - How would you feel if you were Max?
- On the next page, when Max tames the Wild Things (pp. 19–20), ask the children to describe how Max and the Wild Things are feeling now.
- When the 'wild rumpus' starts (p. 23), show the six pages which have no words and, for each double-page spread, ask the children (with a partner) to be 'authors' and come up with a sentence which could go in the book. Ask some of the children to come up and say their sentences out loud to the class.
- At the end of the book, discuss the last few pages of the story. Discuss the different things that might have happened to Max. Encourage the children to use the evidence in the pictures to support their views.
  - What happened to Max?
  - Where did he go?
  - Did he fall asleep? How do you know?
  - Did he imagine it? How do you know?
  - Did it really happen? How do you know?
- It is important to leave the children with an open ending here, not to state that 'It was all a dream'. You may want to give your own view of what happened and say why. Sendak leaves the conclusion open to interpretation and it is nice to do the same with children. As long as the children are beginning to use evidence from the text (both visual and written) then the discussion will be valuable.
- Put one of the pages you have scanned in advance up on the interactive whiteboard. A good example is the picture of Max chasing the dog (p. 4).
- Ask the children to discuss the picture in pairs, talking about what they notice. Ask them to pay particular attention to Max and the dog's facial expressions. When the children have their responses ready, ask them to share what they have noticed. As each child comments on the picture, use the interactive pens to write on the picture, circle details

and add notes with arrows to the outside of the picture. Feel free to make the notes look as informal and rough as you like, for example:

- Max looks angry/Max looks like he is being naughty/The dog looks scared/There is a picture of a Wild Thing by Max/Max is dressed up

- When the children have seen how you have done it, put up another picture on the board (the more things going on in the picture, the better). Some good examples are the page where Max meets the Wild Things (pp. 17–18), where he is made king (pp. 21–2) and where Max is sad after the wild rumpus (pp. 29–30).

- Ask the children to work on their own this time. If they can, the children could write down what they see, but they can simply respond verbally if it is easier. Share the responses. If the children do this quickly, then use several pictures, giving them a few minutes on each.

Using drama to develop visual literacy with *Where the Wild Things Are*

Learning objectives

- To explore a text by recreating key scenes and characters through role-play
- To understand how moods and emotions are shown through body language and facial expression
- To link body language and facial expressions in pictures with body language and facial expressions in real life
- To work in groups, discussing their own and each other's ideas
- To present their work to an audience and offer opinions on other groups' work.

Resources

- Book: *Where the Wild Things Are* by Maurice Sendak
- A3 enlargements of selected pictures from *Where the Wild Things Are*
- Tambourine.

- Start with some warm-ups to get the children moving and using their bodies:
- Walking around the room (without talking) and freezing when they hear the tambourine is a good way to establish the rules of the session.
- Stop/Go: The children have to do the opposite of your command, so if you say 'Go', they have to stop and vice versa – this is more tricky than it sounds and very enjoyable!
- Children have to walk without speaking as if they are in the park, waving and miming a greeting at each other.

- Shoe activity: Children sit down in a space. Sit in front of the children and tell them that yesterday you went for a walk. It helps if you mime putting on your shoes, carefully tying up the laces. Then tell them that they were just your normal walking shoes.

- Ask the children to do the same as you, miming putting on their shoes carefully. When they have got their 'shoes' on, ask them to walk around the hall as if they were going out for a stroll. Again, if they are asked to do this in silence, it helps to transmit to them that Drama requires vocal and bodily control and that it is not simply playtime.

- Ask the children to sit down again and mime taking off their walking shoes. Then ask them to put on a pair of wellington boots. Demonstrate this if necessary. Ask them to walk around as if there were lots of muddy puddles for them to splash in. Choose some children who have mimed this well to show the class as a model. This activity can continue for as long as you wish. Other types of footwear are trainers (running), heavy boots (stomping) and socks (tiptoeing).

- Ask the children to think about how their faces and bodies can show how they feel. It is a good idea to demonstrate how you might look if you were feeling glum (sloping shoulders, sad face, slow walk) and ask the children to guess how you are feeling.

- Using the space, get the children to walk around (again in silence) showing a happy mood, then an excited mood, angry mood and so on. After each mood, pick out the children who have done this particularly well and ask them to show the others. Encourage feedback from the children by saying what you like about the children's work.

- Ask the children to think about an activity they like doing (skipping, running or reading, for example) and to mime doing it. As you count down from five to one then bang the tambourine, ask the children to freeze as statues showing them doing their activity.

- Inform the children that you (and any other adults supporting the session) have taken on the role of a visitor to a museum and that you are going to go around and look at them as statues and try to guess what they are doing. The idea of a teacher in role helps the children to become more comfortable with the idea of drama.

- Try and guess what the children are showing as their statues and then ask them. When you have asked some (or all) of the children, ask the best examples to remain as statues while the others guess what they are doing.

- Divide the children into groups of four or five and hand out an A3 enlargement of a selected picture from *Where the Wild Things Are* to each group. Try to use three or four different pictures, so that each group is not doing the same picture. As there are at least four children in each group, choose pictures which have at least four characters in. Some good examples are: pp. 17–18, where Max first meets the Wild Things; pp. 19–20, where Max tames them; pp. 21–2, in which Max becomes king; and pp. 29–30, where Max sits outside the tent. Ask the children to decide in their groups who is playing which character and then recreate the picture as a frozen image, paying particular attention to body and facial expressions. The children might need about five minutes, during which time you can circulate and help groups.

- When the children are ready, line the class up in a row facing forward so that they have an idea of sitting as a formal audience and then ask the groups to come up and recreate their pictures one group at a time. As each group freezes, hold out the original picture above them, so that the class can see and comment on how accurate their representation is. If there is time, you can swap the pictures and ask each group to recreate a different picture.

- As a cool-down/plenary, ask the children to find a space, lie on their backs, relax and think about what they have done and learned in today's session. Remind them about reading body and face as an indicator of emotion.

Hot seating

Learning objectives
- To develop empathy with the characters in a text
- To develop comprehension of a text through role-play and improvisation
- To ask appropriate questions, give suitable answers and listen to the questions and answers of others in a whole-class situation.

Resources
- Book: *Where the Wild Things Are* by Maurice Sendak
- A crown (paper, card or plastic).

- The use of hot-seating activities, where children are asked to adopt the role of one of the characters from a text and answer questions from the other children is commonplace in primary schools. It is an excellent way to assess and develop children's comprehension of texts and help them to consider things which the text only implies. Of course, if we view the child who is in role as the only pupil who is active in the session with the questioners as relatively passive, then the activity becomes somewhat pointless. Therefore, it is important to really encourage the children to ask effective questions and model some yourself.

- Ask one child to come and sit at the front of the group (or at the centre of a circle) and take on the role of Max. They can wear Max's crown if you have one. While it is important at some point over the course of these sessions to allow all children to be the interviewee irrespective of their speaking and listening capabilities, it is a good idea to first choose a child who will model this role well.

- Some questions for Max:
  - How did you get to the strange land?
  - Why did you want to go there?

- Why did you want to go home?
- Why were you so naughty?
- How do you feel about your mother?
- Were you scared of the Wild Things?

■ Ask another child to adopt the role of one of the Wild Things:

- What are you?
- Where do you live?
- Have you always lived here?
- How do you feel about Max?
- Did you want Max to leave?

■ Another child can take on the role of Max's mother. The difference between this character and the others is that Max's mother is 'offstage' in the book and is never seen. Taking on this role will require well developed inference skills and the child may even need to invent appropriate information where necessary. Therefore, select a child who will be capable of doing this. Some questions you may wish to ask are:

- Why did you send Max to his room?
- Where is Max's father?
- How do you feel about Max?
- What happened when you went to bring Max his food?
- Is Max always naughty or was it just this time?
- What happened after Max ate his dinner?

1.3

Reading Visuals

Further Ideas and Resources

These lists of resources and ideas for activities supplement the teaching ideas in Chapter 1.2 and offer suggestions for teaching visual literacy activities with other age groups.

Reading and discussing images

This activity (which asks pupils to look at images and write down or discuss what they notice) is self-differentiating and can be undertaken with any age group. The only differences between a Year 1 and a Year 6 version of this activity are the images used. While it may be more straightforward to use a page from a picture book with younger children, older pupils can develop their visual literacy skills through studying paintings and photographs. Images of suitable paintings can be found by searching online or in art books and can easily be displayed on the whiteboard while the children note down and discuss their observations. Try to encourage the children to relate their observations to narrative and character, concentrating on the facial expressions and emotional states of the people or animals in the images and considering what story the pictures might be telling. With older children, you may wish to ask them to look at an image and develop their observations in different ways:

- Write a first person monologue, expressing a character's inner thoughts
- Write a short story explaining the events which happened after the ones shown in the image
- Write a playscript detailing the dialogue between the characters
- Write down what the figures in the image could be saying or thinking (in the form of speech bubbles), then come and place them on the whiteboard by each character as if it were a giant comic.

The following lists give resources which you might wish to use as images to base activities on:

Key Stage One

Books:
Elmer by David McKee
Lost and Found by Oliver Jeffers
Not a Box by Antoinette Portis
Diary of a Wombat by Jackie French and Bruce Whatley
Wolves by Emily Gravett
Emily and the Big Bad Bunyip by Jackie French and Bruce Whatley
The Dark, Dark Night by M. Christina Butler and Jane Chapman
The Bear by Raymond Briggs

Images:
A selection of artists' work can be found at Arena's website (www.arenaworks.com).

Key Stage Two

Paintings:
An Experiment on a Bird in the Air Pump (1768) by Joseph Wright (www.nationalgallery.org.uk/artists)
Les Raboteurs de Parquet (1875) by Gustave Caillebotte (www.musee-orsay.fr/en/collections/index-of-works/home.html)
Ferdinand Lured by Ariel (1850) by John Everett Millais
Speak! Speak! (1895) by John Everett Millais (www.tate.org.uk/collection)

Photography:
Mitra Tabrizian (www.mitratabrizian.com).

Drama

The resources above are also excellent starting points for Drama work with children. A model of a Drama session for a Key Stage One class is shown in Chapter 1.2 and this can be altered slightly for a Key Stage Two year group. Whereas with younger children the session culminated in the pupils recreating an image, older children should perhaps be asked to do this earlier in the session and should then be asked to further develop their understanding of body language and emotion. If, for example, we use a painting as an image to base a Drama session on, the following model could be employed:

- Start with warm-ups:
    - Stop/go (children have to do the opposite of the command you give them)
    - Remote control (children walking around or miming an activity for which you

have the remote control and can therefore pause them, fast-forward or rewind as if they were on television)

- In pairs, children have to create a tableau of an image or a scene and the other children have to guess what it is
- Children are given a word to say, such as 'spaghetti' or 'toast', and have to say it in a variety of different ways (angrily, excitedly)
- Children are given a word on a piece of paper (such as 'lead'), which they then have to describe to the rest of the class, without using the word itself.

- After the warm-ups, divide the children into groups of two, three or four (depending on the number of characters in the image you are using) and hand each group a large photocopy or poster of a painting or photograph (see 'Paintings' list above for suitable images). It will be easier if at first you give the same image to every group. Ask the children to recreate the image, giving them a couple of minutes to organise this.

- After they have held their friezes in position ask the children to discuss the image in their groups and try to work out a story that goes with the image, assigning names and personalities to the figures in it. Giving the children sufficient time, ask the groups to create a short piece of drama (with speech) which shows the events preceding the image. The improvisation should finish with a frozen tableau of the image as seen in the previous task.

- Show these examples to the rest of the class, commenting on the best aspects of each. Then ask the children to create a second piece which shows the events that happened after the image, beginning with the frozen tableau that the last piece ended on.

- These two pieces can then be put together as one continuous performance based around the image. If the children find this activity challenging, then this drama work can be undertaken over two or even three sessions. Having explored the image through drama, the children can then write down their improvisation as a playscript or produce some written monologues for the figures that they portrayed in the image.

Note

1 Mark Rothko (1903–70) was a twentieth-century American artist, born in Latvia. Although his work is diverse, he is best known for his stunning canvases which are often characterised by a 'compositional arrangement of . . . [a] vertical stack of colour blocks' (Fer 2008: 37).

2.1

Picture Books

The idea that picture books are an often complex fusion of art and literature which are not only educationally valuable but are also able to be aesthetically appreciated and enjoyed by both adults and children is now an established notion within educational circles. The last twenty years in particular have produced a great deal of significant research focusing on the wide range of picture books available, the unique ways in which they function and the sophisticated reading skills which they require from their readers in order to be fully appreciated (Nodelman 1988; Meek 1991; Doonan, 1993; Baddeley and Eddershaw 1994; Watson and Styles 1996). A picture book offers a reading and, indeed, a looking experience unlike any other. The best picture books are, as Evelyn Arizpe and Morag Styles state, 'composed of pictures and words whose intimate interaction creates layers of meaning, open to different interpretations and which have the potential to arouse their readers to reflect on the act of reading itself' (2003: 22). Traditionally, the picture book has relatively little written text and instead places a greater emphasis on pictures due to the fact that the medium as a whole was, and still is, primarily aimed at younger children and emergent readers. Yet in recent years, picture books have begun to move out of the realm of children's literature and emerge as a valid art form in their own right. As with any medium, the strongest examples demonstrate a clever ability to employ the accepted conventions of the format as narrative and thematic strengths rather than considering them to be limitations. One such convention is that picture books often contain very little written text, some perhaps consisting of only fifty or sixty words. Yet why should this be considered detrimental to a reader's enjoyment of the text? After all, a poem or a song may contain a similar amount of words, yet both have the ability to move us profoundly and engage us intellectually. Similarly, in many picture books, the emphasis is placed on the artwork to help tell the story but this does not necessarily mean that it is a simplistically constructed narrative. Indeed, if we went to an art gallery and looked at paintings which contain no written text, we would not consider them to be simplistic or childish for this reason. Picture books, of course, have not achieved the crossover into the mainstream adult book market to anything like the same degree as the fiction read by older children, such as the *Harry Potter* series and Phillip Pullman's *His Dark Materials* trilogy.[1] It is highly unlikely that you would glimpse an adult reading a picture book on the train, and they are certainly not read by many who are not parents nor even read by older children (who may well view reading picture books as taking a step backwards in their literacy development). Yet the reading of a picture book – with or without a child present – can be a delightful and often moving experience and one which provides a refreshing alternative to a novel. As with any sophisticated art form they can, as Margaret Meek states, offer 'ways of presenting the world' but can also offer 'scandalous, excessive, daring possibilities' (1988: 19).

I recently discovered Antoinette Portis's *Not a Box* which proved to be an incredibly satisfying and enjoyable reading experience. The book tells the story of a young rabbit who plays with a cardboard box, transforming it into a multitude of wondrous things through the power of imagination. While the written text is minimal, with just one sentence every two pages, and the crayon-like line drawings delightfully simple, Portis deploys both words and pictures to great effect. By the end of the book, the lovable protagonist has been effectively and affectionately brought to life and is arguably as well realised a character as any we might find in a novel. In addition, the lack of words does not prevent the author from infusing the text with a warm and witty tone and the fact that I was able to read it in a matter of minutes was a strength of the text – it meant that I could reread and enjoy it again immediately (something which is much less easy to do with a novel). On a technical level, *Not a Box* proves to be far from simplistic. Portis uses a small range of colours with a symbolic consistency which underscores the ideas contained in the narrative. The black lines are used to denote the rabbit and the box throughout the text because in the story both are real and tangible, whereas on the pages where we are privy to the rabbit's imagination, Portis introduces red lines to show what the box has become. For example, a wonderful illustration shows the black-outlined rabbit sitting in the box with the red outline of a racing car overlaid onto the box and a pair of red goggles drawn on the rabbit's face. Similarly, the pages which show the pedestrian real world are brown (like a cardboard box), whereas the fantasy pages are bright red and yellow, Portis using colour to represent the liberating and exciting power of imagination. Even the book as a whole is aesthetically pleasing and designed with sophistication. The paperback edition has a grainy brown cover with the texture of a cardboard box, the title is printed in unelaborated red font such as you might find on the outside of a box used for shipping goods and, in a delightful touch, there is a 'Net Wt. 148g' on the front cover and a 'This Side Up' instruction complete with arrows on the back. A good picture book, therefore, has the ability to engage and move any reader on its own terms, simply by employing the medium's conventions effectively.

Previously, I proposed a three-part classification system for picture books and comic books (Stafford 2009) which I will reiterate here. This model is an attempt to clarify the distinct ways in which visual texts construct the relationship between words and pictures. It lists the following three categories: the illustrated storybook, the picture book and the comic book. In terms of this chapter, I wish to elaborate on the first two categories and explain this distinction further.

I use the term illustrated storybook to describe any fiction book which contains both words and pictures but in which the pictures merely illustrate the written text. In other words, a book where the pictures do not add any new information to the story but simply support what has already been written. This is perhaps most clear in a text such as C.S. Lewis's *Prince Caspian* where Pauline Baynes's classic illustrations visualise what Lewis has written. However, the illustrated storybook's relationship between pictures and words can also apply to books where the ratio of text to pictures is much lower. A book such as David McKee's *Elmer*, for example, which has a relatively small amount of words in comparison to the pictures which fill every single page, would nonetheless also be classed as an illustrated storybook. This is due to the fact that analysis of the images reveals that they do not add any additional narratives to McKee's written text. Traditionally, *Elmer* would be described as a picture book, but I make the distinction here because the very term 'picture book' implies that the pictures are of central importance to the narrative. Of course, it is undeniable that in a book such as *Elmer*, the pictures *are* important – they are a huge part of the book's appeal and it is impossible to imagine the text without them. In narrative terms, however, they merely reflect, or illustrate, what the words have already told us. It is for this reason therefore that I describe a text such as this one as an illustrated storybook.

The second category, picture books, is reserved for books whose pictures go beyond, or deviate from, the words, breaking free from the constraints of the written text. A good example of this is the perennial favourite *Rosie's Walk*, Pat Hutchins's story of a hen who takes a stroll through the farmyard. While the sparse text provides a simple commentary on Rosie's journey ('Rosie the hen went for a walk … across the yard … around the pond'), the pictures show that the unwitting hen is in fact being pursued by a predatory fox, whose attempts to devour her are consistently thwarted (he steps on a rake for example and falls in a pond) (Hutchins 1970: 1–10). The significant point here is that the written text never once refers to the fox or his slapstick escapades and it is only by looking at the pictures that we realise the full humour (and the full danger) of Rosie's walk. Similarly, in the aforementioned *Not a Box*, the pictures carry unique and independent narrative information which when added to the words complete the overall message of the book. The words relay a discussion between the book's rabbit protagonist and an unseen questioner ('*Why are you sitting on a box?* … It's not a box.') which inform us that the rabbit is insisting that the cardboard box is more than it appears. It is the pictures, however, which brilliantly provide us with an insight into the central character's mind and show us what the box actually becomes through the transformative power of imagination (a race car, a mountain, a rocket) (Portis 2008: 1–8). Again, the pictures provide new information which we cannot possibly gain from the written text.

A final example of this relationship between words and pictures is exemplified in Maurice Sendak's classic *Where the Wild Things Are*. The picture book tells the story of Max and his journey to a strange land where he befriends a group of monsters and becomes their king. Although the written text provides us with some information about the story and the characters, it is limited. We are told, for example, that Max 'came to the place where the wild things are' and that he 'tamed them with the magic trick of staring into all their yellow eyes' (Sendak 2000: 17–20), but there are no descriptions of the individual monsters. It is Sendak's artwork which truly brings these iconic characters to life with their big claws, chimerical bodies and beautiful faces which are capable of being both extraordinarily fearsome and extraordinarily tender. Here, it is the pictures, not the words, which allow us to view the creatures as more than just a generic group and encourage us to see the Wild Things as differentiated individuals, perhaps even prompting us to choose a particular favourite. Indeed, when we think about the Wild Things it is surely not the words that chiefly define our relationship with the book, but the pictures. In short, the pictures in all of the examples above add a whole new dimension to the narratives.

No value judgement is made here when differentiating between the illustrated storybook and the picture book. The fact that the former does not use its pictures to advance the narrative in the same way as does the latter, does not mean that it is in any way inferior as a format. Aesthetically speaking, the pictures in both textual models are invaluable parts of the reading experience. The point of the above distinction, however, is to show that different books employ illustrations in different ways. The examples demonstrate that the pictures in a book such as *Elmer* have a radically different function from those in *Not a Box*. The way in which a book constructs the relationship between words and images should therefore affect not only how we read and appreciate it, but also how we teach it.

Look closer: *Mungo* and *Charlie and Lola*

In recent years a number of writers and illustrators have produced texts which have played with the format of the picture book and self-reflexively examined their own narrative processes. This in itself is a measure of just how sophisticated the picture book can be and illustrates how a deceptively simple medium has the potential to explore some very complex ideas. In short, we have seen the advent of the postmodern picture book. While the term 'postmodern' has become a label which is far too readily thrown at any artistic product that displays even the faintest glimmer of irony or self-awareness, it is evident that some contemporary picture book authors are in fact producing texts to which the term could accurately be applied. Of course, the label of postmodernism is subject to debate and constant reinterpretation, yet I use it here in order to describe the ways in which some picture books show an awareness of their own form (in both a pictorial and a written sense) and play with the act of storytelling itself.

Lauren Child, creator of the *Charlie and Lola* books, is one author whose work displays postmodern features. While her stories about the eponymous brother and sister are, on the whole, linear in terms of their narratives, the accompanying artwork and layout of the books are anything but traditional, fusing real photographs with hand-drawn illustrations, resulting in collages which give the impression that we are in fact looking at a cut-and-paste scrapbook. In *I Am Too Absolutely Small for School*, Child presents Lola as a girl with a drawn and painted head atop a body made up of a dress which is in fact a photograph of a real printed fabric (and, consequently, looks different in every picture as Child has deliberately used various sections of the same fabric). If we look closely we can see that, in some illustrations, the characters look 'cut-out' and the white paper behind each illustration is evident, as if a child had done the cutting. One spread, which shows us Lola's imagination as she tries to count, depicts elephants made up of photographed fabric, wallpaper and even wooden flooring, while another is simply an enlarged photograph of felt-tip pens and a toy telephone with a drawing of Lola at its centre (Child 2007: 6–9). Child adopts a similarly eclectic approach to the written text, breaking all the traditional rules of books by alternating font style and size (sometimes within words) and allowing sentences to flow freely and dizzily over the page, unconstrained by the usual straight-line format of print. Her approach is clever, mimicking the random, unpolished and often chaotic way in which we learn to write and draw on a page and allowing children to identify powerfully with what they see as if they had created it themselves. Child's artwork, if not her narrative, draws the reader's attention to the fact that they are reading a book, the paper collages reminding us that the text we hold in our hands is made of the same material. She thereby fulfils one of the criteria of postmodernist texts (as identified by Peter Barry) by presenting the text as a text, not reality, and denaturalising it (2002: 91).

This postmodern reinvention of the picture book reaches its zenith in Child's *Beware of the Storybook Wolves*, wherein the protagonist, Herb, has to deal with characters who escape from his fairy-tale books, and its sequel *Who's Afraid of the Big Bad Book?*, which sees Herb being sucked into one of these same books. Here the pictures once again remind us that not only is Herb a reader who encounters unruly characters that have sprung from the pages of a book, but that he, too, is a character in an actual book that we are reading. Child goes to great lengths to reiterate the tangible, physical experience of reading. Just as Herb's beloved books 'usually had bits of banana, biscuit and the odd pea squashed between the pages', so too does the very page we read these words on, marked as it is by the liquid from the bottom of a milkshake glass and a squashed pea. Later, Herb runs through one of his books, finding a door 'difficult to open because the illustrator had drawn the handle much too high' and evading capture 'by snipping a hole in the palace floor', the evidence of which comes in the form of an actual hole in the page (Child 2003: 1–18). Even the front cover of *Who's Afraid of the Big Bad Book?* utilises the 'Chinese box' approach to narrative (where a story is contained inside another story and so on) by showing Herb reading a copy of *Who's Afraid of the Big Bad Book?*, which has the same front cover as the one we are holding in our hands. Our relationship with the text and its protagonist is therefore a complex one: on one level we identify with Herb as a fellow reader (who, like us, imagines what it may be like to interact with fictional characters), but on another level, we are forced to view Herb as just a character in a book which we are reading and are therefore distanced from him as readers. This continual self-referencing of the book and its tendency towards intertextuality (shown through Herb's encounters with a range of famous fairy-tale characters and an appearance by the Little Wolf who still wears the same dress that he did in the book's prequel) further cements its status as a postmodern text. Both of the books in which Herb appears anarchically reject not only the traditional rules of narrative but also the rules which govern the physical act of reading a book. In this sense, they display a somewhat mischievous postmodern attitude wherein narrative and artistic 'fragmentation is an exhilarating, liberating phenomenon, symptomatic of our escape from the claustrophobic embrace of fixed systems of belief' (Barry 2002: 84).

This same attitude is evident in Timothy Knapman and Adam Stower's *Mungo* series. These witty and inventive picture books tell the story of the titular Mungo and the adventures that ensue when he too becomes part of the books that he reads. Even though the device of the protagonist stepping into a book remains consistent in all three titles, the *Mungo* books explore a range of literary genres and, indeed, a range of media. In *Mungo and the Picture Book Pirates* Knapman and Stower play with features of the picture book and the storybook, *Mungo and the Spiders from Space* utilises some of the narrative and visual elements of comic books and in *Mungo and the Dinosaur Island*, the dinosaur book in question (The Amazing Secret of the Lost Island) is based on an old monster film. The books therefore work extremely effectively as explorations of the concept of genre for young children while also functioning as deconstructions of the picture book medium itself. This is seen in *Picture Book Pirates* which begins with the pirate-obsessed Mungo begging his mother to reread his favourite book to him. Knapman (who was inspired to write after having to reread a beloved story several times to friends' children on holiday[2]) then begins to play with the established rules of reading by telling us that Captain Fleet, the protagonist of Mungo's favourite book, is actually so exhausted from having to re-enact the story 'SIX TIMES in one night that he'd decided to take a holiday' (2006: 14). With the Captain abandoning the book, the villainous Barnacle Bill (who is, of course, usually defeated in the tale) will go unchecked and become victorious unless Mungo changes his role from that of passive reader to active participant in his favourite story. In the sequel, *Spiders from Space*, Knapman employs a similar technique, where the science fiction story which Mungo is reading is unable to end happily because the last page is physically missing from his book. Mungo must therefore again intervene in the events of the narrative he is reading in order to defeat the evil Dr Frankenstinker and achieve narrative closure. As these examples demonstrate, Knapman's work proves that the picture book format does not necessarily have to be simplistic. Mungo's adventures encourage children to celebrate but also question the act of reading even as they are doing it, laying bare the narrative process and the relationship between author and reader, an idea which is echoed through Adam Stower's artwork. In *Picture Book Pirates*, the artist cleverly differentiates between events in the 'real world' and events which take place within the pages of Mungo's favourite book by showing us full-page spreads which have tattered and ripped corners and give the illusion that there are other parchment-like pages behind them for the scenes where Mungo is inside his book. Similarly, in *Spiders from Space*, Mungo's discovery of the missing page is presented to us as an almost entirely black void with just a few torn remnants remaining, allowing us to temporarily share Mungo's perspective. In addition to such details, Stower also varies the overall visual style of each book in order to make it appropriate to the genre. *Spiders from Space*, for example, uses the layout and conventions of the comic book medium, eschewing the more traditional watercolour artwork of the previous adventure for the bold and dazzling colours of a science fiction comic from the 1950s. The third book in the series, *Dinosaur Island*, draws from the imagery of cinema, telling the story through accurate representations of silent film reels (which alternate images with captions) and long rectangular panels which mimic the widescreen format. The artwork, like the narrative, deconstructs the various media in a visual sense, making us aware of how each genre or type of text tells its story. The *Mungo* books, therefore, constitute an exploration of how stories are told and how genres meet reader expectation while playfully disrupting established forms. Like Child, Knapman and Stower have created texts which, on one level, are self-reflexive and complex, but on another are simply exciting and accessible stories for children. The books' younger readers are, after all, unlikely to be interested in how or why these texts are postmodern, and Knapman correctly asserts that children tend not to read the books on a theoretical level but rather view them simply as 'a game' in which the process of reading the book is akin to the author saying 'Here are the rules'.[3] The most sophisticated picture books are successful because they work on two levels simultaneously. While they can be enjoyed by children for their exciting and stimulating mix of words and pictures, older readers can appreciate the way in which this unique art form can deliver complex and emotionally satisfying reading experiences.

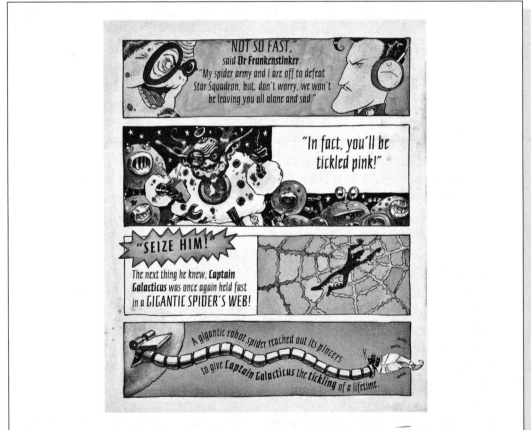

Figure 2.1 From *Mungo and the Spiders from Space* by Timothy Knapman, illustrated by Adam Stower

Interview with Timothy Knapman

Timothy Knapman is the writer of the *Mungo* series of picture books: *Mungo and the Picture Book Pirates*, *Mungo and the Spiders from Space* and *Mungo and the Dinosaur Island*. He has also written a play, *The Smallest Person*, and the librettos for a number of operas. Here, he discusses his inspirations for the *Mungo* stories and explains why he views creating a picture book as a collaborative process akin to writing a screenplay.

TS: What were your inspirations for the first *Mungo* book, *Mungo and the Picture Book Pirates*?

TK: The reason I wrote the book is basically because I went on holiday with some friends. They've got three boys and I read them picture books and there were certain ones they wanted to have over and over again. So the premise was 'Well, I'm getting bored doing this, what would it be like if the characters got bored doing this?' and out of that I got the story. Then the question was 'What book is it going to be?' and, at that point, there had been no successful pirate films or books for ages.

TS: I assume this was before the appearance of Captain Jack Sparrow[4] then?

TK: It took two and a half years between my book being written and it coming out. So, in those two and a half years I think they had at least two *Pirates of the Caribbean* films. So I did slightly think 'Oh!' But the inspiration for the pirate part of the book is all the pirate clichés; all the Errol Flynn movies and the Burt Lancaster movies and *Treasure Island* of course. But the actual Pirandellian[5] aspect of *Mungo and the Picture Book Pirates*, the postmodern part, comes from *Monty Python's Flying Circus*.[6]

From a very young age, I watched *Monty Python's Flying Circus* – I remember watching the last series of it when I was seven. So that idea of breaking the narrative frame, of taking a form and turning it inside out, all of that comes from them. They also associated it with humour, after all that idea [of playing with narrative conventions] isn't necessarily a humorous idea. Pirandello doesn't use it as a humorous idea in *Six Characters in Search of an Author*; he uses it as a tragic idea.

TS: You seem to have a very confident sense of the audience for your books as an author. There are some great references and jokes in the books which would almost certainly go over the heads of your child audience.[7] Could you talk to me about this?

TK: Picture books, unlike most other books, have two very specific audiences they have to address simultaneously: the adult reading the book and the child who is being read to. All of my books are written as much for the grown-ups as they are for the children. They are written to be good things to read out. I have written plays as well, so I'm used to the things I write being said out loud. I put in things like tongue twisters and funny names because I'm writing for the 'actor' as well as the 'audience'. It's almost like writing a play. Therefore, if the adults reading it can identify with it, that's another useful hook. Also, in commercial terms, the impulse for me is to think 'I am writing for children', but in between the child and the author, there is the parent, the shop and the publisher. I have to please all of these people before my book gets to the child – all those other considerations!

TS: So all these things are bubbling away under the surface while you're writing?

TK: Well, not when I write. When I write, I'm writing absolutely for the child and for the parent. But the moment you finish and hand your story in, you have to think 'Will a publisher take this?' You also have to consider the age of the child audience. The children's literature market splits up into age groups because bookshops want to know where to put things. So, picture books go in one place in the shop and books for older children are basically split into 5–8 year olds and 9–12 year olds. Nowadays, unfortunately publishers are putting age bandings on books more and more which is something the bookshops want them to do.

TS: The books have a quite specific relationship with genre. Each of the *Mungo* books explores a clearly demarcated genre or sub-genre: pirate stories, sci-fi and dinosaur adventure stories. How did this come about?

TK: The *Mungo* books are all based on long-established genres (pirate stories, SF comics, monster movie books-of-the-film), genres that have been around so long that they've been parodied to death and come out the other side, as it were. As a writer, this gives you two things: a well defined space with a set of accepted rules to play with and something that you're able to enjoy (by using all the conventions of the genre) without 'sending it up' – being dismissive, or smart, or too good for it. You have a clearly delineated form and the fun is to be had in using that as a framework and then twisting things around and hanging your ideas from it. You can do this because someone else has previously 'sent up' the genre ad nauseam and it has survived and, by reason of its enduring appeal, risen above that sort of criticism. I think children would pick up on it very quickly if I didn't like the genres I was writing in and they might be put off – and quite right too! The *Mungo* books, like all children's books in different ways, should be fun. Reading them should feel like 'Whoopee! Look at all the toys in this toy box, and I can play with every one of them!'

TS: They are quite sophisticated books. You are getting children to consider ideas such as postmodern narratives, intertextuality and self-conscious storytelling.

TK: But actually what I'm *not* doing is asking them to consider ideas. I'm saying 'Here's a game. Let's play this game. These are the rules.' That's it ... and they get it. Grown-ups conceptualise these things, see them in terms of ideas. Obviously I hope children get pleasure from them and also they might start to think about things like unreliable narrators and all that stuff. But hopefully they'll be interested in the books as a practical thing, not a theoretical thing.

TS: I love the idea of Mungo interacting with the books he reads as they come to life. Why did you use this narrative technique?

TK: If you're reading a book there's a sense that you're looking at a window. The idea in the *Mungo* stories is that he opens the window and climbs through – the idea of the 'rabbit hole'.[8] Because children live in a world where the world of imagination and the world of reality are much less clearly delineated than they are for grown-ups, a lot of children's books are about how you get from one to the other (through the wardrobe, down the rabbit hole) but the thing about the *Mungo* books is that the rabbit hole is the book itself. Once you've sorted out the genre, the difficulty is getting Mungo into the book. The first one was okay because the character was so bored that the story goes wrong and the second premise was that somebody tore the last page out, so that there's no ending to the book he's reading.

TS: Can you tell me about the process of picture book creation? At what point does Adam [Stower, the artist] come in?

TK: Once the publishers agree to buy my manuscript, then there's a little bit of 'back-and-forth' about the text with the book's editor. They question things and you have to fight for some things. There's certain things that you have to explain why you mean what you mean and you can't – so that's probably a good reason to get rid of them. Then there are things that you know are good but you can't explain them so you have to fight for them. But I do not think that, in the end, the text that is in the final book and the text that I submitted to Puffin were very different.

Then the illustrator, in this case Adam Stower, comes on board and I didn't meet Adam for the whole of the making of the first book. It's structured so that I communicate with the editor, she communicates with the designer (who also works at the publishers) and the designer then communicates with the illustrator. The illustrator draws the pictures of the characters and we all have a look at them and decide whether they look like what we thought the people would look like. Then Adam does 'roughs' of the scenes. We decide which words go on which pages and which scenes he should illustrate. Then Adam goes away and paints them and then you have a finished book.

TS: So, do you decide in your head how it should look when you're writing it?

TK: No, I had no conception of how it was going to look. I think if [the writer] does, then he's on a hiding to nothing. If you can see it, then you should draw it. Up to that point, I'd written song lyrics and plays, things where I'm in collaboration with somebody. If you write a play that can only be played by one actor and that actor isn't available, what are you going to do? So, while I'm writing the words, I leave a space for somebody else to come along and do something else – I collaborate. If you're lucky, the sum of what you do will be better than what you did on your own and it is usually much, much better than you have imagined. So it's leaving a space for the visuals and the design. It's like writing a screenplay for a film. Rather than being the director, you write the screenplay and then someone else comes in and casts it. Things can go horribly wrong with films of course and they can be miscast but that hasn't happened to me so far, so I'm relieved about that!

TS: The *Mungo* books seem to be inspired variously by other media, such as film (*Mungo and the Dinosaur Island*) and comic books (*Mungo and the Spiders from Space*). Was this a conscious decision?

TK: I had to define the different worlds which Mungo enters as strongly as I possibly could – part of that's in the design of the books. The whole *Spiders from Space* comic book thing wasn't my idea; it emerged during the whole process of putting it together. We had to make it different from other picture books. Also it was partly that there were so many words in it, the only way to get all these scenes in was to put them in little frames and therefore it became a comic.

TS: Finally, what are your favourite books, films and television programmes?

TK: Books: *Where the Wild Things Are* by Maurice Sendak, and *Zeralda's Ogre* by Tomi Ungerer.

Films: The Pixar movies, *Star Wars*, *The Man Who Would be King* and the new *James Bond* films.

Television programme: *The Wire*.

Interview with Adam Stower

Adam Stower has been an artist and illustrator for over eighteen years. In addition to his extensive work illustrating books for children of all ages, he is the artist of the *Mungo* series of picture books and the creator of *Slam!* and *Two Left Feet*. Here, he talks about how he works with the writer to create a picture book and how his illustrative art differs from his picture book art.

TS: How did you become an artist?

AS: I've always loved drawing ever since I was a kid. I've always done it. My first published work was for my school magazine when I was nine and then later on in the student newspaper. My first public published work was some cartoons for posters when I was fifteen. I didn't do Art A-Level, but I was lucky enough to get on to a foundation course in Cambridge, which I was very pleased about because it set me on the path. I went on to do a BA Honours at Norwich in graphic design and illustration and then came to Brighton to do an MA in narrative illustration. I've been illustrating professionally for eighteen years.

TS: Which artists and illustrators inspired you?

AS: I remember books like a wonderful version of *The Sorcerer's Apprentice* by Barbara Hazen and Tomi Ungerer, Richard Scarry's work and the *Asterix* and *Tintin* books. Also Maurice Sendak (*In the Night Kitchen* in particular), as well as Raymond Briggs's *Fungus the Bogeyman*. There's also a great book called *Captain Slaughterboard Drops Anchor* by Mervyn Peake. These books all had great characters and detail – I used to pore over them a lot and I include lots of detail in my work now. During college I became aware of classics by people such as Heath Robinson and Arthur Rackham – they had a great impact on me. I am also a big fan of Chris Riddell – he's a big influence on my work.

TS: How did you become involved with the *Mungo* books?

AS: I was approached by [publishers] Puffin with the written text for *Mungo and the Picture*

Book Pirates and I really liked it. I didn't actually meet Tim [Knapman, the writer] throughout working on the first book – it wasn't until the second book that we met. I loved his written text, particularly the conceptual aspect of characters leaving their tale and book and the planned narrative getting changed. I'd explored those themes in my MA project, so that was something that really excited me.

TS: Can you tell me about the process of creating a *Mungo* book from start to finish?

AS: I am provided with a written text and often this version will be slightly changed afterwards because the illustrations take over some part of the job of describing things. I will do some character studies of the main characters, which get sent back to the publisher and the author. Once those are established, I go to thumbnail drawings – very rough, loose sketches to show which parts of the text to put on the pages. This helps with where the page turns should go, which should add tension and surprises to the book. After that, I go to full-size roughs, where I draw it out in greater detail and the designer will drop the written text into the rough pictures, so we can see that there is plenty of space left. You actually have to leave more space than you think you'll need because of foreign editions – some languages tend to use more words than English. Once that has been approved, you go to final artwork. It's quite lengthy – like creative tennis! On average, it takes about a year (while I'm working on other projects). A painting for a double page would take about four days on average.

TS: The *Mungo* books show him jumping into books. How did you decide to represent this process through art?

AS: It was something I had experimented with on my MA. We had to come up with visual devices to separate the different places where the narrative takes Mungo: there's Mungo in his reality, then we have the reality of us sharing reading the book with Mungo and then him jumping into the story. When I was showing Mungo sharing the book with us, I used a *trompe l'oeil* effect around the edges where I gave the impression of several tatty pages. But when he jumps into the story, those edges were left out because once he's in the book, it becomes his reality. Each one has been exciting – the story structure is essentially the same but the detail changes. It's challenging to keep a sense of constancy but keep it looking fresh and interesting.

TS: How does your illustrative work differ from your picture book work? Do you feel more of a sense of narrative responsibility with picture book work?

AS: Yes, I definitely do. I do illustrative work for fiction for slightly older children and because there's much more text in those, the weight of responsibility of describing everything isn't so much on the illustrations. In picture books, there's much more responsibility on the illustrator to describe things because you want to minimise the text if you can. It's nice – it allows the text the freedom to focus on the story and the illustrations can take the burden of describing the characters and the world off of the text, because you can just see it. Picture books are unique because you can really use the pictures and the text together or you can use them in contradiction. The pictures definitely have equal weight with the text – I don't think either should be dominant. They benefit from one another – it's symbiotic.

TS: The style of the *Mungo* books' artwork changes depending on the genre of the book he is reading. How does genre impact on your artwork?

AS: In a variety of different ways I think. With the dinosaur adventure, I was thinking of the old King Kong movies from the 1930s and 40s and with *The Spiders from Space* it was very much late 40s, early 50s comics – early sci-fi fantasy with jumpsuits and moustaches and Brylcreemed hair. The rocket ship, Vroom 101, was based on all those American 1950s cars – the bullet lights and the chrome and its open top as well. For the *Pirates* story, I used the old classic adventure tales. They always have a certain look – they use certain colours for things: golden clouds and seascapes. You just have fun with all these things really and I also really enjoy costume – dressing my characters up. It's fun setting things in slightly different times and environments and with Mungo jumping in and out of different storybooks, that's one way we kept it fresh.

TS: The second book, *Mungo and the Spiders from Space* adopts the style of a comic book in certain places. What was it like using this format?

AS: I used 1940s and 1950s comics as an inspiration. They had a certain palette – pinky reds and yellows and mauves. I've noticed that in a lot of picture books, there's more of a graphic novel aspect coming into them and into younger children's books. I think people are starting to cotton on that children have a much more sophisticated understanding of graphic representation than they are given credit for. The challenge we had was that comic books are designed to be read on your own but our book also needed to be able to be read aloud to a child. For instance, when it came to a speech bubble, I'd have to put some sort of exclamation inside it and then next to it, we'd have to write 'said Captain Galacticus'. So it was sort of combining picture books and comic books and that was one of the challenges – making it all flow. When Mungo was actually within the comic book world, I wanted to illustrate a world where there were these speech bubbles with text in – 3D panels which would float about and cast shadows. I wanted to show that if you went to that world, the features of the comic book such as speech bubbles would be there, like physical entities. That is another visual device to separate the worlds, to try and avoid confusion.

TS: What are your favourite books, films and television programmes?

AS: Book: *The Code of the Woosters* by P.G. Wodehouse.

Films: *Play It Again, Sam, The Incredibles* and *Belleville Rendez-Vous*

Television programmes: *Battlestar Galactica, Black Books* and *Jeeves and Wooster.*

2.2

Picture Books
Teaching Ideas

The following sessions aim to help pupils develop their responses to picture books in terms of both the visual and the narrative aspects of the medium. The sessions can be taught individually or as part of a longer programme. The activities in this section are aimed at Year 2, but can be adapted for any age group. For further extension ideas and resources, see Chapter 2.3.

Speaking and listening: *Mungo and the Picture Book Pirates*

Learning objectives
- To explore a picture book text, noticing and commenting on how the pictures tell the story as well as the words
- To use the book as the basis for their own imaginative verbal description
- To describe and explain the plot, characters and visual elements of books they have read as a class and on their own.

Resources
- Book: *Mungo and the Picture Book Pirates* by Timothy Knapman and Adam Stower
- A piece of A3 paper
- A selection of the most popular picture books and reading books in the class.

- Introduce the book *Mungo and the Picture Book Pirates* to the children, asking them what they think the book might be about and who might be in it from the illustration on the front.
- Read the story, encouraging the children to answer questions which require them to look closely at the pictures:

- On p. 1 ('This is Mungo'), how can we tell Mungo likes pirates?
- On pp. 4 and 5 ('Once upon a time'), how would you describe Barnacle Bill?
- Direct the children's attention to the edges of the pages of the book (pp. 4–10). Why has the artist drawn yellow pages at the sides? Here, Adam Stower has painted the edges of the pages in Mungo's book. Some children may understand that this is to show that Mungo is reading a book.
- On p. 8 ('Captain Horatio Fleet'), why are the words 'DARING' 'DASHING' and 'DAZZLING' bigger than others?
- On pp. 18 and 19 ('Head over heels'), why are the sentences in curvy lines?
- Do you think the story was a dream? Here, you can make links with the ending of *Where the Wild Things Are*.
- On pp. 28 and 29 ('When Mungo's mum came back'), what do you notice? The evidence on the page (Captain Fleet's sopping footprints, the bird feathers and Mungo's medal) implies that the adventure really happened but children can, as always, decide for themselves.

- Go back to p. 17 ('"Oh, Christopher Columbus!" cried Mungo') to show Mungo leaping into the book. Ask the children to think about a book they would like to jump into.
- Ask the children to go and choose a book of their own or from the class reading resources (one which they are familiar with) and ask them to sit in a circle, with the books hidden behind their backs. Explain to them that they are going to imagine that they can jump into a book like Mungo did. The children do not have to have a physical copy of the book each – some may wish to choose the same book, for example, and some may know their favourite book so well that they do not need to bring it.
- Place the piece of A3 paper (folded like a book) in the centre of the circle and tell them that when they jump 'into' the magic book, they can imagine that they have entered their chosen book. The child in the centre then has to imagine and describe what they can see and the other children have to guess which book they are in. It might be useful to model it yourself first by jumping onto the piece of paper and giving a short description such as 'I can see a jungle' then pause to allow children to guess. Then give another sentence: 'There are large creatures there with animals' bodies' and so on (*Where the Wild Things Are*).
- Try to give all the children a turn at jumping into the magic book in the centre. You can deepen the level of response by questioning the children and encouraging them to really describe their surroundings.

Reading and continuing the story: *Mungo and the Spiders from Space*

Learning objectives

- To explore the picture book medium and understand the ways in which it combines pictures and words to tell a story
- To read the first part of a story, then predict, plan and create a suitable ending
- To continue a story using the appropriate features of its textual form.

Resources

- Books: *Mungo and the Picture Book Pirates* and *Mungo and the Spiders from Space* by Timothy Knapman and Adam Stower
- A4 paper (torn down the right hand side to resemble the page torn from Mungo's book on p. 15 of *Mungo and the Spiders from Space*).

- In preparation, read *Mungo and the Picture Book Pirates* to the children a few days beforehand, so that they understand the plot device of Mungo having to jump into the book and save the day. This could form part of a week's focus on authors Timothy Knapman and Adam Stower where you can look at the *Mungo* series and other books they have written/illustrated separately.
- The day before the activity, ask the children to verbally retell the plot of *Mungo and the Picture Book Pirates* (directing their attention to the aspect of the plot where Mungo leaps into the book). Read the children the sequel, *Mungo and the Spiders from Space*, taking time to look at the detailed illustrations and consider some of the different features of this text such as:
  - Speech bubbles ('"We've hit something!" said Captain Galacticus' on p. 7)
  - Panels (such as the 'Story so far' section on p. 5)
  - Narrative boxes ('And this is the story it tells' on p. 4)
  - The onomatopoeia ('Ba-doink!', p. 7).
- Ask the children what each of these things does – especially the speech bubbles and the onomatopoeia. Ask the children where they might have seen features such as these before (in a comic book).
- You may wish to ask some of the children to take on the parts of Captain Galacticus and Gizmo and ask them to say the parts in the speech bubbles aloud.
- When you reach p. 15 ('The last page was missing!'), stop reading (ensuring you have covered over the facing page (p. 16) with a piece of paper or card) and show the

children that the page has been 'torn out'. Ask the children for their initial responses to the story and to predict what will happen next (in pairs/talk partners). Some of the children may suggest that Mungo will enter the book so focus on these responses more and make links to the previous *Mungo* book. Then, if possible, ask the children to go home and think overnight about what will happen next in the story.

- The next day reread the story to p. 15 and then have a brief discussion of the children's ideas.

- Show them the pages of A4 paper with the right-hand side torn away (if possible try to make it resemble the jagged edges of Stower's illustration on p. 15) and tell the children that they have to finish the missing page and complete the story.

- The A4 page should have two horizontal lines on it, dividing it into three equal-sized rectangles. Show the children how each can be used as a panel to tell three steps of the story from top to bottom, similar to p. 13 (for a simpler version of this activity, just provide the children with a blank piece of A4 so that they only have to draw one large image). The children should be encouraged to use one or two written sentences (or speech bubbles) to accompany their pictures, but some children may find it easier to just use pictures.

- When the children have finished their pages, ask them to come up and align their page with the jagged tears on p. 15 and describe to the rest of the class how they finished the story. Some children will have used Mungo in their story but they do not, of course, have to.

- Read the rest of the story, emphasising that it is only one way of continuing the narrative, not necessarily the only way. Compare Timothy Knapman and Adam Stower's ending to the children's own ones and encourage them to comment on the different versions. The torn-out pages can also make a superb display afterwards.

Figure 2.2 Work by Darcie

Figure 2.3 Work by Thomas

Figure 2.4 Work by Macie

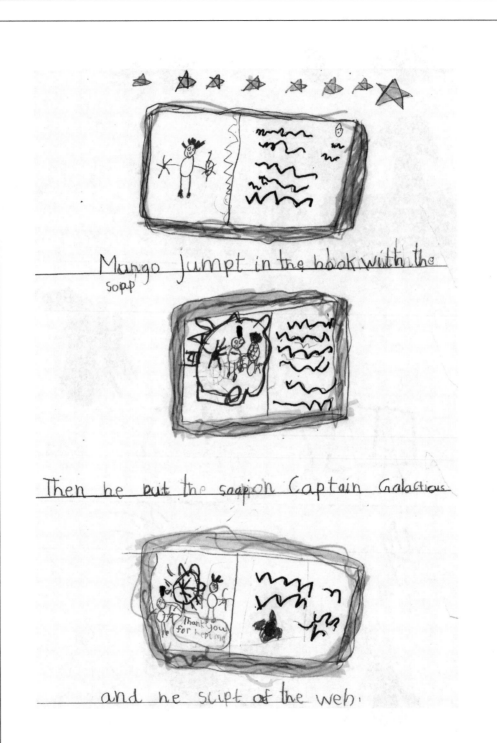

Figure 2.5 Work by Kavleen

Figure 2.6 Work by Kwame

Constructing a story: the *Mungo* series

Learning objectives

- To use an existing narrative as a model for a new and original story
- To combine pictures and words to tell a story
- To consider the effects of the visual aspects and layout of a text on its audience
- To select appropriate and interesting words and pictures to tell a story
- To use word-processing software to create stories.

Resources

- Book: *Mungo and the Dinosaur Island* by Timothy Knapman and Adam Stower
- A selection of classroom picture books
- Computer word-processing software.

- Read the third Mungo adventure, *Mungo and the Dinosaur Island*, to the children. Take time to discuss the features which make it different from a prose text, such as:
  - The 'WANTED' poster on p. 4
  - The film cell comic on p. 6
  - The panels on p. 8
  - The onomatopoeia and the curving sentences on pp. 13 and 14.
- Ask the children why the author and artist have included these things – try to encourage them to view the visual flourishes as deliberate and adding to the feel of the story for the reader.
- Tying in to the two previous sessions (where children imagined themselves jumping into a favourite book and also completing one of the *Mungo* books), ask the children to think about one of their favourite picture books and imagine entering its pages. If some children find this difficult, you may wish to limit their choice to one book which the class have read recently so that the children will not struggle to think of a suitable text. Some good examples are *Where the Wild Things Are* by Maurice Sendak, *Not a Box* by Antoinette Portis, *Elmer* by David McKee and *Wombat Goes Walkabout* by Michael Morpurgo and Christian Birmingham.
- Tell the children that they are going to try to write and illustrate a two- or three-page picture book showing what happened when they jumped into their favourite picture book.
- On the board and using the *Mungo* book, suggest some different ways in which they might make their pages visually interesting. For example, if they were to jump into the book *Elmer*, there might be a sentence curved into the shape of Elmer's trunk such as 'Ben slid down Elmer's trunk and landed with a SPLAT in the coloured berries'.

- Children first need to decide on their picture book and then use it to plan out their page. They can draw the pictures, colour them and then decide where the text needs to go. They could type out their text on the computer and print it off so that they are able to cut it up into individual words and play with the shape of the sentences on their illustrated page. This also makes the finished work look more like a page from a book.

- Encourage the children to make the finished page visually interesting but not overly complex and to play with the layout and text in different ways (even if the book they are jumping into has a regular sentence format). This will take some planning and may not necessarily be finished in one session.

- The children can show their pages to the rest of the class. Comment on the visual aspects of the work and question the children as to why they have made the decisions they have in the design – prompting an awareness of reader.

- The work can be displayed on a board or made into individual picture books to give the children a sense of authorship.

CHAPTER

2.3

Picture Books

Further Ideas and Resources

These lists of resources and ideas for activities supplement the teaching ideas in Chapter 2.2 and offer suggestions for teaching picture book-based activities with other age groups.

Drama activities based on picture books

Drama is an effective medium through which to explore picture books with any age group due to the fact that both tell stories in part through visuals. If children are taught to appreciate the complexity and sophistication of the best picture books, even older pupils will accept that they can be the basis for some challenging work in Literacy and Drama sessions.

Key Stage One

Antoinette Portis's *Not a Box*, which shows how an ordinary box can be turned into something more through the power of imagination, is an excellent way in to Drama for a Reception or Year 1 class.

- Read the book with the class and talk about all the different things which the rabbit turns the box into. In the hall, with the children sitting in a large circle, put a large cardboard box in the centre and ask the children to come forward and mime using the box as something else (for example, a car, a house or a dog). Model the first few examples yourself so that the children get the idea.
- If the children are able to work independently in groups, divide the class into groups of four and provide each group with a similar cardboard box. Ask them to devise a short piece of drama based around the box. They may wish to show the box as a car or as a spaceship. This activity will hopefully begin to develop children's imaginative play into a Drama session without over-formalising it. The children can show their piece back should they wish to, at which point you can praise elements of each piece.
- In a follow-up session using the same text, ask the children to draw a picture illustrating how they used the box. The children can use Antoinette Portis's illustrations as a model, showing the box in black and the imaginary changes to it in red. On the computer, type

a sentence for each child's picture in the style of the book: 'It's not a box! It's a...' and then put this sentence on the bottom of each child's illustration. You can then compile a class version of the picture book to display.

Key Stage Two

- Discuss the idea of making a living picture book with the class (your class will need to be accustomed to Drama work in terms of body language, facial expression and improvisation). Show them some examples of picture books which have counter-narratives (where the words and images contradict one another or tell different stories). Some good examples of these are *Rosie's Walk* by Pat Hutchins and *Gorilla* by Anthony Browne. If these are introduced to the children on the basis of how the pictures and the written text construct different narratives, older pupils will see that the texts are certainly not childish.

- Ask the children, in fours, to discuss and plan a simple picture book in which the pictures and the words are giving different messages. If the children find this difficult, it may help to give them the basic premise of the story. For example, a family party where the sentences state that everyone is having fun and getting along, while the pictures show disagreements and feuds. Ask the children to sketch stick-figure versions of the pictures and write the sentences underneath. Three or four pictures will suffice.

- Using these picture book plans, ask the children to devise three tableaux recreations of the 'pages' for their picture book in their groups of four. As each group re-enacts its three pages from the book, one of the group can read out the sentence that accompanies each picture. For example, one of the children reads a sentence such as 'The family all got on with each other very well' and then the group creates a tableau showing the family in the middle of an argument. An activity such as this can help older children understand how to contrast words with images to create a message and an ironic tone in a visual narrative.

More Drama activities

Picture books can also form a simple introduction to Drama skills by being used as the basis for tableaux. Children can take a favourite picture book with them into a Drama session and, individually or in groups, recreate pages from them. These can then be photographed and displayed with the text underneath them to make a version of the picture book featuring the children. This serves as a good introduction to Drama work because the children become accustomed to using their bodies and faces imaginatively but are provided with a stimulus so that they do not have to invent a narrative immediately. After recreating picture books, the work can be developed by asking children to extend the story by devising a short sequel to the picture book and improvising an original piece of storytelling.

Creating picture books

Even a Year 6 class can benefit from working with picture books if they are presented in the right way. As with the Drama sessions, if older children are introduced to complex picture books which deal with mature themes or have a sophisticated narrative structure, they will be able to develop their understanding of literary concepts such as parody, irony and a sense of audience. You may wish to ask children to plan and create their own picture books with the requirement that their work should tell the story through a combination of words and pictures and that it should show an understanding of counter-narrative. This is a somewhat challenging task and will require a solid understanding of how texts are structured and operate effectively. If the book they create is focused around a more mature subject (such as Emily Gravett's *Little Mouse's Big Book of Fears* which explores phobias), children can develop their ability to write for a specific audience by considering how to present such material for younger children. The following picture books and illustrated storybooks are, due to their contents, structures and narratives, especially appropriate for children at Key Stages One and Two. They can be used as the starting points for Drama work and as models of well-constructed texts which will sustain further analysis:

Key Stage One

Not a Box by Antoinette Portis
Not a Stick by Antoinette Portis
Lost and Found by Oliver Jeffers
Guess What I Found in Dragon Wood by Timothy Knapman and Gwen Millward
The Night Pirates by Peter Harris and Deborah Allwright
Little Boat by Thomas Docherty
The Incredible Book Eating Boy by Oliver Jeffers
Rosie's Walk by Pat Hutchins
Penny and Pup by Linda Jennings and Jane Chapman
Little Ogre's Surprise Supper by Timothy Knapman and Ben Cort

Key Stage Two

Wombat Goes Walkabout by Michael Morpurgo and Christian Birmingham
Diary of a Wombat by Jackie French and Bruce Whatley
Seal Surfer by Michael Foreman
It's a Secret! by John Burningham
Gorilla by Anthony Browne
Little Mouse's Big Book of Fears by Emily Gravett
The Great Paper Caper by Oliver Jeffers
The Lost Thing by Shaun Tan

Notes

1 Sales of picture books and consequently the number of new picture books published in Britain have, in fact, declined over recent years. Madelyn Travis (2008) cites the fall in demand from libraries and overseas markets as reasons for this decline. In order to tackle this problem, the Big Picture campaign was set up (www.bigpicture.org.uk).

2 See interview with Timothy Knapman later in this chapter.

3 See the following interview with Timothy Knapman.

4 Captain Jack Sparrow is a pirate played by Johnny Depp in the *Pirates of the Caribbean* (2003) film trilogy. The films were phenomenally successful across the world, reigniting interest in the concept of pirates and taking over $2.5 billion at cinemas (IMDb 2009). Depp earned an Oscar nomination for his incredible performance.

5 Luigi Pirandello is the writer of a play entitled *Six Characters in Search of an Author*, in which characters from an unfinished story seek help to finish the tale they are part of. The play deals with postmodern ideas such as a self-referential analysis of the playwriting process.

6 *Monty Python's Flying Circus* is a British television comedy series famous for innovatively playing with the format of traditional comedy sketches and radically disrupting established forms of television comedy in the late 1960s and early 1970s.

7 In *Mungo and the Spiders from Space*, Captain Galacticus's spaceship is named Vroom-101 (in a reference to Room 101 in George Orwell's *Nineteen Eighty-Four*). We are also told that the villainous Dr Frankenstinker's 'shocking behaviour was blamed on a nasty case of asteroids he'd had when he was small' as Adam Stower's illustration shows him clutching a tube of haemorrhoid cream (Knapman and Stower 2007: 10).

8 The 'rabbit hole' is the means by which Alice journeys into Wonderland in Lewis Carroll's *Alice's Adventures in Wonderland*. The idea of a child travelling into a faraway magical world is now an established trope of children's literature.

3.1

Comic Books

The rise of the comic book

It is an exciting time for comic books. To say that this literary form is beginning to move out of its specialist niche and step, blinking, into the sunshine of the mainstream is not merely wishful thinking on the part of comic book readers. The medium as a whole has always struggled to be accepted as a respectable part of Britain's artistic culture and is often characterised as the *enfant terrible* of literature, the mischievous and somewhat immature younger sibling of the novel. Yet in recent years, there have been subtle yet undeniable indicators of a surge in the popularity of comic books and graphic novels in both Britain and America and sales figures reflect this.[1] André Breedt, a representative for Nielsen BookScan, a book-sales data organisation, identifies Manga (Japanese comic books) and graphic novels as the literary market's 'most spectacular area of growth in recent years', adding the impressive statistic that recently 'sales have increased by almost 100 per cent year-on-year' (cited in Brown 2009: 11). Elsewhere, the demand for comic book characters and stories is also evident, albeit in different media forms. In 2008, the biggest film worldwide was Christopher Nolan's Batman adaptation *The Dark Knight* (which took over $1 billion), and Jon Favreau's *Iron Man*, based on the Marvel comic, was also one of the ten biggest films of the year (Box Office Mojo 2009a).[2] Evidence of the increasing popularity of the comic book, however, is more than just pecuniary. Recently, the School Library Association published the latest in its series of recommended reading for boys. Subtitled *Boys into Books*, the lists of titles are divided into age-differentiated sections such as 5–11 and 11–14. The author of the former, Chris Brown, recognises that 'pictures are important', noting that they 'often add far more to the information than is relayed by the words alone' and later goes on to identify comics as a valuable medium, criticising snobbish attitudes towards them. While both Brown's list and the 11–14 version do include some graphic novels and recommend that picture books can and should be read by older children, neither list is ideal. Brown's acknowledgement of the popularity of comic books and their 'ever-eager readership' is not truly reflected in the list, where the titles which are comics in the purest sense of the word in fact constitute only a tiny proportion of the recommended reading (2008: 11–12). In addition, many of the comic books selected (such as *Artemis Fowl: The Graphic Novel* and *Point Blanc: The Graphic Novel*), while good quality, are adaptations of existing novels, not original stories, which seems to imply that comic books are only really to be used as vehicles to retell prose narratives. Another negative aspect of the lists is their stubborn and unhelpful gender assumptions when there is absolutely no reason why comic books cannot be enjoyed by girls as well as boys. To be fair, the School Library Association has not yet published a corresponding publication for girls, but the boys' lists do reinforce the traditional view that comics are primarily for males. Of course, it is easy to criticise the *Boys into Books* project but it should be reiterated that any officially sanctioned document which shows even a minute awareness of the existence of comic books, let alone promotes their use, is certainly a positive thing. The publication can only be considered a step in the right direction by those who recognise the potential which comic books have for literacy work.

Perhaps the most significant educational change in terms of comic books has been the introduction of the renewed *Primary Framework for Literacy* in 2006. At Key Stage Two, it is a pleasant surprise to find that the framework suggests that teachers use comics and even correctly identifies them as 'texts', although there are some missed opportunities evident here. Surely the unit exploring 'Stories set in imaginary worlds' (Year 4, Narrative Unit 2), for example, would benefit from close exploration of science-fiction or fantasy comic books in addition to, or even perhaps instead of, the 'photo-editing software' which is suggested? At Key Stage One, the framework is more reticent to promote the use of comic books directly, although it is unclear why. Perhaps it is because comic books are considered too complex for this age group, although anyone who has watched even the youngest child read a comic would be able to argue the opposite. Similarly, comic books might have been considered too much of a distraction from the task of teaching pupils how to read and construct more traditional, written narratives. If this is the case, however, why then are teachers advised to show Year 1 pupils 'film version[s] of a familiar traditional tale'? In fact, the Year 1 and 2 units do provide some excellent opportunities to explore comic book modes of storytelling by consistently linking narrative with visuals even if the medium itself is not explicitly mentioned. According to the framework, opportunities should be given to Key Stage One pupils to tell a story through 'a sequence of pictures', 'use a sequence of photos' to help plan a story (Year 1, Narrative Unit 1) and 'create a digital text combining words, images and sounds' (Year 2, Narrative Unit 2) (Department for Children, Schools and Families 2008). It is somewhat frustrating to see that the opportunity to explore the comic book form is hinted at but not fully followed through, especially as we may well be able to combat cultural prejudice against comics if children at an early age see how sophisticated and interesting these texts can be. On the plus side, however, at least the framework leaves teachers some room to incorporate comic book-based activities (such as the ones featured in the next section) into their literacy teaching. By adapting and extending the storyboard and picture-sequencing work, children can be introduced to the ways in which comics tell stories and transmit information. The signs suggest, then, that the framework is finally beginning to recognise something which comic fans have always understood: comics are a valid art form in their own right and can be as sophisticated and satisfying a reading experience as any other form of literature.

Technical aspects of comics

The unique and often complex ways in which a comic book can tell its story are deserving of closer examination. We may assume that children have knowledge and prior experience of reading comics but this is not necessarily true and, even if they have, it is still vital that we take the time to ensure that they fully understand the technical aspects of comic book narratives. This section discusses some of the central elements of comic books and how they operate.

Panels

Panels are to comics what prose is to the novel. They are the fundamental building blocks of the text, the static images which tell the story through their sequencing. They usually take the form of vertical or horizontal rectangles but can also be square, circular or any shape imaginable and, in all but the most basic comic texts, are liable to change shape over the course of the comic or even over the course of a page. Each panel is read as a complete, self-contained image, usually forming part of a row which we read across the page from left to right, before moving down to the row immediately underneath. The most exciting and liberating aspect of panels, however, is that writers and artists may choose to vary the traditional format and change layouts from page to page, so that even the most experienced readers have to pay careful attention in order to work out the correct sequence. Previously, I linked panel sequencing with the critical theory of structuralism (Stafford 2009) and I wish to expand upon this here. Structuralist theorists attempt to understand and derive meaning from any given utterance or act of speech by placing it within the wider context of language as a whole, thereby imbuing this individual example of language (termed the *parole*) with meaning and allowing us to understand it more effectively due to the fact that we are able to position it within a wider spectrum (the *langue*) (Barry 2002). We can apply this theory to the comic book panel. Here, the meaning of any individual panel (*parole*) is dependent on its position within the sequence of panels in which it appears (*langue*). While this is true of any panel, it is particularly true of a panel which contains images but no speech bubbles. Figure 3.1 demonstrates the inter-panel relationship. The sequence, comprising four panels, shows a woman pouring a drink, which is then revealed through close-up to be poison. She later hands the drink to another woman who is unaware of its contents, after which the sequence concludes with the poisoner cruelly thinking 'Cheers!' While the sequence's narrative is quite clear, the tone, plot and characterisation can be drastically changed by simply removing one panel. If the second panel with its close-up of the poison were to be removed, the sequence would become an innocuous story about a woman pouring a drink for another and our whole understanding of the remaining panels would be changed on a fundamental level. This is particularly true of the final panel. Depending on whether or not the second panel is included in the sequence, we will read the facial expression and the thought bubble depicted in panel four in radically different ways. If we know that the woman is intending to poison

Figure 3.1 A four-panel comic narrative

someone, we read her smile as disingenuous, sinister and cruel and her 'Cheers!' as being bitterly ironic. If, however, we have not seen the second panel, we have no reason to assume that the woman is being anything but friendly and welcoming. Of course, what is significant here is that the final panel is identical in both versions of the story – it is only our perception and interpretation of it which has changed. Therefore, through the inclusion or removal of a single panel, the text is radically altered in terms of its narrative (from a tale of attempted murder to a simple meeting between friends), its genre (changing from a sinister thriller to a light drama or even, perhaps, a social comedy) and its characters (the woman in white has changed from a deceitful villain into a diligent hostess). Panels, therefore, are not simply a neutral technical feature of the narrative. The way in which they are ordered and structured is absolutely crucial to our understanding of the text as a whole and they are often inextricably linked with the tone and emotional effects of the story. For example, if the pace of the story is frantic and exciting, the panels, like sentences in a book, might be small and numerous, showing a number of images which the reader can scan quickly to create an impression of speed and action. Conversely, a scene which requires a more sombre tone might employ fewer panels but make each one larger, forcing the reader to spend longer looking at each and thereby slowing down the pace of the narrative. In addition, the shape of the panel can create its own feeling. A moment of particular violence or aggression may be depicted within a jagged frame evoking an explosion or broken glass, whereas a gentler image may be contained by a softer, curved and less rigid line. Similarly, the power and strength of characters such as superheroes can be reinforced when artists depict them transgressing the boundary of the frame around them, as if the panel has failed to contain them. Comics expert Will Eisner terms these variations in framing 'the "language" of the panel border' (2001: 44).

Speech balloons, narrative boxes and sound effects

Comics show speech by depicting the words coming out of a character's mouth contained in what are commonly known as speech balloons or speech bubbles. These are one of the fundamental elements of comics and one which the majority of readers understand from even an early age. The understanding that speech balloons represent spoken dialogue is not to be taken for granted, however. In a visual medium such as the comic book, it shows quite a sophisticated level of understanding in children who can quickly ascertain that while the other icons in the picture are supposed to be actual 'real' visible elements within the world depicted (for example, a dog), the speech balloons and the words within them are not and are in fact merely representing what can be *heard*, not *seen*. Like panels, speech balloons can vary in appearance so that extra information can be provided for the reader. A jagged balloon outline could imply a loud noise or a jarring screech and a large or small font size within the balloon often tells us if the character is shouting or whispering. In the Marvel comic *The Ultimates*, the stereotypical square-jawed hero Captain America is depicted in one panel leading the charge into battle. As he yells at his troops: 'What are you waiting for, ladies? Christmas?', the final word breaks out of the confines of the oval speech balloon and is in a different font which is twice the size of the other words, showing not only that he is yelling but also emphasising the strength and power of the superhero – he is so dynamic that even his words cannot be contained! In addition, the white speech bubble has a red surround which, combined with the fact that 'Christmas' is in big blue letters, links the dialogue with the red, white and blue of Captain America's patriotic, flag-based uniform and suggests that this hero is fighting for his country (Millar *et al.* 2002: 15). Therefore, speech balloons can provide us with character information as well as reporting dialogue. Another popular technique is to make the speech balloons jagged when showing dialogue spoken through a radio or telephone (as seen in Derek Watson and Kit Wallis's *Wonderland*). Here, the jagged lines of the balloon visually represent the static and crackly sound quality of the radio (Watson and Wallis 2004: 19).

Another related feature of comics is the thought balloon. This is like the speech balloon but instead shows what a character is thinking – their inner monologue. Traditionally these are demarcated by a bumpy, cloud-like shape to the balloon, as opposed to the usually smooth line of the speech balloon. In contemporary comics that are aimed at a more mature audience, writers and artists have tended to employ thought balloons less and they are now something of an outdated convention. The thoughts of the protagonist Sarah in *Wonderland*, for example, are shown in rectangular boxes which are placed in the corners of panels and do not float above the character's head, stylishly giving the impression of a 'voice-over' narration because the boxes are not explicitly visually linked to Sarah. Having said this, children, however, are almost always able to identify thought balloons which proves that they are still used widely in children's comics and that they are another convention which we should discuss with children.

Another way in which written text is used in comics is through what I term narrative boxes. These are the small rectangular boxes which appear in the corners of panels to help provide extra information which the dialogue or thoughts of the characters cannot. They might be used to show where the scene is set (for example, 'London') or the time – especially if the story is telling a flashback to many years before. A stereotypical example of a narrative box would be 'Meanwhile' or 'Later'. Again, these have tended to fall out of favour as a modern comic book convention and many writers, such as Derek Watson in the above example, conflate the thought bubble with the narrative box to make a more sophisticated hybrid of the two.

A final, but important, combination of words and pictures in comic books is the sound effect. Again, comic readers quickly learn that the often large and colourful examples of ono-matopoeia splashed across panels are not supposed to be objects which are visible to the characters in the story but are ways in which the writer and artist compensate for the fact that comics, unlike films, have no aural element. The most obvious example of this would be the 'POW!' of a punch or the 'CRASH!' of glass breaking. However, far from simply being a humorous or stereotypical part of comic aesthetics, the sound words often constitute extremely creative and novel ways of representing specific noises. *Wonderland* shows the readers that soil is being dug out from a tunnel with 'SKRITCH' and drugged darts hit an elephant's ear with a 'THWAP' (Watson and Wallis 2004: 45). It is also interesting to note here that the better comics tend to use onomatopoeia sparingly, thereby increasing its effectiveness.

Interview with Christian Slade

Christian Slade is a writer, artist and illustrator. He writes and draws the *Korgi* graphic novels, which tell of the adventures of a young girl called Ivy and her beloved compan-ion, a Corgi dog called Sprout, in a magical realm. Here, Christian talks about the chal-lenges of telling a story using images only and the similarities between comic books and animated films.

TS: Approximately how long does it take you to finish a page of *Korgi*?

CS: First I sketch out the whole book in small drawings called thumbnails. This can take a few weeks. Next I move to final art in which I average about a page a day. I usually have anywhere between three and five pages going at the same time in various stages – more complicated scenes and spreads can take longer. I have worked on some spreads of *Korgi* for weeks. It depends on how complicated the scenes are and how many char-acters are in them.

TS: You have deliberately chosen to tell the story of *Korgi* without using words, which works excellently. Why did you make this decision?

CS: I have always been a fan of 'silent' stories since I was a kid. It probably goes back to an early appreciation for animated films which tell their story in a visual language first. Another reason, which is very simple, is that I did write out dialogue and some text boxes, but I had a hard time deciding on what font to use and where to place the text. My original vision for the books was to have them wordless so I removed all the text and I felt that the whole story was still able to be read, so I simply left them out.

TS: What challenges do you face as a storyteller when you decide not to use written text in a comic book? Do you have to compensate for the lack of words in other ways?

CS: Yes, I sometimes have obstacles that I have to overcome by choosing to tell a story with pictures only. For example, *Korgi Book 3*, which I am working on now, has a flashback scene which takes place quite a bit in the past. How do I convey this? The answer was well thought out and we have decided to use a slightly different style of art along with some clever use of panel work which has the reader look through an old book. In *Book 2*, Ivy explains to Lump and Scarlet about how she had her wing shot off. I did it in three panels of pantomime. It is actually very natural for me to tell a wordless story and I find it more liberating than I do challenging.

TS: The pictures in *Korgi* are sumptuous. You do not use colour in your pictures. Why is this?

CS: *Korgi Book 1* was my final thesis project for my MA from Syracuse University in 2005. I was under a tight schedule and so I decided, by keeping the art in black and white, I would be able to focus on the drawing and story and still get the book done in a reasonable amount of time. It also just felt right. By not having any colour or words, I can focus more time on the drawings and the story.

TS: What techniques and materials do you use for your artwork in *Korgi*?

CS: I use Bristol smooth paper and various ink pens and brushes.

TS: The *Korgi* books are an exciting mix of genres such as fantasy and science fiction. Was this a conscious choice or did the story simply develop of its own accord in these areas?

CS: The *Korgi* books and the whole world of *Korgi* is everything I love. Woodland fantasy and science fiction are two of these things, so they set the stage for this tale. Whether it's the way a certain tree grows or a cloud formation moves, or simply the way my dog tilts his head, everything that goes into *Korgi* are the things I love and find interesting.

TS: You have worked for Disney as an animator. How do the mediums of comic books and animated films compare? What are the main similarities and differences?

CS: They are very close at their core and I think that is why I see a lot of crossover in the field. Many animators work in comics and many comic artists draw in animation studios – to me it's all the same: visual sequential storytelling. The biggest difference between them though is that animation is usually much more of a group effort, whereas comics and graphic novels can be done by one or two people. I also find animation very cutting edge in terms of technology and it is a newer medium which utilises motion and music. I don't have a favourite. I love them both!

TS: Sprout, the heroic Corgi, has some wonderful facial expressions throughout both books. How do you strike a balance between expressing recognisable human emotion on his face and yet still ensuring that he looks like a dog?

CS: Sprout is based on my own Welsh Corgis, Penny and Leo. I have drawn these dogs more than anything else and it is second nature to me to act out their expressions. It comes very naturally, yet sometimes it is a big struggle to get the perfect expression for the scene.

TS: What is your favourite film, book and television programme?

CS: Book: The *Harry Potter* series.

    Film: *Star Wars*.

    Television programme: *The Sopranos*.

Figure 3.2 Sprout and Ivy wake up in *Korgi Book 2: The Cosmic Collector*, by Christian Slade

Look closer: film and comic books

If we examine the comic book in terms of the other media we are exploring in this book, it seems natural to consider its specific relation to film. As I stated in the beginning of this chapter, film and comic books are enjoying an increasingly synergistic relationship, the products of which have captured the imagination of many children and adults. Many younger pupils may well encounter characters such as the X-Men, Batman and Tintin through the medium of a cinema or television screen long before they do so in the pages of the comics in which they originated. It is therefore important to consider the nature and history of the relationship between film and comic books. Given the film industry's voracious appetite for material to adapt, it seemed logical that, sooner or later, cinema would turn to the comic book to feed its hunger. Indeed, the two mediums seem to be a perfect marriage. Both are primarily visual in nature, relying on imagery to drive the narrative, but also combining this imagery with additional elements (sound for film and written text for comics). The two mediums are not identical, however. The way in which we watch a film, for example, is arguably more passive than the way in which we read a comic book. In its purest form, a film is designed to play out its story once it has begun and when a scene is finished we cannot immediately revisit it – it has passed us by and (if we are watching the film in a cinema and not on DVD) we are unable to pause or rewind it. In short, the filmmaker determines the pace at which we experience their film and even though we may be intellectually engaged with the work, we are essentially passive observers. Comic books, on the other hand, are like novels, they require us to take an active part in the process by reading the words and panels, which we can do at our own speed. We might choose to read a page in one minute or twenty, skim through in a rush to find out what happens or pore over the page savouring every last pencil line and exclamation mark. In fact, the reading of a comic book is even more of an active process than the reading of a novel. The accepted Western convention of reading text from left to right while moving down the page means that we do not have to think about the order in which we should process the information. Providing we are literate, the reading order is automatically understood by both author and reader. A comic book, on the other hand, is rarely as straightforward. Certainly, there are comics which subscribe to a traditional layout of regularly sized and spaced panels and mimic the reading order of a novel: laid out on single pages, reading each panel in its entirety while moving along the row from left to right and then moving down to the row beneath. However, many comics (particularly in the last twenty years or so) play with this format, alternating single pages of panels with double-page spreads (where the narrative flows left to right across both pages before moving downwards) or perhaps moving the action diagonally across the page from bottom left to top right or even vice versa. A comic book therefore requires a greater degree of audience interactivity than a film does. An additional difference between the two is the time spent with each art form. A 200-page comic book will most likely take longer to read than the two hours required on average to watch a film. We might read such a comic over days or even weeks, inevitably giving ourselves far more time to digest and contemplate the material as we progress through the comic than we would whilst watching a film. My point in stressing these fundamental differences is that we should not necessarily assume that the two media are identical. It is, however, fair to suggest that they are related on at least a basic level.

In theory, filmmakers who adapt a comic for the big screen may find that much of their preparatory design work has already been done for them by the original comic book artwork. The look of the characters and the costumes they wear have already been designed, as have the sets, lighting and overall visual style of the piece. In fact, many 'making of' documentaries reveal that even films which are not based on comics often have their screenplays converted into comic-like storyboards so that the director and camera crew know how to shoot the film. This highlights the similarity between the framing devices of a comic book's panels and that of a camera (and, later, that of the cinema and television screen). Again, to be precise, this is not necessarily an automatic or natural link between comics and film. Early-twentieth-century comic narratives such as Windsor McCay's *Little Nemo* are told mostly through square or long, slim vertical panels, the horizontal rectangular panels reminiscent of a cinema widescreen featuring relatively rarely. Similarly, as the comic book progressed through the decades, even the action-packed Marvel superhero stories of the 1960s and 1970s such as *Captain America* and *Uncanny X-Men* generally kept to the same page layout of square panels with the occasional wide rectangle. This avoidance of the widescreen panel is possibly for practical reasons; while a wide, thin panel is suitable for showing a landscape or an image which needs to depict a number of simultaneous events (for example a battle between two armies), a comic book which has limited pages cannot employ this panel format too often purely because it takes up too much space. In terms of the ratio of plot to panels, a large number of small square panels are more effective in advancing the narrative and delivering as much dialogue and plot to the reader as possible. It is only relatively recently that many comic writers and artists have truly shown evidence of the influence of cinema in the pages of their comic books. Marvel's *Astonishing X-Men* employs cinematic widescreen panels as its primary visual mode of storytelling, meaning that the dialogue is often minimal but giving the comic a somewhat epic feel. This is perhaps due to the fact that Joss Whedon, the writer, comes to the title with a great deal of prior experience in film and television. Similarly *The Ultimates*, a Marvel comic first published in 2001, features cinematic widescreen panels as the rule rather than the exception, reflecting the increasing success that films based on Marvel characters had begun to enjoy worldwide by this point.[3]

Just as many comic book artists and writers have only recently begun to emphasise the visual parallels between comics and film, it is only in the last few years that filmmakers and movie studios have begun to properly realise both the financial and artistic potential of films based on comics. As Matt McAllister argues, 'comic book materials attract a youthful movie-going demographic, appeal to nostalgic older audiences, and offer thrills and well-defined archetype characters' (2006: 110). Accordingly, films such as *Superman* (1978) and its sequel *Superman II* (1980) were huge hits, but it was Tim Burton's *Batman* (1989) and *Batman Returns* (1992) which provided the template for the contemporary superhero film. By presenting his vision of Batman as a terrifying, sinister vigilante and his alter ego Bruce Wayne as a troubled, brooding loner who struggles with his grief for his murdered parents, Burton returned to the noirish roots of the character as created by Bob Kane in the 1930s. With both films, Burton broke the mould for comic book adaptations by rejecting the notion that the hero figure is an untroubled, clean-cut and morally simplistic champion of the people. Here, Batman was a personification of the suppressed darkness and violence of Bruce Wayne's personality, born of depression and a desire for vengeance; a solitary hero who, crucially, had more in common with freakish villains like Catwoman, the Penguin and the Joker than he did with the average citizen. At the conclusion of *Batman Returns*, he acknowledges to Catwoman that 'We're the same, split right down the centre' – the tortured superhero had arrived.

It was not until 2000 that Burton's model was developed further in the form of Bryan Singer's *X-Men*, which took the popular Marvel superhero team created by Stan Lee and Jack Kirby and launched them as a highly successful film franchise. *X-Men*'s central premise, which Singer cleverly exploits, is the idea that rather than gaining special powers through an accident or mishap, a small number of humans are born as 'mutants', whose amazing and sometimes terrifying abilities are realised at puberty. While some of the powers are highly desirable, such as Wolverine's healing factor and the villainous Magneto's ability to control metal, others are viewed as little more than a curse; for example, Rogue's deadly touch means that she is unable to make physical contact with those she loves and Cyclops cannot open his eyes without releasing destructive blasts of energy. The films eschew the traditional comic book fantasy that superpowers are something to be desired and coveted and instead argue that if superpowered beings did exist they would more likely be distrusted and regarded with suspicion, becoming marginalised figures who prowl on the edges of society. *X-Men* and its sequels *X2* and *X-Men: The Last Stand* achieved something which no other comic book movie had done – they politicised superhero characters, demonstrating that the material was capable of offering a sophisticated commentary on relevant, real-world issues.[4] Singer's films intelligently explore this metaphor for individuals who are members of a disenfranchised minority not through choice but simply as a result of their fundamental genetic make-up, establishing powerful links with sexuality, gender and disability and echoing the battles for social acceptance which continue to be fought by groups such as those involved in the gay rights movement. The powerful prologue of *X-Men* breaks new ground for comic book movies with its concentration-camp setting, boldly yet sensitively situating the film's themes of discrimination and intolerance against the background of the Holocaust. As we watch Erik Lensherr, a young Jewish boy who will ironically later grow up to become the Fascist mutant leader Magneto, being separated from his parents by guards, the tone of the film could not be clearer: this fantasy premise serves as a timely reminder of the logical conclusion of the politics of prejudice and oppression. Due to the quality of the storytelling, the films also attracted a prestigious cast which included Patrick Stewart, Ian McKellen and Hugh Jackman, all of whom clearly responded to material which transcended its genre-based origins. Perhaps it is the combination of Singer's 'commitment to the seriousness of the themes' (Hughes 2003: 211) and characters who, despite their superpowers, are easy to identify with, which has made the *X-Men* films such a huge hit with audiences worldwide. The trilogy took over $1 billion in cinemas (Box Office Mojo 2009b) and, as I write, a prequel, *X-Men Origins: Wolverine* which focuses on the early life of Hugh Jackman's Wolverine character, is currently celebrating the biggest opening weekend of the year (McNary 2009). Significantly, Singer helped establish the tone for future comic book movies, mixing action and spectacle with a serious treatment of social and emotional themes, paving the way for films such as Ang Lee's *Hulk*, Christopher Nolan's *Batman Begins* and *The Dark Knight* and Sam Raimi's *Spider-Man*, each of which attracted a wealth of prestigious filmmaking talent both behind and in front of the cameras. It is certainly encouraging that these films reach a mass audience but refuse to compromise in terms of their thought-provoking content, thereby prompting children to consider concepts such as prejudice, discrimination and acceptance of difference. Statistics for the last decade confirm the immense popularity of comic book-based films: the *Spider-Man* trilogy alone has amassed box-office receipts of around $2.5 billion (Box Office Mojo 2009b) providing undeniable proof that audiences worldwide are responding to, and engaging with, these stories, characters and themes.

Interview with Dave Gibbons

Dave Gibbons has been a comic book artist and writer for over thirty years. He is one of the most well-known artists in the industry and has worked for DC Comics, Vertigo and Marvel. In 1985, he created *Watchmen* with Alan Moore, a serious and sophisticated re-examination of the superhero myth. A huge critical and commercial success, it is argued by many to be the most influential graphic novel ever written. Here, Dave shares his extensive knowledge of the comic book medium and its potential for storytelling, and explains how he felt when his work was adapted for the big screen.

TS: How did you start in the comic book industry?

DG: I've always loved comics. I can remember getting nursery comics when I was a kid. I clearly remember being bought my first ever *Superman* comic when I was seven years old. My granddad bought it for me – I still have the comic – and I've just loved comics ever since. I always liked to draw when I was a kid. From a very young age, I started off by copying from comic books, that's how I really learned to draw. I've got a very vivid memory of being in primary school and the teacher in the art lesson saying 'Okay children, you can paint whatever you like today' and other people painted a car or some flowers. But I did a guy in a space suit manacled to an asteroid. The teacher was slightly baffled by this! Then when I was older, I did amateur stuff for fanzines and then I started working in mainstream, professional comics. I did lettering first of all and then joke cartoons and then eventually I 'ghosted' for an artist – I imitated his style while he was on holiday and then I started to get work on my own. I've now been doing it for more than thirty years.

TS: Why do you like telling stories in the comic book form?

DG: When I was a kid, it was clear to me that with a piece of paper and a black pen, you could do anything that a professional could do. The only thing to stop you was your talent. It wasn't like getting into music, where you had to have a musical instrument; getting into film where you had to have a camera and an editing suite – it was cheap and democratic. You could draw all these pages, staple them together and it was exactly the same experience as reading a comic book. I do think there's something quite primal about telling stories in pictures – people always cite things like the Bayeux Tapestry and cave paintings. There's something basic about showing a series of pictures and telling a story with them. It's how we tend to think and remember things as well. Comics have that extra dimension: that you're moving through time as well. Rather than just showing somebody a static picture, you're giving them an experience – there's a narrative quality. The immediacy of comic books always appealed to me – the way the story can go straight from your head to the reader's without the need for a huge amount of technology.

TS: What are the challenges of conveying a narrative in this form to the reader?

DG: I suppose like any storytelling medium, you have to have a good story – something that's worth telling. Some comics fail because the story isn't quite well thought-out enough, just as many movies fail. Then there's the actual telling of the story: like with any work of art, you have to draft and reshape. Also in comics, you're limited by the format of the page and maybe the number of pages you've got, so you have to cut the story down into modules that fit within it. I've always had the theory that a page of comics is the unit of storytelling. I try to start a scene at the top of a page and end a scene on the bottom, but that doesn't mean you should only have one page per scene. I always find page turning a very clear signal: it's the end of one scene and the beginning of another. So once you've broken your story down into scenes, you then break the scenes down into the number of pages, then you break the pages down into the number of panels. That's the craft of comics – it's not the drawing. It's taking the story and chopping it down into units. Of course, there's always that feeling when you sit down to do anything on a blank page! So I start informally by just doing doodles and then you turn those into thumbnails – little versions of the page – and then the final ink drawing.

TS: Why do superheroes have such enduring appeal?

DG: They are a modern mythology. Just as you had Zeus and Achilles, there have always been stories of godlike beings and their interaction with mankind. There are also the wonders and the downside of having great powers, the relationships between the good gods and the bad gods – these are things which relate to the human psyche. Personally, I like comics which aren't necessarily about superheroes. There are some wonderful things you can do with comics that don't have to feature superheroes. Some superhero comics are looked upon as being juvenile and I don't think there is anything inherently juvenile about the medium of comics. You can tell any kinds of stories in comics.

TS: Many people think that comics and film are very similar mediums but you have previously stated that you do not think that this is necessarily the case. What is your view on the relationship between the two?

DG: I think, superficially, comics do seem to be like films because they are both telling stories in a succession of images. But there are obvious differences: comic books don't move, the reader has to supply the closure – take one still image and another and infer what has happened between them in that space between the panels we call the 'gutter'. In a movie, however, it unfolds for you. Comics are a reading experience – you do it at your own pace, you can go back and reread things, flip over some bits quickly or very slowly, whereas movies are for spectators – the moviemaker sets the pace. But in comics we do use the same terms as moviemaking – 'cut to', 'long shot' or 'close-up' and in panels you can imitate movie terms such as panning and tracking over a series of panels. In some ways, they mimic what movies do but movies don't have the dimension which comics have, which is that comics are a design on a page. The relationship of the panels in a comic book is not only the relationship in time but also a graphic relationship – when you're designing a page of a comic, you always intend to give it a variety. You'll have a close-up if it's an important emotional thing; you'll have a long shot if you need to establish a place; simply drawn pictures if you want the action to be the most important thing and very densely drawn pictures if you want atmosphere. You have to consider the graphic impact of what you're doing in a different way than when you're composing shots for movies. So I don't think the two mediums are exactly equivalent. It's the same as if you listen to a dramatised novel on the radio, it's the same story and the same scenes but the way it's expressed is very different.

TS: *Watchmen*, which you created with Alan Moore in 1986, was recently successfully turned into a film. As someone who has had their work adapted for the screen, can you describe how you felt about the process?

DG: When we first did the comic book, we didn't have it in our heads at all that it would ever be adapted to be a movie so we didn't make any concessions at all to its 'filmability'. Over the years, there were several directors rumoured to be attached then it was mentioned that Zack Snyder was in the frame to direct it. It was at the premiere of his film *300* that I first spoke to Zack. I had just come out of seeing the movie and was absolutely thrilled by what a wonderful and true adaptation it was of Frank Miller's graphic novel. I thought 'This guy might just be able to do *Watchmen*!' and we ended up speaking for half an hour. Sometime after, I was given the opportunity to comment on the first draft of the script and I was really quite flattered – they didn't have to consult me. The thing moved on and I got invited to the set when they were shooting. When I was there I was looking at it and saying 'Wow!' – I was actually in the presence of characters that I had drawn, actually in three-dimensional flesh which is very surreal. They had made a full-size Owlship[5] and to stand inside that, which had been an image inside my head, was really dream-like and surreal. When I finally got to see the movie, I really enjoyed it. The first time you see it, it's just 'Oh wow! They're on the screen! It's real! They're saying that line!' The second time, you've got past all that – it was that wonderful thing where you forget you're watching a movie and you just experience it. I think it's a very faithful adaptation in the overall feel and meaning of the original graphic novel. I think the extra stuff they invented for the film is wonderful, particularly the opening title montage.

TS: What are your views on the future of the comic book medium – will it embrace other technologies and change?

DG: I am very interested in the possibility of new technologies, both for executing the work and reading it. Comics have been digitally coloured for ten or fifteen years. There are some very interesting things on the internet where you read digital comics. I think that's where I'm interested in going. It's essentially a slideshow where you juxtapose images. I'm really interested in being able to deliver stuff on phones, particularly the iPhone. It seems to me that the technology is in place to actually deliver comic-style material to people for them to read anywhere and in any format.

TS: What are your favourite books, films and television programmes?

DG: Books: *Tiger! Tiger!* by Alfred Bester, *Carter Beats the Devil* and *Sunnyside* by Glen David Gold.

Films: *The Godfather trilogy, Dr. Strangelove.*

Television programme: *The Sopranos.*

3.2

Comic Books

Teaching Ideas

The following sessions aim to help pupils become familiar with comic books and understand how they operate as texts. The sessions can be taught individually or as longer programmes of study. The activities in this section are aimed at Year 4, but can be adapted for any age group. For further extension ideas and resources, see Chapter 3.3.

Reading and discussing comic books: *Korgi*

Learning objectives
- To read and understand a comic book narrative and the ways in which it transmits plot and character
- To introduce children to a range of text forms, understanding that each transmits information and story in different ways
- To create a narrative using a combination of images and words.

Resources
- Book: *Korgi* by Christian Slade
- A selection of scanned pages from *Korgi* as saved images on the computer
- A4 sheet with three blank panels (see Figure 3.4).

- Ask the children to think about any comics that they have read or know about. Most children have a very good knowledge of the multitude of comics which are available in shops and of the characters in them.
- Ask the children in pairs to think about the features of comic books that are different from books and write them up on the board:
  - Speech bubbles
  - Narrative boxes

- ■ Panels
- ■ Thought bubbles
- ■ Sound effects
- ■ Pictures.

■ Show the children some scanned pages from *Korgi* on the whiteboard (the sequence on pp. 24–9 – Figure 3.3 shows one of the pages in this sequence). Although *Korgi* is ideal because it has no words, you can of course use any comic here as long as it is suitable for the age group. Do not tell the children the title of the comic or the premise as the point of this activity is for them to derive as much information as possible from the pictures.

■ Go through the pictures with the children without explaining them, then leave the images on the screen and ask the children to either discuss or write down what they think is happening in the story.

Figure 3.3 Sprout chases a dragonfly in *Korgi Book 1: Sprouting Wings*, by Christian Slade

- When the children have done this, ask two children to read aloud their version of what they think is happening. Encourage the class to discuss and refine the two versions. Ask the children to consider:
  - What is happening in the pictures and how they know
  - How they feel about the characters (and why)
  - The emotions the characters are feeling (supported by evidence)
  - How the fantasy setting has been indicated in the story.
- Take one or two of the pages in the sequence (pp. 27–8) and ask the children to write down speech bubbles and/or thought bubbles for the girl (Ivy) and her dog (Sprout). As *Korgi* contains no written text, this is an effective way to help children become accustomed to using the conventions of comics (if you number the panels on the board, the children will find it easier to write down the corresponding speech bubbles for each panel). The children then read out their speech and thought bubbles to the class.
- Ask the children to continue the story of the comic you have been looking at, using the A4 sheets with three blank panels (Figure 3.4). They will need to plan their story, using the characters and plot of the example you have provided, before they draw and write the finished panels.
- As a plenary, discuss how some of the children have continued the story, how they have incorporated elements of the fantasy genre and how they have used some of the features of comics. In later sessions, share all of the *Korgi* books with the children, encouraging them to discuss how the fictional world has developed in terms of genre (a move from fantasy to science fiction).

Using drama to explore comics

Learning objectives
- To understand how body language and facial expression can be used to relay plot and character information in visual narratives
- To explore how static images can tell a story
- To combine words and images to tell a story through role-play
- To work in small groups, sharing ideas effectively in order to plan and perform a piece of drama.
- To see others' work and provide constructive feedback as a member of an audience.

Resources
- A4 sheets with three blank panels (Figure 3.4)
- Large card speech bubbles, A3 size (Figure 3.5). These can be photocopied onto paper but it will be more practical to back them with cardboard.

Figure 3.4 Three-panel sheet

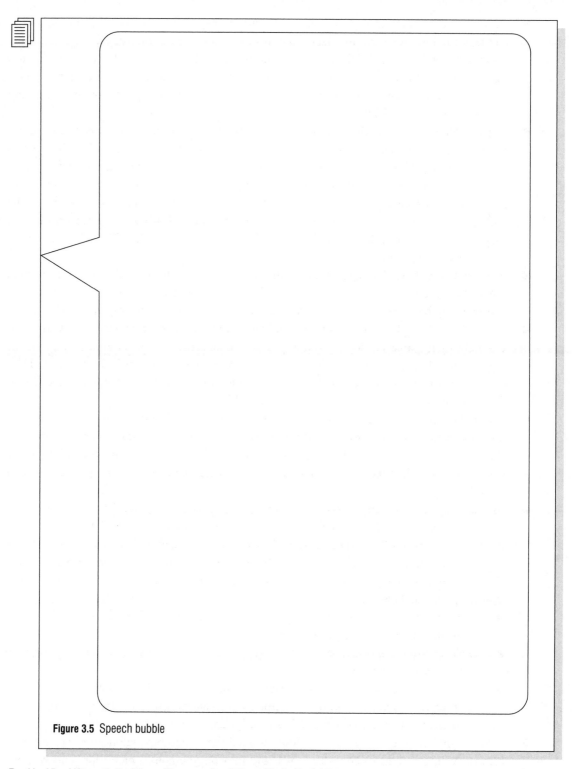

Figure 3.5 Speech bubble

- This activity will be more effective as two sessions: first, a classroom-based planning session and later the Drama session in a hall space. If this session follows on from the previous one, remind the children of the features of comic books and how they tell a story. If this is a one-off session, then simply show the children an example of a comic book on the white-board and discuss some of the basic features of the medium (speech bubbles, thought bubbles, narrative boxes, the artwork).

- In pairs/talk partners, ask the children to plan a three-panel comic book story and hand out the A4 three-panel sheets. You might wish to give them a theme such as 'The Chase' or 'A Discovery'. Explain to the children that this plan is going to be used as the basis for a 'real' comic book, which they will re-enact in their pairs. It therefore needs to be simple, not require complex props or sets and only have two characters. In addition, explain to the children that they will be given one speech-bubble card each (two for each pair) but that they can write on both sides of the card and therefore the comic plan should have no more than four speech bubbles in total.

- The children will need a substantial amount of planning time to make sure their comic plan meets these requirements and still tells an effective story, but if they are told from the start that they will be recreating these comics, then they should be able to plan appropriately.

- When the children have finished their comic plan and it is has been checked, allow them to write out their comic's dialogue on the speech-bubble cards in large, clear lettering (enlarge the speech bubble in Figure 3.5 to A3 size, cut out and back with card). By the end of this session, each pair should have a three-panel comic drawn on their sheet and the dialogue from their comic copied onto their A3 speech bubbles.

- The following Drama session, which constitutes the second part of this activity, can be undertaken in a separate session later in the day or even some days after the session detailed above. This session will need a larger space such as the school hall and the children will need to bring their three-panel comics and large speech bubbles from the previous session with them.

- As warm-ups for the drama session, ask the children to move around the hall, using the space and focusing on movement rather than voice. Many of the warm-up activities detailed in Chapter 1.2 (Using Drama to develop visual literacy with *Where the Wild Things Are*) can be used here. Even the Year 1 Drama activities can be repeated with Key Stage Two children if they are presented in a manner which is more suited to older pupils. Warm-ups can include:
  - Stop/go: children have to do the opposite of the commands 'Stop and go'
  - Mirroring: in pairs, facing each other
  - Walking around in different moods: conveying a range of emotions silently, using only body language and faces
  - Remote control: pretend that you have a remote control which controls the children, and that, as they walk around the room, you can alternately fast-forward them, rewind them, speed them up, slow them down and mute them.

- Ask the children to get into threes or fours and tell them that they will need to create a tableau (they might want to consider it as being in a photograph) which represents the title you will give them. They have one minute, and no longer, to work out how their picture will show the theme and then get into their positions. When the time is up, shout 'Freeze' and ask the children to hold their positions. They will most likely find this difficult at first but will become more competent at it with practice, so it is better to start with easier titles and then make them more challenging (you may also want to give them only thirty seconds each for the last few tableaux). Titles might include:

- The classroom
- The argument
- The race
- The shipwreck
- A party
- A game of basketball.

- Ask the children who have made the best tableaux from the groups to show them to the rest of the class, accentuating the body language and the facial expressions and how they give the audience information.

- Now ask the groups to make up their own idea for a tableau and show it clearly. When they have had enough time (two or three minutes), ask each group to show their frozen scene to the rest of the class, who then have to guess what it represents.

- Ask the children to get into the pairs they worked in to plan the comic book in the earlier session. Using their plans and their large speech bubbles, the children will need to turn their three panels into three separate tableaux, so that each pair has recreated their comic book narrative. Restate that they need to give thought to facial expression and body posture and that they will need to hold up the speech bubbles clearly near their mouths, so that the audience can read them.

- As they rehearse, it is useful to circulate among the groups in order to ensure that they are holding up their speech bubbles correctly and that their frozen tableaux show the story clearly.

- When the children have had enough rehearsal time, ask them to sit in a row (this helps to create a sense of a formal audience) and ask each group to perform their living comic book in front of the audience. Each group can announce the specific title of their story and tell the audience who their characters are. Each panel should be frozen for ten seconds or so in silence before the pair adopts the next position. As the children show their tableaux, you can represent the role of the comic reader, reading the speech bubbles aloud clearly for the audience and commenting on what the panels show.

- Encourage the audience to give feedback on what they liked about each comic and draw the audience's attention to particularly strong examples of body language and facial expression. If you have a digital camera, photograph each pair's series of tableaux/panels and these can then be used as part of a display or bound into a class comic book. They can also be put up on the interactive whiteboard for a short session at a later date where the children can view their tableaux and see them presented in the form of a three-panel comic narrative.

- As a cool-down to the Drama session, ask the children to think about what they have learned in terms of the ways in which a story can be told without sound or movement.

3.3

Comic Books

Further Ideas and Resources

These lists of resources and ideas for activities supplement the teaching ideas in Chapter 3.2 and offer suggestions for teaching activities which use comic books with other age groups.

Lesson ideas

The following sessions are intended as general models for teaching comic books with children that can be adapted as necessary to fit any class.

Year 1

Resources
- A selection of comics aimed at younger readers, most of which can be supplied by the children themselves
- Visualiser.

- In preparation, ask the class to bring in comics that they might have at home. Begin the session by asking the children, in pairs, to discuss their favourite comics and the characters they like also. Make a list on the board of favourite comics and characters.
- Ask the children some questions about comics:
  - What are comics?
  - Are comics just about superheroes?
  - What makes a comic different from a written book or a picture book?
  - What might we expect to see in a comic book? (List features such as speech bubbles, panels, sound effects – let the children decide the terms for these features.)
- In their pairs, ask the children to take a few minutes to look at a comic either that they have brought in or that you have supplied. Ask some of the pairs to present their comic to the class. Each pair can read out a page of their comic, explain what is happening and perform the dialogue (while their comic page is on the visualiser). They can review the comic and say what they thought about it also.

- Choose one of the comic pages and ask the children to come up and point to each of the features on the list if they can see it. For example, a child can come up and identify a speech bubble, narrative box or sound effect. Take some time to discuss sound effects with the children. Ask some questions:
  - What are these letters for? What do they show?
  - Why aren't they proper words?
- Ask the children as a class to try to recreate the noise that the sound effect is showing ('CRRRASHH!' or 'BLAMMMM!').
- Looking at each panel individually, ask the children to come up to the front in their pairs (or threes) and recreate a panel from the comic, using their bodies and freezing in position.

Year 2

> ## Resources
> - A selection of comics (supplied by the children or yourself)
> - A visualiser
> - An empty comic grid (see Figure 3.6).

- If the children are unfamiliar with comic books, then begin the session with an introduction similar to the Year 1 session above. After the children have identified some of the features of the comic book and can confidently recognise them, ask them to work individually or in pairs and produce a short comic book story.
- Before children are given their final grid sheet (Figure 3.6), tell them that a comic, like any other story, needs to be well planned and thought out. The children might like to sketch out a rough, six-panel story briefly. When the story is planned appropriately, the children can then work on their final version. Tell the children that you will expect to see speech bubbles and sound effects in their story. They will most likely find it quite difficult to plan out a six-panel story, so it might be helpful to give the children a story or some key words. Some examples could be: 'the chase', 'the argument', 'the storm' or a simple storyline with characters which they can interpret as they wish such as 'the wolf and the rabbit'.
- Share the children's work with them, commenting on the use of features such as sound effects and speech bubbles.

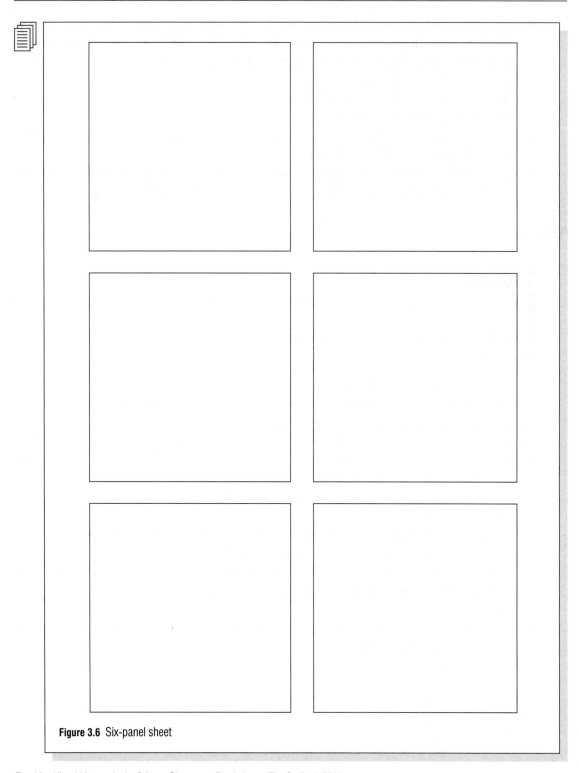

Figure 3.6 Six-panel sheet

Figure 3.7 A range of panel shapes

Year 3–4

> **Resources**
> - A scanned page from a comic
> - Interactive whiteboard
> - Comic panel sheet (see Figure 3.7).

- Show the children a scanned page from a comic on the whiteboard or on the visualiser. Choose a page from a comic which has a variation of panel shapes and sizes (this can probably be found in the pages of most Marvel or DC comics – a popular character like Spider-Man may be a good choice).
- Ask the children to discuss the page in their pairs and report back as to what they think the page is showing and why. Ask them how the characters are feeling and why (requiring them to come up and point to visual evidence to support their opinion). Discuss the panel layout and ask the children how it adds to the mood of the page (excitement and a sense of action possibly).
- Hand out the comic panel sheet (Figure 3.7) to the children and ask them to plan a short story (perhaps even continuing from the page you have used with them). Ask them to think about how they will best use the panels to create an exciting feel in their comic. Ideally, they will use the more unusual panels for the most exciting parts of their story.
- As the children work on their pages, ask them to consider what images might suit the bigger panels best. For example, the top horizontal panel might depict a landscape and the long vertical panel at the bottom a person or a shot of someone running away from the reader's viewpoint.
- When the children have finished drawing their comic, share some of the better examples, exploring how the children have used the jagged and long panels.

Year 5–6

> **Resources**
> - Scanned pages from a comic book
> - Interactive whiteboard.

- Begin by showing the children some sample pages from a suitable superhero comic (or any type of comic story) which you or one of the children has supplied. Ask the children to discuss in pairs the features of the comic which make it unique from other media and make a list on the board.
- Explain to the children that comics start from scripts and that there is a writer before there is an illustrator. The structure of a comic script is very much like a play, with

instructions on what we can see and dialogue for the characters, to show what they are saying. At this point, select one of the panels from the comic book you have been studying and demonstrate how the script might look for it. The layout of a comic script is as follows:

- Description of what we can see in the panel
- Sound effects
- Dialogue.

For example:

PANEL ONE: A long horizontal rectangle. We see a wide shot of a field on a sunny day. There are trees and birds flying in the sky – a traditional country scene. We can make out two people in the distance, located in the middle of the field, facing one another. They are no more than silhouettes but they stand formally.

FIRST FIGURE (on left of scene): So, we meet again!

SECOND FIGURE (on right): Yes, it would seem we have.

- When you have demonstrated this, ask the children in their pairs to choose one of the panels on the board and write the script. Emphasise that the process would usually be reversed, with the script coming before the art, so the script has to be extremely detailed in its description so that the artist knows what to depict in the panel.
- Share some of the panel descriptions with the children and see if each of them can be improved upon and added to by the rest of the class.
- Ask the children to plan out and write a simple six-panel script for a comic page. They should use the format discussed (panel description, sound effects and dialogue). Explain to them that they will be sharing their scripts with a partner when finished, who will then be responsible for drawing their script as a finished comic. In this way, the children will be encouraged to write for an audience and will hopefully be as accurate as possible in their descriptions so that their written work can be interpreted correctly.
- The writing of the scripts will most likely take more than one session, so allow two sessions for the writing. When the scripts are finished, ask the children to swap the scripts with a partner and then to draw the comic books for their partner's script.
- When the comics are finished, encourage the children to discuss the process (offering suggestions for how their partners' scripts could have been improved) and talk about any difficulties they encountered while creating the scripts and the comics.

Comic book resources

With many comics aimed at teenagers and adults, it is not always easy to locate suitable comic book resources for use with primary school children. The following is a list of material which will generally be suitable for children to study in school. It is divided into Key Stages One and Two but much of the material in the Key Stage One section (such as *Owly* and *Korgi*) can, and should, be used with older children as well.

Key Stage One

Owly by Andy Runton

A charming series of adventures based around a group of animal friends. There is no dialogue as the story is told through pictures only:

- Volume 1: *The Way Home and the Bittersweet Summer*
- Volume 2: *Just a Little Blue*
- Volume 3: *Flying Lessons*
- Volume 4: *A Time to be Brave*
- Volume 5: *Tiny Tales.*

Korgi by Christian Slade

A delightful fantasy story set in a magical world where a young girl and her dog have a series of adventures. With no words, this is told through pictures only.

- Book 1: *Sprouting Wings!*
- Book 2: *The Cosmic Collector.*

Little Mouse Gets Ready by Jeff Smith

The adorable Little Mouse shows how to get dressed in this introduction to comic book narratives, designed especially for young readers.

Tiny Titans by Art Baltazar and Franco

DC Comics produce this monthly title which follows the exploits of super-children (including Robin and Batgirl) at school.

- Volume 1: *Welcome to the Treehouse*
- Volume 2: *Adventures in Awesomeness.*

There's a Wolf at the Door by Zoë B. Alley and R.W. Alley

Five traditional children's stories ('The Three Little Pigs', 'The Boy Who Cried Wolf', 'Little Red Riding Hood', 'The Wolf in Sheep's Clothing' and 'The Wolf and the Seven Little Goslings') retold in comic form and presented in a big-book format, ideal for sharing with a class.

Key Stage Two

Wonderland by Derek Watson and Kit Wallis

In a dark, plague-ridden future, Sarah, a brave young girl, sets out on a thrilling journey with her brother Poncho to find their father with help from her brother Edison, and her trusty elephant, cat and robot.

The Arrival by Shaun Tan

A beautifully illustrated, surreal tale which relates an immigrant's experience, told through pictures.

The Snowman by Raymond Briggs

The classic and moving tale of a boy's magical journey with a snowman. Employing pictures only, this is an example of the visual narrative at its finest.

The Bear by Raymond Briggs

The story of a giant bear that comes to live in a small house with a family and the adventures that ensue. A funny and poignant comic.

Mouse Guard: Fall 1152 by David Petersen

A fantasy tale of warrior mice in a medieval world. A comic narrative full of adventure and excitement.

Internet resources

There are some excellent resources on the web which can be explored with the whole class via the interactive whiteboard or by individual pupils on the computer:

www.dccomics.com/dckids
Provides free issues of children's comics which can be read and studied onscreen.
www.marvel.com/digitalcomics
An online library of Marvel comics, a subscription to which gives you access to thousands of titles. There are also some samples which can be read for free. Marvel provides its own ratings system for its comics which reflect the suitability of their content. This is discussed in the next section.
www.bbc.co.uk/doctorwho/comicmaker
An excellent, beautifully designed resource which allows children to create their very own *Doctor Who* comics.

Comic ratings

Some of the larger comics publishers provide ratings with their comics to clarify the suitability of the titles. DC Comics does this by producing a dedicated range of children's titles under its DC Kids banner while Marvel gives each of its comics a rating according to the subject matter (www.marvel.com/catalog/ratings.htm). These ratings can be found on the front or back cover, next to the barcode. They are rated as follows:

ALL AGES – suitable for all children.
A – suitable for nine years and over.
T+ TEENS AND UP – thirteen years and over. Parents/adults may wish to read these comics before giving them to children.
PARENTAL ADVISORY – fifteen years and above. Will contain more mature themes and storylines.
MAX: EXPLICIT CONTENT – comics which are aimed at an adult readership.

When using comics with primary-age children, the 'ALL AGES' comics will be suitable for study. The vast majority of the 'A' titles will also be suitable, although, as with all material, you should check them through carefully before using them with children.

Notes

1 A recent newspaper report also cited the surprising fact that 'Marjane Satrapi's *Persepolis* [an autobiographical graphic novel which tells the story of the author's childhood in Iran] outstripped Harry Potter to become the best-selling novel in Foyle's bookshop last year' (Martin 2009). Similarly, Alan Moore and Dave Gibbons's graphic novel *Watchmen*, now over twenty years old, had its print run increased to one million copies in 2008 after the trailer for Zack Snyder's film adaptation hit cinemas (Gustines 2008).

2 A recent magazine feature estimated that there are currently seventy films based on comic books which are in varying stages of development (Day *et al.* 2009).

3 *The Ultimates* has proven to be somewhat influential in terms of recent Marvel films. In the comic the team's general, Nick Fury, was given the likeness of the actor Samuel L. Jackson, who was cast in the role some years later, appearing at the end of the 2008 *Iron Man* film looking identical to the comic book version. In addition, a sequence in *The Ultimates Volume Two* in which Bruce Banner is dropped from a helicopter and lands, transformed into the Hulk, was copied in the recent film *The Incredible Hulk*.

4 The *X-Men* comics in fact have often been read as a metaphor for America's civil rights movement, with the pacifist Professor X and his nemesis the terrorist Magneto created to be fictional representations of Martin Luther King and Malcolm X respectively. Over the course of the trilogy, the plots continue to be firmly rooted in very real issues. The X-Men have to fight against Senator Kelley, a powerful politician who wishes to introduce an Act which will require all mutants to be 'registered'. While Magneto's solution is to kidnap the senator and turn him into a mutant, Professor X understands that the only way forward is through persuasive argument and by convincing the public that they have nothing to fear from mutants. In the final film of the trilogy, *X-Men: The Last Stand*, a 'mutant antibody, a way to suppress the mutant X gene' is developed by a pharmaceuticals company and the emotive term 'cure' is applied. Opinion is divided among the X-Men: while Rogue wishes to be cured of her affliction, claiming that 'You don't know what it's like to be afraid of your powers', Storm demonstrates her sense of pride, stating 'You can't "cure" a mutant. Since when did we become a disease?'

5 The Owlship, or 'Archie' as it nicknamed, is the hi-tech flying ship of one of *Watchmen*'s central characters, Nite Owl.

4.1

Film

Film, in the way in which it presents images to the viewer as moving, seemingly living entities, is a distinct medium with a particular terminology and specific analytical approach all of
its own. Film is principally defined by the dynamism of its moving images but does, however, share some qualities with the picture book and the comic book. When these three
seemingly disparate media forms are reduced to their most basic compositional units, they
are surprisingly similar to one another: the picture book page, the comic book panel, the television screen and the individual film cell are all, in their simplest forms, an image presented
within a rectangular or square frame. The difference lies in how they are presented to their
audiences: on a technological level, film is simply hundreds of thousands of these individual
pictures shown to the viewer in rapid succession to create the illusion of a single moving
image. When extra elements are added to the process, the differences become even more
pronounced and film moves further away from comics and picture books to become a
unique and powerful medium in its own right. These elements include music, dialogue,
sound effects, editing, lighting and acting and, when a skilled director assimilates these elements effectively into one film, it is inevitably true to say that the whole is greater than the
sum of its parts. Film can connect with its audience in a way which no other medium can.
Paintings, photographs or music alone can undoubtedly evoke strong emotions in us, but the
combination of watching a film with a soundtrack, be it music or dialogue, has the capability
to move us profoundly. Consider the memorable opening sequence of Anthony Minghella's
The English Patient, where panoramic shots of the desert are combined with haunting vocal
chants, or the scene in Tim Burton's *Edward Scissorhands* where Kim Boggs (Winona Ryder)
dances in the flakes from Edward (Johnny Depp)'s ice sculpture to the accompaniment of
Danny Elfman's beautiful music. Yet film does not just move us to appreciate beauty – it can
also both terrify and thrill on a primal level. The visceral shock of our first glimpse of the
killer's mask in Wes Craven's *Scream* is heightened by Marco Beltrami's tense score and the
deafening roar of the Tyrannosaurus Rex as it menaces the visitors to *Jurassic Park* creates an
unforgettably exciting viewing experience. The vast majority of children also seem to derive
great pleasure from cinema and television, often returning to their favourite films and programmes repeatedly. The advent of home-cinema technology, replete with surround sound,
vast screens and the eminently collectible format of the DVD, with its accessible viewer-
friendly navigation and 'making of' documentaries, means that children are now more than

ever immersed in the moving image in their own homes. By giving them the tools to analyse what they see, we can ensure that not only will they enjoy what they watch but that they will also learn from it.

Film and television: a comparison

It is important to note here that, for ease of reference, I am grouping both cinematic and televisual texts under the banner of 'film' or the 'moving image'. It is undoubtedly true that cinema and television are in fact quite dissimilar from one another. While they both trade in the moving image, there are significant differences in the technology which each employs and in the scale, budget and format of their respective products. For too long, television has been viewed as cinema's poor relation, with many actors, writers and directors moving inexorably in one direction, viewing the jump from small screen to big screen as a graduation of sorts. James Monaco reasonably argues that 'because [television] is much less intense than cinema … action and spectacle come off more poorly than in the movie theater' but the flip side of this is that television is, by its nature, a smaller, more personal and certainly more intimate medium. Indeed, Monaco also argues that because many television dramas and comedies are presented in the format of a longer, ongoing series, television is 'better equipped than most other media to deal with subtle development of character' (2000: 488). In recent years, this has been superbly demonstrated by the resurgence in quality and popularity of the television drama series. Shows such as *Doctor Who*, *Lost*, *Desperate Housewives* and *Six Feet Under* have consistently shown the ability to retain large audience figures across multiple episodes and series through their writing, characterisation and plots which are undoubtedly the equal of (and in many cases are superior to) the best films. Writers such as Russell T. Davies, Alan Ball and Marc Cherry are craftsmen who both love and understand the medium intimately and are able to shape the characters and the storylines of these series into excellently paced, ongoing narratives.

At more advanced levels of media study, the differences between cinema and television are themselves worthy of analysis and the two media need to be clearly distinguished. While primary-age children are certainly capable of recognising at least some of these differences, at this relatively early level of study it is unnecessary to differentiate between the two and better instead to simplify the approach by amalgamating cinema and television under the umbrella of the moving image. It will suffice here to briefly examine the differences between the two media, so that older children can consider them, should they wish to. Table 4.1 shows the main differences.

Mise en scène: what we look for when studying film

Like comic books, the study of film requires at least a basic understanding of the main techniques and methods which are used in filmmaking. As with all analyses, in order to engage more deeply with the text, it is necessary not only to identify these techniques when they

Table 4.1 Main differences between film and television

ASPECT	CINEMA	TELEVISION
The product or text	Film, and then after a cinema release, DVD	Programme or a series of programmes broadcast weekly
Average length of product	Anywhere from 70 to 210 minutes	Programmes most commonly appear in 30- or 60-minute episodes
Content of product	The vast majority of films released in cinemas are fictional stories	A mixture of fictional dramas and comedies, combined with, among others, light entertainment shows, documentaries, news programming and sports
Advertising	In the cinema, advertising is shown before the main feature film, but none on DVD	All channels except the BBC divide programmes up into parts, between which they have advertising breaks
Makers of product	A film is financed and released either by one of the major Hollywood studios (Fox, Warner Bros.) or an independent film company (The Weinstein Film Company)	Television channels such as BBC and Channel 4 either make their own programmes or commission companies to make programmes for them
Costs	Costs vary widely from film to film, with the biggest blockbuster films regularly costing over $200 million, but the average mainstream American film budget is roughly estimated at around $65 million (The Numbers 2009)	Again, costs vary depending on the programme, but the BBC's budget for their entire drama programming for the year was recently estimated at £200 million (Wright 2009)
Audience for products	Films are rated and classified by the British Board of Film Classification and then given an age appropriate certificate of either Universal, Parental Guidance, 12A, 15 or 18.	On most channels, it is the responsibility of the viewer (or the viewer's parents if they are a child) to decide what is suitable or unsuitable for viewing. Terrestrial channels broadcast programmes they deem unsuitable for a younger audience after the 'watershed' at 9 p.m.

are being used but also to consider how they affect the overall tone, theme and feeling of the film for the viewer. The concept of '*mise en scène*' is an important one in film studies. The French term literally translates as 'putting on stage', originally referring to how any given scene in a theatrical production might be staged in terms of lighting, set, costume and positioning of the cast. It is now commonly used as appropriate terminology for reading film. Marilyn Fabe defines it as:

all the elements of film direction that overlap with the art of theatre ... the director's choice of actors and how they are directed, the way the scene is lit, the choice of setting or set design, props, costumes, and make-up.

(2004: 3)

This is a useful definition but I prefer Andrew Dix's description which 'considers not merely the elements cinema shares with theatre but also visual properties that are distinctive to film as a medium'. Here, Dix argues that when reading film, we must take into account the unique techniques of filmmaking which go beyond the experience of watching a play in a theatre. These include 'the implications of the camera's proximity to [its object]' and what is 'indicated by the texture of the image itself' (2008: 11). Of course, younger pupils are not necessarily required to use terms such as *mise en scène*, but are certainly more than capable of observing features such as camera angles, lighting and use of colour and commenting on how these aspects of the film affect them as viewers.

Camera techniques

The camera's position is one of the primary sources of information regarding the tone of a scene for the viewer. For example, if the image, or 'shot' as I will refer to it here, is at a low angle, looking up at someone or something which towers over the camera, the director is most likely wishing to emphasise the power and dominance of the object and the relative powerlessness of the viewer. Conversely, an overhead or 'bird's eye' shot which looks down over buildings and people will invoke a feeling of power and even detachment from the scene below. The positioning of the shot is one of the most fundamental signifiers of narrative information in a film and yet it is sometimes the easiest to overlook. When we watch films and television passively in order to be entertained, we may pay little attention to camera angles and therefore when we come to critically analyse the moving image, it is important to remain aware of even the most routine camera angles and how they can contribute to our understanding of mood or character. We should ask children a number of questions when considering camera angles:

- Is the camera close to or far away from the people or objects?
- Is it low down and near the ground, or high up above the action?
- Is the camera moving fast or slowly, or is it static?
- How does the shot make us feel?

Two of the most important types of camera shot to explore with children are the close-up and the long shot. Close-ups and long shots constitute opposite ends of the cinematographer's spectrum. A typical close-up might show an actor's head filling most of the screen, while a typical long shot might show a landscape or a whole building. Between these two extremes lies the medium shot, which is neither particularly close to or far away from the action, perhaps framing half, or all, of an actor's body onscreen. A simplified explanation of these shots is that the close-up portrays emotion whereas the long shot portrays action. While this is certainly not always the case, it is a solid enough starting point for use with children. Just as any piece of fiction needs to incorporate descriptions of what a character is feeling with what a character is doing, so too does a film, ensuring a balance of close-ups and long shots for a satisfying viewing experience. If a film was composed solely of close-up shots, the effect would be overwhelmingly claustrophobic and would not reveal enough information about the characters' surroundings. Conversely, if we were given nothing but long shots, there would be no opportunity for the audience to identify with the characters intimately because we could not see any of the emotions that their faces were registering.

Long shots are used for a number of reasons. A director might wish to show a shot of the outside of the building or the wider landscape in which a scene is set, termed an 'establishing shot' because it sets up the location of the scene which immediately proceeds from it and helps create atmosphere for the audience. For example, we might see the exterior of a castle or the villain's headquarters. In *X-Men* and *X2*, Bryan Singer frequently introduces the scenes set at Professor Xavier's School for Gifted Youngsters by showing us the outside of the building from the ground or above. By taking a few seconds to show the splendid, ivy-covered exterior of the formal but beautiful building, Singer is not only indicating that the location of the following scene is different from the previous one, but is also adding to the tone by showing a setting which radiates an atmosphere of calmness, safety and protection, echoing the characteristics of its founder. Therefore, the establishing shot can provide information which is at once factual, emotional and intrinsically connected to the plot and the characters. Another filmmaker who uses establishing shots excellently and suffuses them with atmosphere is Peter Jackson, director of *The Lord of the Rings* trilogy, who alternates beautiful establishing shots of the gentle green hills and lush countryside of the Hobbits' beloved Shire with the terrifying, nightmarish and lethally sharp architecture of the seats of evil in Middle Earth such as Minas Morgul and Isengard. Here, Jackson also expertly determines appropriate camera movement: the establishing shots of the Shire are calm and largely static, creating a relaxing and idyllic atmosphere, while many of the evil army strongholds are introduced with vertiginous camera angles and dizzying swoops which take us up and over the towering buildings, reinforcing both the power and the unnatural appearances of these fortresses. Long shots are also an effective way for a director to show action scenes, in which visually spectacular stunts or effects take precedence over emotions and dialogue. Again, Jackson uses wide shots to show the amassed armies of the villainous Sauron, reinforcing the sheer scale of the conflict and the numbers of warriors it involves. Here, a vista populated by tens of thousands of soldiers deliberately prevents us from seeing the emotions of individual characters and instead creates a general sense of awe and fear in the audience by overwhelming them with a legion of creatures.

The close-up, on the other hand, is often our primary method of emotional engagement with a film. Béla Balász notes that:

close-ups are often dramatic revelations of what is really happening under the surface of appearances. You may see a medium shot of someone sitting and conducting a conversation with icy calm. The close-up will show trembling fingers nervously fumbling a small object – sign of an internal storm.

(2004: 315)

On a practical level, a close-up shot of an actor forces us to consider their character's emotions purely because their face fills the entire screen, leaving us with no choice but to read it for visual indicators of their mood (as Siegfried Kracauer puts it: 'it serves to suggest what is going on behind [a] face' (1997: 46)). In fact, the close-up is a powerful way for the director to ensure that an audience notices anything that he or she wants them to observe, whether that be an emotion, a movement or an object crucial to the plot which could easily be missed within the multitude of visual information provided in a long shot. It is useful here to establish a link between the written and the visual text. On a basic level, close-ups tend to reflect the sentences which detail the emotions or the interior world of characters, whereas medium and long shots would show their actions and could be used to portray the sections of the text which describe setting and place. This can be illustrated with an example from a novel. In Kate DiCamillo's wonderful and moving *The Miraculous Journey of Edward Tulane*, the titular character, a toy rabbit, goes on a heartbreaking journey, part of which he undertakes with a boy called Bryce:

> The walk to town took all night. Bryce walked without stopping, carrying Edward under one arm and talking to him the whole time. Edward tried to listen but the terrible scarecrow feeling had come back … the feeling that nothing mattered, and that nothing would ever matter again.
>
> (DiCamillo 2006: 147–8)

If adapted into a film, the first sentence could be represented by a long shot establishing the small figure of Bryce walking along a winding road at night, perhaps hinting at his destination by showing the twinkling lights of a town in the distance. Here, a long shot would be particularly evocative because the figure of Bryce would be relatively small in the shot, reinforcing his vulnerability as he walks through an unpopulated landscape, alone but for Edward. The second sentence might be represented by a medium shot, showing the viewer that Bryce is in fact carrying Edward with him. The final sentence would, however, require a close-up of Edward's face in order to convey the sadness and grief which he feels.

Of course, close-ups, medium shots and long shots can be connected visually through the 'zoom', in which the camera moves from a long shot to a close-up or vice versa in one fluid movement. This technique might be used to zoom in on one particular member of a crowd in a long shot, or to zoom out from one person's face to situate them in a wider context, revealing, for example, that the character is surrounded by seemingly insurmountable forces or is perhaps in the middle of a hostile landscape. A particularly effective example of the latter can be seen in an episode of *Doctor Who* entitled *42*, wherein Martha Jones (Freema Agyeman) is trapped in an escape pod and propelled away into outer space. Beginning on a close-up of Martha's frightened face as she beats at the thick glass of the spacecraft's door, we see her gradually fall away from us until the pod is a small speck surrounded by the vast expanse of space, poignantly reinforcing the terror and loneliness of her situation and suggesting that it will be nearly impossible for her to return safely. Ang Lee also uses the zoom albeit in a more frenetic manner in his adaptation of the Marvel comic *Hulk*. Here, Lee employs a technique known as the crash zoom where the camera zooms from close-up to long shots so rapidly that the images in between are little more than a blur. The effect here is to link the wider action and locations with the intimacy and emotion of the individual. Lee recognises that, just as a wide shot is needed to show the army's planes firing weapons as they swoop over the Golden Gate Bridge, we also need an immediate zoom in on their target, the Hulk, so that the camera can register the painful effect of the missiles. In doing this, Lee never lets us forget that every violent action has a consequence for its recipient and thereby helps us to identify with the misunderstood Hulk who is at the centre of the army's frenzied and impersonal attack.

Other ways in which the camera moves that deserve a mention here are panning and tracking. These are both types of shot for which the camera is not static, but the difference lies in how it moves. A panning shot is when the camera moves from left to right or up and down, but remains on a fixed base. It helps here to imagine the camera on a tripod or stand. The camera itself can swivel vertically or horizontally but the base it is on does not move. The panning shot is often used as a slower, gentler introduction to a scene, perhaps used as an establishing shot to sweep over a landscape. An impressive example of this comes in the early stages of Steven Spielberg's *Jurassic Park*, when Dr Grant and Dr Sattler (Sam Neill and Laura Dern) first witness the majesty of a Brachiosaur. At one point the camera pans upwards from them to show the full height of the dinosaur. The use of the pan is particularly effective here precisely because the camera remains fixed at a human level but tilts up from its base to give the viewer a feeling of the towering dinosaur's immensity. A second panning shot moments later moves from left to right with the doctors as they walk alongside the Brachiosaur, Spielberg understanding that the slow pan is the most suitable type of shot here. Not only does it allow the two characters to remain at the centre of the shot as they move but it also keeps the pace of the scene consistent due to the fact that the slow graceful motion of the camera reflects the gentle yet inexorable progress of the dinosaur.

A tracking shot is when the whole camera, including its base, moves along in a shot. It derives its name from the fact that camera operators often literally build a track along which the camera can run to maintain a constant height and speed, although it can also be hand-held. This is used to create a sense of movement on film, the camera perhaps keeping pace with a character who is being chased or, conversely, moving slowly alongside characters who are having a conversation while walking. Table 4.2 summarises these different shots.

Editing

An essential and unique element of film is the way in which it is edited or cut. The process of editing is where the film footage is put into the correct order to make the finished film.

This is not, however, to imply that it is a purely mechanical endeavour, as editing plays a key part in creating the tone of the finished film. The editor (usually under the guidance of the director) is responsible for determining how long each camera shot will last, which shot will follow the previous one, how the transition between scenes will occur (fade in to the next scene, fade to black or simply cut to the next scene) as well as integrating the soundtrack and special effects with the existing footage. As Joseph M. Boggs and Dennis W. Petrie argue, this 'must be done with artistic sensitivity, perception, and aesthetic judgment as well as a true involvement in the subject and a clear understanding of the director's intentions' (2008: 186). It is often true that the shorter the length of the camera shot and the more cuts between shots there are, the more thrilling and action-packed the scene is, whereas sequences which are edited to have longer shots and less cuts tend to be calmer and emphasise emotional content over physical content. Here, again, a link with the written text can be established. Often, when describing action in a story, a writer may employ short sentences to heighten the excitement for the reader and maintain a fast-paced narrative. A good example can be seen in Michael Morpurgo's excellent novel *Kensuke's Kingdom* when the protagonist Michael and his dog Stella Artois are swept overboard:

> Then a sudden glimpse of white in the sea. The breaking of a wave perhaps. But there were no waves. Stella! It had to be.... Only then did I realise my mistake. Stella's head was mostly black. This was white.
>
> (Morpurgo 2000: 46)

If we imagine for a moment that each one of Morpurgo's sentences is a shot in a film and that the full stops represent the cut from one shot to the next, we can see how the effectiveness of the short sentences in a written action scene is mirrored in the short shots and numerous cuts of a filmed action scene. Alternatively, we can see how scenes which create a slower, more reflective feel often require longer sentences. This is evident in *Kensuke's Kingdom* when Michael surveys the beautiful island on which he is marooned:

> There was a long swathe of brilliant white beach on both sides of the island, and at the far end another hill, the slopes steeper and more thickly wooded, but not so high as mine.... Even as I stood there, that first morning, filled with apprehension at the terrifying implications of my dreadful situation, I remember thinking how wonderful it was, a green jewel of an island framed in white, the sea all about it a silken shimmering blue.
>
> (Morpurgo 2000: 53)

In a film version of this scene the shots, like the sentences, would need to be much longer with fewer cuts, making the pace more gentle and effectively conveying Michael's relaxed state of mind. The editing, therefore, is a key determinant of a film's pace and tone.

Table 4.2 Types of camera shot

SHOT	DESCRIPTION	USE
Close-up	When a face or an object fills the screen	To direct the audience's attention to an important detail or to make them consider the emotions of a character
Medium shot	A shot that shows an actor's whole body or perhaps the top part of their body in the frame	To show body language or action such as running and ensure that the audience can still see what the actors are doing but not in minute detail
Long shot	A shot which shows an entire landscape, crowd or building from a distance	To establish the wider physical surroundings of a scene and contextualise it geographically. Also used to reinforce the size and scale of a place or a crowd in order to create a sense of spectacle
Zoom in and zoom out	When a camera closes in from a long shot to a close-up (zoom in) or pulls back from a close-up to a longer shot (zoom out)	To move the audience's attention from the wider setting to a specific detail or character in a crowd. Also used to dramatically establish a character's dangerous or hopeless situation by focusing on an individual and then zooming out to reveal where they are
Panning	When the camera moves from left to right or up and down but the camera is on a fixed base	To slowly show the viewer a wide landscape. Also used to reflect the point of view of a person who is standing still but moving their gaze across a scene
Tracking	When the whole camera moves along, keeping pace alongside the object of the shot	To follow movement and create a sense of dynamism without having to cut away to another shot

Lighting and sets

Elements such as lighting, sets, costume and make-up are vital to our reading of film, but are sometimes taken for granted by an audience. Of course, these elements do not always need to be dramatic and overt. If we are watching a scene set in a restaurant during the day where two people are having a conversation and we do not notice the lighting or setting because the scene looks 'normal', then the lighting technicians and set dressers have done their job well. It is therefore important to remind children that nearly every scene, interior or exterior, has been lit and its set designed or dressed in some way – even a scene set in a dark forest needs to be lit with the correct balance between light and dark and may require the trees to be fabricated in order to fit the feel of the scene. It is easier, of course, to examine scenes with more obvious or stylised uses of lighting and sets, for it is then that we realise just how intrinsically these elements are linked to the tone of the film. Whether we see a bright and sunny spacious apartment or a dark and gloomy cave, the lighting suffuses almost every frame of a film and often, consciously or subconsciously, determines how we feel in any given scene. Consider, for example, how the differing settings within one film can make us feel. *Harry Potter and the Goblet of Fire* takes us on a journey from the dramatic yet warm-hued surroundings of Hogwarts Castle (the sets and lighting stressing the mysterious yet ultimately safe nature of Harry's school) through the harsh, rocky and coldly lit outdoor arena where Harry faces the dragon, to the overwhelmingly dark and foreboding graveyard where Harry must confront Voldemort. Each of these key locations helps to engender the appropriate feelings within us, both while we are watching the film and when we remember it afterwards, and plays a central part in defining the tone of each scene.

Acting, make-up and costume

Just as camera shots and lighting are the filmmaker's primary method of establishing the emotional tone of the narrative, acting, make-up and costume are the ways through which character is explored on film. Due to the visual nature of the medium and the prevailing cult of celebrity, actors often become the dominant feature of a film in terms of marketing and promotion and, at least initially, we may well notice performance before direction, lighting or other technical features. While it is not the purpose of literacy studies to explore the craft of acting, it is important to discuss performance in class not only because it is a subject on which nearly all children feel they can offer an opinion, but also because it leads to a greater understanding of character. When I taught the sessions on Tim Burton's *Charlie and the Chocolate Factory*, for example (see Chapter 6.2), I took some time to question the children about Johnny Depp's performance as Willy Wonka. What began as a relatively simple chat about Depp as an actor led to some interesting points about how his take on Wonka differed from the novel's. Many of the children preferred Depp's portrayal of the sweet-maker because of its inherent strangeness and sinister undertones. One child claimed that he liked the performance because he could not tell initially whether Willy Wonka was good or evil and that Depp kept you guessing as to Wonka's true intentions. While this is certainly also true of the way Dahl writes Wonka, the children felt that the written version of the character was, at least initially, far more welcoming and open, leaving less intrigue for the reader. The discussion evolved naturally from this point, and the fact that I had started by asking a straightforward question about a popular actor of whom they were all aware meant that more of the children engaged in the discussion. In fact, Johnny Depp is an excellent actor to study. One of the finest-ever screen performers, Depp displays 'astonishing dramatic range' (Dix 2008: 218), with his ability to play serious, realistic characters (J.M. Barrie in *Finding Neverland*, John Dillinger in *Public Enemies*, Sweeney Todd) as well as unusual and strange figures through highly stylised, nuanced and often witty performances (Captain Jack Sparrow in *The Pirates of the Caribbean* trilogy, Edward Scissorhands and Ichabod Crane in *Sleepy Hollow*). Depp is highly skilled at expressing emotion and character through his face and eyes, and figures such as Willy Wonka and Jack Sparrow are worth examining with children precisely because they are deliberately odd but also because their surface behaviour often belies their true intentions and motivations – as Tim Burton says, when acting, Depp is always 'doing a lot under the surface' (Burton and Salisbury 1995: 94). When children are given such good examples of intelligent performance and the opportunity to explore facial expression and body language for themselves in drama sessions, they will be better equipped to read character through acting.

Added to performance, we must also take account of costume and make-up when examining a character. Although we would not judge a person's character solely by what they wear in real life, we are likely to consider it as a signifier of personality on some level. On screen, however, costume forms an even more central part of our judgement of character. This is due to the fact that film is a primarily visual medium and therefore as an audience we tend to be more visually discriminative, consciously or subconsciously. In addition, with a running time of only two hours for the average film, we do not have the luxury of getting to know a character over days or weeks and we must therefore use every piece of information available to us when analysing them. Often costume designs in film employ stereotype as cinematic shorthand, knowingly using colour, style and fashions to quickly convey ideas about the wearer to the audience. This is not to say that the filmmakers and designers are necessarily guilty of stereotyping in the negative sense of the word but simply that the onus is on them to transmit ideas to their audience quickly and effectively. This can be seen clearly in the film *Enchanted*, a comedy in which the animated Disney character Giselle (Amy Adams) stumbles into the very real world of contemporary New York en route to marrying a prince (James Marsden). The costume designer Mona May draws on elegant dress designs typical of Walt Disney classics such as Cinderella and Snow White, which are not only appropriate to the story but which also allow more well versed viewers to draw conclusions about Giselle's character, namely that she is elegant, kind, feminine in a traditional sense and, also, somewhat naive. In addition, the casting of the superb Adams, with her red hair and fine features, visually cites one of Disney's most famous heroines, Ariel, the eponymous *Little Mermaid*.

Similarly, studying any character on screen encourages deeper insight into how information is transmitted visually, usually on two levels: the *implicit* and the *explicit*. We can see how this is done if we visually analyse a well-known character such as Wolverine as played by Hugh Jackman in the *X-Men* trilogy and its prequel *X-Men Origins: Wolverine*. In terms of explicit visual information, we can see that Wolverine is tall and muscular, reflecting his abilities in combat and his history as a warrior. When his deadly adamantium claws are displayed, we clearly understand that the fact that weapons are an inseparable part of his body tells us that violence and aggression are elements of his character. This is confirmed by his body language throughout the films which tends to be tense and alert and radiates power and strength. Any visual reading of a character must, however, also take account of other, more implicit visual information which requires the observer to make slightly more subtle connections. For example, Wolverine often wears a leather jacket, which traditionally carries connotations of a tough, rebellious masculinity. In addition, Wolverine has a distinctive hairstyle that is raised into fins at either side of his head. As well as echoing the mask worn by the character in the original comic book source material, the hair also mimics the head shape and pointy ears of an animal such as a wolverine. This, combined with his profusion of facial hair, suggests that the character has a wild, untamed and animalistic side to his personality. While we would not perhaps expect many primary school children to pick up on all of these visual hints when looking at a picture or clip of a character, they can still be encouraged to draw conclusions about character from what they see. The explicit/implicit approach can be applied to any character be they on screen, in a comic or in a picture book and helps to encourage both a surface and a deeper reading of visuals. Here, the explicit information is that which has a direct or demonstrable link to characteristics, in *Doctor Who*, for example, the fact that David Tennant's Doctor wears a brown pinstripe suit as opposed to an outfit designed for physical combat proves that the Doctor is more likely to think his way out of situations rather than fight, and the fact that he wears casual Converse trainers proves that his love of adventuring frequently requires him to be on the move. The implicit information is that which suggests information about a character but does not necessarily prove it, for example the way in which the Doctor pairs his suit with his trainers implies that he has an irreverent and unconventional approach to life and suggests a refusal to play by established rules.

Look closer: *Jurassic Park*

In order to demonstrate how these various aspects of film are combined by a director to form a cohesive whole, it will be useful to examine a scene from a well-known film. Directed by the legendary Steven Spielberg, *Jurassic Park* (1993) is not only the tenth most successful film of all time (Imdb 2009) but is a definitive example of a blockbuster which has mass appeal yet is also sophisticated and engaging. The scene I have chosen to focus on comes in the latter half of the film (beginning at 1:30:17) and follows Dr Alan Grant (Sam Neill) and two children Lex and Tim Murphy (Ariana Richards and Joseph Mazzello) as they are caught in the middle of a Gallimimus stampede in the park. The scene begins with an establishing shot of the field through which the tired characters are walking, the lighting and location showing that it is a warm sunny day. As the characters get nearer to the camera we can see that their faces and clothes are caked in mud and that they sport numerous wounds, demonstrating that they have already had a difficult time in the park. The next shot, a long shot, puts the trio on the left of the screen, revealing the rolling hills and the distant herd of dinosaurs that is heading in their direction. This provides the audience with a sense of scale and subtly suggests the impending threat; the inclusion of the distant rumble of hooves on the soundtrack adding to the rising tension. Spielberg and his editor Michael Kahn then alternate long shots of the dinosaurs running nearer with close-ups of the anxious Lex, fascinated Dr Grant and terrified Tim as he announces 'They're ... uh ... they're flocking this way!' Here, the close-ups prevent us from forgetting about the humans, thereby ensuring that characterisation is not lost in the action. When the three individuals are finally engulfed by the herd and have to run, Spielberg uses medium shots at ground level placing us inside the stampede as the beasts narrowly miss the children and Dr Grant and charge past the camera as if also avoiding us. The tense and thrilling atmosphere is also heightened by the deafening gallop of the dinosaurs which has now reached a crescendo and drowns out any other sounds. At the climax of the scene, when the Tyrannosaurus Rex attacks the fleeing herd and kills a Gallimimus, Spielberg places the camera at a point behind the characters as they watch from their hiding place. The shot is framed by the back of their heads, accentuating their proximity to the predator. The final image of the scene closes in on the three observers and stresses character once more by showing us Dr Grant's professional interest in the attack, Lex's shock and Tim's somewhat humorous fixation with the gore. Here Spielberg, like all good storytellers, reminds us that action, tension and thrills only matter to an audience if we care about the characters involved.

4.2

Film

Teaching Ideas

The following sessions aim to help pupils become familiar with reading and responding to film as a medium. The sessions have been planned as a progression from static images to short films without dialogue and then finally to an examination of longer, more complex film narratives. They can be taught individually or as part of a longer programme of study. The activities in this section are aimed at Year 5, but can be adapted for any age group. For further ideas and resources, see Chapter 4.3.

Film and character

Learning objectives

- To read images as texts, discussing how they transmit information
- To explore how character is represented visually
- To develop comprehension and inference skills using explicit and implicit visual cues
- To compare how a written text and a visual text present the same information
- To use images as the basis of written work about character.

Resources

- Book: *Harry Potter and the Chamber of Secrets* by J.K. Rowling
- Still image of Alan Rickman as Professor Severus Snape from the *Harry Potter* films (images available on Harry Potter Official Website, www.harrypotter.com)
- Still images of characters from film and television from the internet or magazines
- Interactive whiteboard or visualiser.

- For this short activity, search online or in magazines for images of characters from a film or television programme. Initially, you may wish to choose characters who are recognisable to the children, as they can comment on them with more confidence. However, showing the children some images of characters they might not be familiar with as the activity progresses will encourage the children to use their imagination more. Images of characters can be found online relatively easily by visiting the official homepage of the film or simply using a search engine.

- Talk to the children about how appearances can influence our views of people's character. Initially, this is a good opportunity to discuss the fact that while we are often told not to judge by appearances in the real world, authors and filmmakers often deliberately use visual stereotypes to make the reader/audience feel a certain way about a character.

- Read aloud the description of Severus Snape in *Harry Potter and the Chamber of Secrets*: 'He was a thin man with sallow skin, a hooked nose and greasy, shoulder length black hair' (Rowling 1998: 62). Ask the children to discuss the brief description and to work out what J.K. Rowling intends her audience to feel about Snape. Again, this is a good opportunity to discuss stereotypes here. Of course, while we understand that in real life, greasy hair and sallow skin do not signify anything negative about a person's character, in terms of the book, these images have been used to evoke specific feelings within the reader (the nose reminiscent of a predatory hawk, the greasy hair symbolising Snape's unlikeable personality).

- Show some still images of Alan Rickman as Snape in the Warner Bros. films of Harry Potter. Ask the children to comment on how the actor's costume, hair, make-up and facial expressions suggest aspects of their personality.

- Next show another image of a character from a different film. Two good examples are Helena Bonham Carter as the Red Queen and Johnny Depp as The Mad Hatter from Tim Burton's *Alice in Wonderland* (available on the Empire website, www.empireonline.com). Ask the children to write down two headings: 'Characteristics' and 'Evidence'. For each observation they make about the Red Queen's or The Mad Hatter's make-up, expression and costume, ask them to consider how it affects their judgement of the character (or, conversely, ask them to describe the Red Queen's character and then back this up with visual evidence). Some examples may be:

The Red Queen

Characteristics	*Evidence*
Eccentric	Unusual make-up, strange hairstyle
Cruel/haughty	Downturned mouth, cold eyes
Powerful	Holding sceptre like a club
Bloodthirsty	Crimson and scarlet hair and jewellery suggest blood.

The Mad Hatter

Characteristics	Evidence
Eccentric	Make-up, hair and costume
Mischievous	Hint of a smile
Wild	Hair and eyebrows are uncontrollable
Accident prone	Stained fingers and bandaged thumb.

- For each character give the class a short time, perhaps four minutes, to note down the things they notice about each character. Use as many different characters as you feel are necessary for the children to develop their character responses.

- If you wish to develop this activity further, select one of the images you have looked at and leave it on the board. Ask the children to write a paragraph, imagining how this character would be described in a book. Try to forge links between the visual observations and the character, as in Rowling's description of Snape. For example, a description of The Mad Hatter might be: 'His green eyes sparkled mischievously under his uncontrollable, flame-coloured eyebrows. His smile was at once kind and full of mystery, as if it were unclear what was going on in his head.' Share the paragraphs with the class, focusing on good examples of the children's work which use the visual aspects to imply character traits.

Beginning reading film

Learning objectives
- To understand that film is a type of text which can be read
- To begin to analyse how facial expression and body language can create tone in films
- To begin to analyse how drama and film techniques such as acting, directing, camera angles and editing can create tone
- To understand how information can be implied to and inferred by an audience.

Resources
- DVDs: *Emma* (Miramax Films 1996); *The Wizard of Oz* (Warner Bros. 1939)
- Interactive whiteboard.

- For this activity, the idea is to get children used to reading moving film without sound and dialogue by watching silent clips. The clips selected here are taken from films which are suitable for children but are not necessarily ones they will be familiar with. Two good examples are *The Wizard of Oz* and *Emma*, but any television or film clip which makes sense when viewed without sound can be used, as long as it is not a recent film which all the children will recognise instantly.

- Start by discussing the ways in which we show how we feel (words, expressions, body language), establishing links with previous drama work if appropriate. If you have done the previous activity on character, re-emphasise how character is shown through costume, make-up and hair.

- Show a clip from *The Wizard of Oz*. Some children might be familiar with this, but try not to give too much information about the film, the setting or even the title. Watch the clip beginning at 45:59 where the three travellers, Dorothy, the Tin Man and the Scarecrow, walk through the woods, but watch it with the sound off so that the clip is silent. Stop the clip at 49:00, where the Lion says 'I am a coward'. Ask the children to write a short commentary on the clip saying what is happening and how the characters are feeling. Watch the clip again, allowing the children to make notes the second time.

- After the second time, allow the children to discuss what they have seen in pairs and then ask five of the children to read back their commentary. You may need to extend their analyses with specific questioning, pointing to evidence to back up what they have argued. Some suitable questions might be:
  - How do the three characters feel at the start of the clip? How do you know?
  - How does the Tin Man feel when the Lion jumps out at him? (Draw attention to his shivering)
  - What is your first impression of the Lion?
  - How does this change and why?
  - How would you describe Dorothy's character?
  - How would you describe the Lion's character?
  - How does the mood of the scene change? (Show how it moves from sinister and scary to humorous.)

- Watch the clip again, with the sound.

- For the second clip, choose something which is a little more subtle in terms of emotion and tone. The scene from *Emma* where Emma (Gwyneth Paltrow) is confronted by Mr Knightley (Jeremy Northam) over her rude behaviour is a good example. It begins at 1:27:21 and ends at 1:29:27. Again, allow the children to watch it with the sound muted and ask them to work out what might be going on. The scene is quite subtle and emotionally complex and therefore the children will not define the exchange between the two characters exactly. It is important to stress that they do not need to 'correctly' guess what is happening but instead use the evidence onscreen to consider how the characters might be feeling.

- After the first viewing, ask the children to consider the following questions:
  - What is happening in the scene?
  - How are the characters feeling?

- ● What do you think the relationship between the two characters might be?
- ● What genre of film might this be?
- ● When is it set?
- ● What music would be suitable for this scene?

■ Play the clip once more. After the second viewing, share some of the children's responses to the questions and, with the class, begin to work out some possible interpretations of the scene. When you have settled on a few different versions of what the scene might be about, ask the children to watch it a third time and, in pairs, to write some lines of dialogue that Emma and Mr Knightley could be saying. The children do not need to write all the dialogue for the characters but can suggest two or three lines for each.

■ Allow some of the children to read back their dialogue aloud as you play the clip a few more times. Afterwards, watch the clip with the sound but again stress that this is not necessarily the 'right answer' to the activity.

Reading short films and understanding tone: Pixar animation

Learning objectives
- ■ To watch a short film and to discuss the plot and the tone
- ■ To consider how sound effects, music and visuals can replace dialogue in a narrative
- ■ To understand how information can be implied to and inferred by an audience.

Resources
- ■ DVD: *Pixar Short Films Collection* (Walt Disney Pictures 2008)
- ■ Interactive whiteboard.

■ Discuss the previous sessions (if you have taught them) with the class and recap some of the ways stories can be told or performed without dialogue. Try to ask the children to think of adverts or shows they have seen where there is minimal dialogue but the story is still transmitted to the audience.

■ Introduce the Pixar short film, *Luxo Jr.* Explain to the children that this was one of the first ever computer-generated short films and that it was made by the company who went on to make *Toy Story*, *Up* and *Finding Nemo*. Watch the short film and then ask the children what the story was. Comment on any words the children use to describe the characters, for example 'mum' 'dad' or 'baby' to describe the lamps, or gendered words such as 'him' or 'her'. If they use terms such as these, ask the children how they knew the characters were male or female, or how they knew the characters were related. The point here is that the film uses two lamps to tell a story and, without adding eyes or faces to them, manages to imbue them with character and personality. Encourage the children to talk about how the lamps express character through movement and gesture.

- Watch the film a second time but ask the children to think about how the mood of the film is established. After the second viewing, write a list of things that help tell the story, including:
  - Music
  - Movement
  - Sound effects
  - Timing
  - Personification of the lamps.
- Next watch the animated short *Knick Knack* twice. Ask the children what the story is and ask them to describe the tone of the piece.
- Introduce the idea of close-ups in your discussion. Ask the children why we need to see close-ups of the snowman and the girl and what these add to our understanding of the story.
- Discuss the music and the way in which it contributes to the light feel of the film. This is a good exercise in studying tone because you can retell the events of *Knick Knack* (a snowman trapped in a snow globe tries to escape) and ask the children to consider why the film is not upsetting or sad. As an extension of this idea, ask the children to think of some ways in which the tone or the atmosphere of the film could be changed to be more sinister or bleak, while keeping the story the same (for example: changing the music, the lighting, the colours or the facial expressions of the main character).
- Finally, watch the Pixar animation *Geri's Game*. This is a more complex film and, while it has a light tone, the story and the way it is told is less straightforward. The plot revolves around an old man called Geri, who is playing chess on his own in the park. When he makes a move, he then gets up and switches sides and plays another move. As each 'player', he takes on a different persona (innocent and scared as the first player, while aggressive and gloating as the second). The film cuts rapidly between Geri's two alter egos, until the first Geri tricks his opponent and wins.
- After watching the film once, ask the children to write a paragraph each, explaining what is happening in the story. After sharing a few of these, discuss with the class what they think is happening and agree on an interpretation. If the children are confused by the story, watch selected scenes or clips again as evidence to explain that Geri is both characters.
- Ask the children to think about how the film is edited to make it seem as if there are two opponents and how the tension increases in the game before watching the film again. Some of the children may observe that the film uses a succession of rapid cuts, quick shots and close-ups of the players and the chess pieces until it builds to the point of Geri's fake heart attack (02:12 to 03:07), after which the shots are longer and the cuts

are less frequent. Here, children might need some help in using terms such as 'cuts' and 'quick shots', so write these on the board.

- Finally, watch the film again and ask the children to note down how the film's tone changes throughout (for example, light and pleasant, then humorous, followed by a section of increasing tension which is then broken with humour once more). You may also want to show the film again after this and allow a child (or the class) to note out loud the points where the feeling or tone of the film changes. This will then help all the children to see how the tone of a film can often vary.

Reading film: *Doctor Who*

Learning objectives

- To learn how to read film and to explore some of the ways in which it creates tone through lighting, editing and camera angles
- To learn about some of the techniques and the terminology of filmmaking
- To analyse selected film sequences and comment on how they transmit narrative information both implicitly and explicitly.

Resources

- DVD: *Doctor Who*, Series 3, Volume 1: episode entitled *Gridlock* (BBC 2007)
- Question sheets (see Figures 4.1 and 4.2)
- Interactive whiteboard.

- This session is based around two clips from the BBC television series, *Doctor Who*. I have chosen this because I believe it to be one of the best-written and -produced programmes on television and also because it is immensely popular with many children. The session, however, does not rely on children being familiar with the programme and will work just as well if they have never seen an episode before. It will help if you have watched the whole episode before showing the extracts to the children. If you wish to use different film clips, look for two sequences from a film or television programme which are noticeably different in tone (a sad or quiet scene and an action scene, for example) and which have a mix of close-up shots, long shots, editing techniques and camera angles.
- The episode I have chosen, *Gridlock*, is rated PG (Parental Guidance). When showing PG material to a class, it is necessary to send out a letter in advance in order to obtain parents' or guardians' written permission for their children to view it.
- Introduce the session by asking children to name their favourite television programmes

and films and explain why they like them. Explain to the children that a film, like a book, can be read but in a different way and that they are going to be asked about how the tone of a clip is established. Tone is a notoriously difficult concept to explain to children and this is where film clips prove extremely useful in terms of the powerful effect they can have on our emotions. Words or phrases which you might prefer to use instead of tone, are 'atmosphere', 'mood' or simply 'the way a clip makes you feel'.

- Introduce the first clip from *Gridlock* by asking one of the children to explain who the Doctor is and what the programme is about. Ask the children to identify the genre or type of programme (science fiction/adventure/action/drama/horror). The clip has a lot of different things happening and it will help, therefore, to establish the context briefly. The episode is set on Earth, far into the future, where the human race spend their lives in flying cars which float on top of one another in an unending traffic jam under the streets of New New York. Prior to the clip, the Doctor's companion Martha Jones (Freema Agyeman) has been kidnapped by a young couple, Milo (Travis Oliver) and Cheen (Leonora Crichlow). The Doctor (David Tennant) must climb down from car to car through the layers of traffic above in order to reach her.

- Explain to the children that you are going to watch the clip more than once and that, on the first viewing, they are simply to watch it and think about what is happening. The clip begins at 24:27 with the Doctor's entrance into a commuter's car ('Capsule open'). A suitable place to end the clip is at 27:27 (where Martha asks 'How long have we got?' and Milo replies 'Eight minutes, maximum').

- After the first viewing, ask the children some questions (but let them discuss the things they noticed and found interesting):
  - What was happening in the clip?
  - Who was in it?
  - Did they enjoy it?

- Give the children the question sheet (Figure 4.1) and read through the first three questions with them. If you are not using the *Doctor Who* clip, you will need to write different questions, but try to keep to the same areas (plot, tone, camera work, lighting and genre). Show the clip again and ask the children to note down the answers to the first three questions as they watch.

- The children may need a few minutes to write their answers down after viewing the clip. Encourage them to share the answers with a partner and then with the class. In terms of the third question on genre, try to encourage the children to discuss how genre is denoted visually and what is expected from a typical science-fiction text.

- Read through questions 4 and 5 and watch the clip again. The reason for this is so that the children can watch it, concentrating solely on tone and filmmaking technique. Give them some time to write down their answers. In the discussion of questions 4 and 5, really encourage the children to back up what they say with examples (showing the example clips if necessary). They should be thinking about lighting, camera movement,

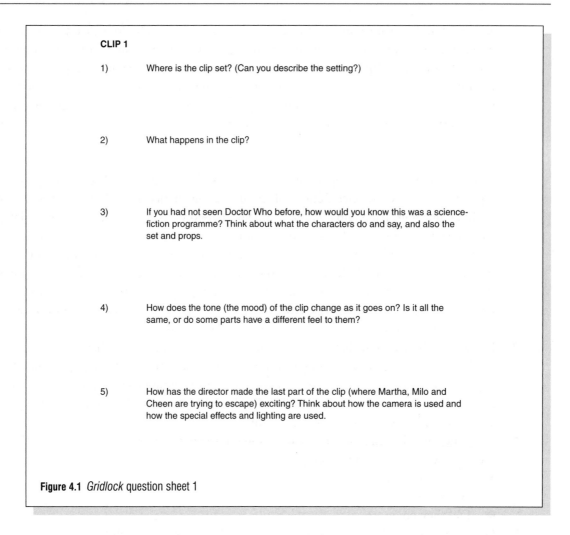

CLIP 1

1) Where is the clip set? (Can you describe the setting?)

2) What happens in the clip?

3) If you had not seen Doctor Who before, how would you know this was a science-fiction programme? Think about what the characters do and say, and also the set and props.

4) How does the tone (the mood) of the clip change as it goes on? Is it all the same, or do some parts have a different feel to them?

5) How has the director made the last part of the clip (where Martha, Milo and Cheen are trying to escape) exciting? Think about how the camera is used and how the special effects and lighting are used.

Figure 4.1 *Gridlock* question sheet 1

special effects and music and, vitally, *how* these techniques affect the audience. Some areas you may want to draw their attention to are:

- The way in which the lighting differs, depending on which car the scene is set in (bright for the first car, then dark at the end to enforce the danger and loneliness of Martha, Milo and Cheen's plight).
- The way in which the tone changes (comic at first, then more serious as the Doctor discovers the Macra monsters, followed by an increasing sense of jeopardy and excitement as Martha, Milo and Cheen escape from the Macra and finally a feeling of quiet threat and danger as they wait in the darkness).
- The way the camera is used (static shots for the early scenes and then dizzying movement and close-ups to create a sense of chaos when the monsters attack the car).

- The editing (draw the children's attention to how long each shot is before it cuts away; at the start of the clip, the shots are relatively long but in the attack sequence, there are lots of very quick cuts to increase excitement).
- The music (no music until the Doctor begins to look under the car at the monsters below and then fast, exciting music for the attack sequence).

- Write on the board the things we look for when reading film:
  - Camera angles
  - Editing
  - Music/sound
  - Lighting.

- When the children have discussed the clip, introduce the second clip. This is from the very end of the episode when Martha and the Doctor have been reunited and the humans have been freed from the underground motorway. Tell the children that the clip is very different from the one they have just seen. Again, allow them to simply watch the clip on the first showing. The clip begins at 40:13 and runs until the end of the episode at 43:33.

- After the children have watched it once, read through the first two questions on the second question sheet (Figure 4.2) and then watch the clip again, allowing the children to take notes as they watch. After they have watched the clip, encourage them to discuss their answers with a partner. Ideally, the children will make the link between the quieter soundtrack and the calm tone of the scene, but it is also worth mentioning the hymn 'Abide with Me' which Martha hears the city singing. This is a good opportunity to ask the children what we would associate a hymn with and how it might make us feel.

- Read through questions 3 and 4 and watch the clip a third time, giving the children time to formulate their answers afterwards.

- When discussing the answers, try to prompt the children to really consider how the scene differs from the earlier ones. While they should not necessarily assume close-ups are only employed during calmer scenes, they may want to think about how this technique allows us to read the characters' faces and think about how they are feeling. They should also consider the fact that the cuts between shots are less frequent and that the camera is more static, creating a calmer and more thoughtful feel to the scene. At the end of the activity, ask the children which scene they preferred and for what reason.

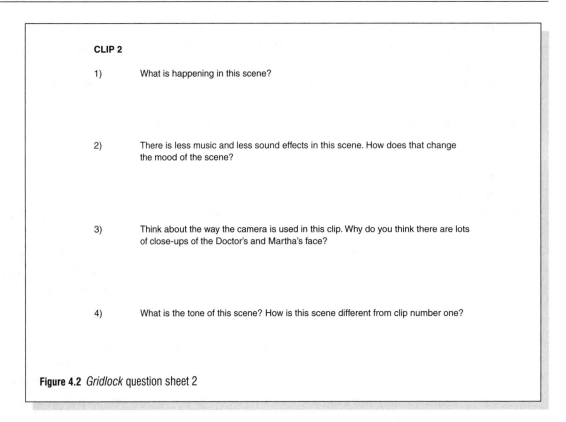

CLIP 2

1) What is happening in this scene?

2) There is less music and less sound effects in this scene. How does that change the mood of the scene?

3) Think about the way the camera is used in this clip. Why do you think there are lots of close-ups of the Doctor's and Martha's face?

4) What is the tone of this scene? How is this scene different from clip number one?

Figure 4.2 *Gridlock* question sheet 2

Film

Further Ideas and Resources

These lists of resources and ideas for activities supplement the teaching ideas in Chapter 4.2 and offer suggestions for teaching activities based around film with other age groups.

Year 1

> ### Resources
> ■ DVD: *The Snowman* (Snowman Enterprises 1982).

■ Show the children the animation *The Snowman* and explain to them that this is a story told without words. Ask the children to watch carefully as they will be asked questions about it afterwards.

■ After the film is finished, ask the children to discuss in pairs what they thought about it. Ask one or two of the children to retell the story briefly to the rest of the class. Allow the class to add to or enhance the retelling with their own observations.

■ In pairs, ask the children to decide upon their favourite part of the film and then ask each pair to come to the front of the class and mime the scene (one taking on the role of the Snowman and the other playing the boy, James). The other children can guess which part they are re-enacting.

■ Replay two sections of the film. First, show the motorbike ride again (12:58–14:42). Ask the children to think about the following questions:
  ● How does the ride feel exciting without using words?
  ● How do we know they are going fast on the motorbike?

■ Allow the children to make their own observations, but you may wish to direct their attention to some specific aspects of the clip such as the music and how its tempo changes when the ride begins, the view from the front of the motorbike, James's facial expressions and the animals running.

■ The second clip is the pair's arrival at Father Christmas's house. It begins at 19:24 and ends at 21:34. Watch the clip twice and then ask the children how the clip feels at the beginning (pause the DVD when the two friends are slowly walking through the dark forest). If the children find this difficult to answer, ask them to imagine how James might feel at this point.

- Watch the clip again and this time ask the children to put up their hand when they think the mood changes in the clip (they might need to watch the clip once more). Explain to the children that the mood changes at 19:40 when the music becomes fast and upbeat.

- To finish, get the children to draw their favourite part of the film and write a sentence or two to explain it.

Year 3–4

Resources
- DVD: *Lilo and Stitch* (Walt Disney Pictures 2002).

- This activity requires pupils to look at a film which is more emotionally and thematically sophisticated and to discuss its meaning. Explain to the children that they are going to watch a clip from *Lilo and Stitch* (many may already have seen it). Introduce the clip but do not give too much information – explain that the clip involves Lilo and her older sister Nani and that Lilo has just upset her sister. The less the children know about the clip, the more they will have to read the film for information, so allow them to work out what is going on. The clip runs from 19:12 to 22:06.

- Watch the clip twice and then ask the children, in pairs, to discuss what they think is happening here. Lilo and Nani's parents have died, leaving Nani to raise Lilo as best she can. Allow plenty of time for a class discussion, asking the children to back up what they think is happening with evidence from the clip.

- Some questions you can ask are:
  - What is happening in the clip?
  - How would you describe the relationship between Lilo and Nani?
  - What do you think has happened to Lilo's parents? Why?
  - How would you describe Lilo? How would you describe Nani?

- This discussion should encourage the children to develop their inference skills. Ask them to focus on the dialogue between the characters, such as Lilo's line: 'We're a broken family, aren't we?' and Nani's comment that people 'just don't know what to say'. These lines imply information about the characters' family life and past events and children can be encouraged to explore their meaning.

- When asking the children to discuss the sisters' relationship in terms of their argument and Lilo's anger, encourage them to look beyond the shouting and chasing and examine their deeper bond, as shown towards the end of the clip.

- As a conclusion, give the children some time to write down in note form or in more formal sentences how they would describe Lilo's character. Share some of the descriptions.
- There is also a second clip to watch from the film. If you have time, this can be done as part of the session, otherwise it can be viewed in a second session. The clip runs from 51:34 to 53:32. It shows a scene with Lilo and her dog/alien Stitch, who has crash-landed from another planet.
- Play the clip twice and ask the children some questions:
  - How is Stitch feeling in this scene? How do you know?
  - How does the scene make you feel? Think about the music and the words.
  - Why do you think the camera pulls back to show Stitch from far away at the end of the scene?
  - What similarities are there between Lilo and Stitch as characters?
- Encourage the children to consider the themes of the film such as family, friendship, loss and loneliness. Also, try to make them consider the way that the music, the muted colours and the camera work (slow fadeouts and wide shots at the end) help to create a sombre and sad tone to the scene.
- If you wish to take this further than the discussion, ask the children to write a list or a few sentences about the things in the film which make the scene sad.

Year 6

Resources
- DVD: *Edward Scissorhands* (Twentieth Century Fox 1990)
- Interactive whiteboard.

- This film session gets children to explore how tone, theme and character are represented in a sophisticated film. It uses Tim Burton's *Edward Scissorhands*. The film is rated PG, so you will need to obtain parental permission before showing it.
- Show the first clip from the film. It begins at 17:13 and runs until 18:58. The scene shows Peg Boggs (Dianne Wiest) bringing Edward Scissorhands (Johnny Depp) to her home from the castle he lived in on his own. Play the clip twice.
- Ask the children some questions which require them to use inference while watching the clip:
  - How does Edward feel when he enters the house?
  - What do you think Edward feels when he sees the picture of Kim? How do we know?
  - How would you describe the characters of Peg and Edward?
  - How do the music and the long shots create a feeling in the scene?

- The second clip runs from 1:12:45–1:14:20 and shows Kim Boggs (Winona Ryder) dancing in the snow which falls from Edward's ice sculpture. Show the clip twice and then ask the children some questions about the tone of the scene:
  - What is the mood of the scene?
  - How is the mood created through the music?
  - What effect does the slow fading between shots have?
  - What do you learn about Edward and Kim's characters in this scene?
  - How are the two clips similar? How are they different?
- Discuss the answers with the children and, if they are able to, extend the discussion to include the thematic elements of the film such as difference, the role of the outsider and the nature of beauty in all its forms.

5.1

Genre

In the previous three sections we have examined picture books, comic books and film as individual types of media, and we will now consider some of the areas within literacy which can be explored through these visual art forms. The concept of genre is a key part of literacy teaching and an understanding of it enables children to develop not only their own writing, but also their critical and analytical reading skills. Genre is one of the many areas in which visually based texts can be linked to the teaching of the traditional written text so that children can concomitantly develop their knowledge of individual media and of genre itself. On a basic level, a genre is a category or a type. Identifying which genre (or genres) a text belongs to is a means of understanding and classifying it based on its form and content while also relating it to existing texts. Considering how an individual text conforms to or contravenes the traditional rules of its particular genre allows pupils to develop a specialised knowledge of both text and genre and encourages them to make connections between texts. This is as true of visual texts as it is of written ones; as Gillian Rose states, 'It helps to make sense of the significance of elements of an individual image if you know that some of them recur repeatedly in other images' (2001: 19). For those pupils who are only just beginning to learn about genre, an examination of how it manifests across film, picture books and comic books can provide a more accessible and memorable way of teaching the subject than exploring it through written texts. For those who already have an understanding of genre in relation to the written text, re-examining the concept through visual texts gives them opportunities to apply their knowledge in different ways.

A visual approach to genre begins with establishing how a given image contains visual cues or triggers which allow us to make associations and comparisons with existing types of images. For example, if the words were removed from an illustrated storybook such as David McKee's *Elmer*, leaving only the pictures, most adults and children would arguably understand that the images are intended for an audience of children – but what precisely is it about these images that allow us to understand this and categorise them so? First, there is the use of *colour*, with many pages employing bright reds, greens, blues and yellows alongside numerous others. We might well associate this uncomplicated and bold use of colour with the colours of children's toys and furniture or even with the colours used by children in their own paintings. Second, the *style* of drawing is simple; objects are delineated by clear *lines* with no attempt to make them anything other than two-dimensional and the *shapes* chosen veer more towards geometric than realistic. Significantly, the animals and scenery could be described as representations of real things, not replications; the trees, elephants and birds possess the features they need to be identifiable (leaves, trunks and beaks) but are stylised and do not closely resemble anything in the real world. Here, McKee's charming illustrations indicate the author's strong sense of audience and are more akin to a naive style of art, deliberately and cleverly mimicking typical children's artwork. This is particularly evident in the look of the title character Elmer, composed as he is of simple patchwork squares of colour, as well as in the scribbled sun whose delineated circumference fails to contain the yellow pencil colouring (McKee 1990: 3). The *content* of the images is also a major factor in determining genre. We can see that the tone of most of the pictures is light and cheerful, with no violence or any images which could be considered distressing, while the focus on friendly anthropomorphic animals also links the images to the popular genre of children's animal stories. While it is not necessarily true that the more child-like a drawing is, the more it is aimed at a young audience, the above elements in McKee's images and the associations they trigger in the viewer have the cumulative effect of enabling us to identify the image as belonging to the genre of a young children's animal story. Therefore, in a painted or drawn image, we can identify genre visually through content, artistic style and the use of colour, line and shape.

In terms of the moving image, the identification of genre in film uses some of the above elements such as content, colour and the style or design of the film but also includes additional features such as costume, dialogue, sets, props and the soundtrack. Here, Colin McArthur's theory of iconography, which discusses how images onscreen create a sense of genre for the audience, is useful. McArthur identifies how many of the films within any given genre display 'continuity … of patterns of visual imagery, of recurrent objects and figures in dynamic relationship' which not only help the audience to quickly identify the type of film they are watching but also aids them in their understanding of the characters and elements of the plot. McArthur refers to this repeated imagery as the 'iconography' of the genre and identifies three main ways in which it is evident: 'the physical presence, attributes and dress of the actors and the characters they play;… the milieu within which the characters operate; and … the technology at the characters' disposal' (1972: 23–4). When studying film with children, McArthur's theory of iconography can be usefully simplified into three categories which will help them to define the genre: the characters (including what they say and how they look), the setting (including set design, lighting and locations) and the props. Discussion and examination of these three elements constitutes a solid, yet simple starting point for any discussion of genre on film. For example, if we look at a film text such as *Doctor Who*, we can see that, in an average episode, we are able to tell that the genre is science fiction due to an analysis of these elements. Many of the settings for scenes in *Doctor Who*, such as the interior of the Doctor's TARDIS with its beautifully futuristic, alien design and complex flight controls, indicate that the programme is not set within the bounds of reality. Second, the props used, such as the Doctor's trusty sonic screwdriver and the various alien gadgets he encounters, would also, by their very look and capabilities, constitute a major element of the science-fiction genre.

The third element, character, would also provide proof that *Doctor Who* is science fiction. Interestingly, the Doctor (David Tennant)'s very human costume of a long coat, trainers and a smart brown pinstripe suit does not in itself suggest the science-fiction genre; his clothes could easily be symptomatic of a contemporary drama, thriller or a comedy. However, were we to listen to his dialogue for clues as to genre, we would soon realise that statements such as 'I'm not just a Time Lord … I'm the last of the Time Lords' (*Gridlock* 2007) explicitly reveal that he is in fact a character from a science-fiction programme. Similarly, if we were to watch a film such as *The Lion, the Witch and the Wardrobe* without prior knowledge of the content, the three elements would again help us define genre. In the film, the fact that we have a range of unusual characters (humans, mythical creatures and talking animals) combined with the props (the magic wardrobe, the White Witch's wand and the children's medieval swords) and the setting (the fictional land of Narnia with its castles and forests) would all strongly indicate that the genre is fantasy. Thus *The Lion, the Witch and the Wardrobe* and *Doctor Who* could both be said to have a strong sense of genre. I avoid using the adjective 'generic' here when describing these texts purely because, in an artistic context, it is something of a pejorative term, implying that a text is derivative or lacks originality, which is certainly not true of either text. In fact, *Doctor Who* and *The Lion, the Witch and the Wardrobe* both stand as excellent examples of their genres, embodying many of the characteristics of science fiction and fantasy respectively while still offering a unique take on them. Hence the description of each as displaying a strong sense of genre.

The concept of genre is inextricably bound up with audience expectation – the two are indivisible. The relationship is a delicate one: when we go to see an action movie at the cinema, pick up a children's picture book about animals or select a superhero comic from the shelves of our local comic book shop the act of selection carries with it expectations. While we may know little about the specific text, it is more than likely that part, or all, of our reason for selecting it is due to genre. It is rare, for example, for a person who detests horror films to knowingly watch one out of choice, just as it is for someone who detests love stories to pick up a romantic novel. Conversely, when we do discover a film, book or comic which seems to belong to a genre we like, our positive prejudice may well encourage us to read or view it regardless of reviews or other people's opinions. When a text is strongly rooted in a particular genre, however, it must strike a careful balance between originality and familiarity. As Roz Kaveney writes, 'Originality in genre work is only some of the time a matter of the completely new plot or idea; it is often a question of the inventive spin put on a stock matter' (2005: 4). Any text which consciously places itself within a genre (or is marketed as such) must be at once different enough to avoid being considered derivative and too similar to previous examples of the genre, and yet retain enough essential features of the genre to meet audience expectation. Discussing typical expectations of genre in films and books before viewing them or reading them with children is a useful way to consolidate genre knowledge. This can be developed further when we ask children after reading a text to think about the ways in which it conforms to genre expectations and, for older children, how it defies them.

A good example to examine here is the comedy film *Enchanted* (2007), which tells the story of Giselle (Amy Adams), a princess-to-be living happily in a fairy-tale world, who is tricked by a wicked witch (Susan Sarandon) and transported to modern-day New York, where she meets and eventually falls in love with a single father, Robert, played by Patrick Dempsey. The film works on many levels: it is not only a romantic comedy, but also both a homage to, and parody of, the classic animated Disney cartoons such as *Cinderella* and *Sleeping Beauty*, and can also be read as a feminist spin on the fairy tale. The interesting thing to note here is that *Enchanted*, like many films, straddles at least two genres: in this case the fairy tale and the romantic comedy. As an example of the fairy tale, it deliberately cites elements of the genre such as the lovelorn heroine and the magical curse placed upon her, the wicked stepmother, the talking animals and the dashing prince. It then deviates from this model, rejecting the genre's conventional rules by placing Giselle in a post-feminist contemporary world where she is forced to become independent, confront the reality of divorce and must ultimately fight a dragon in order to rescue her true love, Robert. While the film delights in subverting the rules of this particular genre, it conforms satisfyingly to the rules of another: the romantic comedy. In this sense, the film deliberately and confidently delivers the required elements of the genre, without deviation. It presents two loveable main characters, who are both in relationships with other people and who initially seem incompatible (Giselle's naive view of love clashes with Robert's cynical view developed as a result of his job as a divorce lawyer and the fact that he is a single father). The audience, however, knows that these characters will overcome all complications and differences and ultimately live happily ever after. As with any romantic comedy, the pleasure comes from seeing *how* this will occur. While we might only expect older or more able pupils to observe how specific texts play with genre in the above manner, the approach and the texts used can of course be varied to suit the age and ability of the class. It is, however, certainly the case that literacy teaching in schools over recent years has been designed to encourage even young children to consider a variety of genres and their features and therefore many will be able to at least begin to explore genre through film, picture books and comics.

Look closer: *Doctor Who*

Doctor Who, first broadcast on the BBC in 1963, has proved to be one of the most popular science-fiction programmes in television history. It initially ran for over twenty-five years until 1989 when it was cancelled, was temporarily resurrected in 1996 in the form of a single, feature-length television film and then triumphantly returned to British screens in a new, updated format in 2005. Since then the programme, or 'New Who' as it has been nicknamed (in order to distinguish it from the late-twentieth-century series), has resonated with both adults and children, regularly drawing millions of viewers in its peak slot of 7 o'clock on a Saturday evening[1] and has become a genuine cultural phenomenon, with two spin-off shows, *Torchwood* and *The Sarah-Jane Adventures*, in addition to an extensive range of merchandise. Under the guidance of executive producer and chief writer Russell T. Davies, the show, like the Doctor himself, has regenerated, retaining many of the established elements from its previous incarnations (the iconic blue police box that is the Doctor's time machine – the TARDIS, the famous theme tune and appearances by infamous enemies such as the Daleks, Cybermen and the Master) while being reinvented and updated for a contemporary, twenty-first-century audience. The show itself is arguably one of the best-written and -acted programmes on television and now stands as an excellent example not just of science fiction but also of drama. Davies, perhaps the best television writer working today, understands the fundamental rule of any good story, be it science fiction, fantasy, horror or any other genre: that it needs to be based first and foremost around believable characters who behave convincingly and display real emotion. Perhaps the most important way in which he has reinvented the programme is that 'he has finally brought into focus the emotional impact the Doctor's adventures have on those around him' and, indeed, on the Doctor himself (Gillatt 2008: 23). Likewise, on a thematic level, *Doctor Who* uses a fantastical premise to intelligently explore a range of ideas which are wholly relevant to its audience such as the nature of friendship, love, loyalty and loss and thought-provokingly examines what it is to be human.

In terms of characterisation, the Doctor exists as a fascinating enigma. A 900-year-old Time Lord who intermittently reinvents both his body and his personality through regeneration, he is in some ways still as mysterious and unfathomable to audiences as he was upon his debut over forty years ago. In his tenth incarnation as played by David Tennant (arguably the greatest Doctor ever), he remains a complex and multifaceted character, a dynamic mix of 'boffin and action hero, schoolboy and professor, hot young guy and ancient wizard' (2009: 11) in the words of Steven Moffat (who took over from Davies as the show's executive producer and lead writer for the fifth series). The Doctor is capable of great compassion and great anger, can be both empathetic and vengeful and both playful and serious, yet his heroic nature is consistently reinforced through his adherence to a strict and just moral code. His potential to constantly surprise us is symptomatic of Davies's belief that 'if characters keep turning, moving, thinking, shifting, if they aren't fixed, then they can do anything. Just like real people' (Davies and Cook 2008: 43). The Doctor is, ultimately, a traveller who is in perpetual motion. His boundlessly enthusiastic love of life conceals his awareness of the fact that, despite the presence of his companions, his journey through the universe will ultimately be a lonely one, defined as much by loss as it is by adventure. This is especially true of Tennant's Doctor, who, when asked by Jackson Lake where 'all those bright and shining companions' are, answers 'They leave, because they should, or they find someone else … and some of them … some of them forget me. I suppose in the end … they break my heart' (*The Next Doctor* 2008). This understanding and emotional articulation of the Doctor's situation is another way in which the programme is elevated above the average science-fiction text; Davies and his fellow writers ensure that the audience is made aware of the very real implications of a very unreal situation. When the Doctor's companion Rose asks him why he has travelled with a number of companions previously, he replies:

I don't age – I regenerate, but humans decay. You wither and you die. Imagine watching that happen to someone that you … You can spend the rest of your life with me, but I can't spend the rest of mine with you. I have to live on – alone. That's the curse of the Time Lords.

(*School Reunion* 2006)

Twenty-first-century *Doctor Who* episodes have tended to cast a more thoughtful light on his adventures and their implications, viewing them less as interstellar jaunts and more as an ongoing series of character-defining moments which are as much an emotional journey as an actual one. Here, the Doctor has more in common with Per Schelde's description of the genius figure popularised by Romantic literature, one who is located forever 'outside the human sphere, constantly tottering on the brink of disaster' and whose brilliance must come at the cost of 'being lonely' (1993: 32).

Yet the Doctor is only one of the programme's protagonists. At the core of the show is the relationship between the Doctor and his human companion. The role of the companion is a vital one for the audience, acting as our way in to the fantastical world of the Time Lord and rooting his adventures in reality. Rose Tyler (Billie Piper), Martha Jones (Freema Agyeman) and Donna Noble (Catherine Tate), the Doctor's companions since the return of the series, are all constructed as very real characters who seek adventure and who, for various reasons, wish to escape their normal lives. The pairing of the Doctor with these women is symbolic of one of the central ideas of the programme: the contrast between the safety of domesticity and the dangers and thrills of adventuring. Within minutes of meeting Rose and being pursued by Autons, the ninth Doctor (Christopher Eccleston), who is especially dismissive of the idea of family and home, tells her 'Don't worry about me, no. You go home – go on! Go and have your lovely beans on toast' (*Rose* 2005). But later, when Rose's mother Jackie (Camille Coduri) tries to prevent her from going with the Doctor by arguing 'It's not safe', it is Rose who says 'Mum, if you saw it out there, you'd never stay home' (*World War Three* 2005). Ultimately, however, despite the fact that the companions regularly resist their loved ones' attempts to pull them 'away from intergalactic wonders and back towards a responsible domesticity' (Chen 2008: 58), family inevitably proves to be a powerful draw. Through this conflict between home and the wide world, the series enables its audience to identify with the events of a science-fiction story and relate to them emotionally. This is powerfully illustrated by scenes in which the various companions decide to call home to speak to their families when they find themselves facing death or in unusual situations – Rose on a space station in the distant future as she watches the destruction of Earth (*The End of the World*), Donna as she prepares to singlehandedly take on the Sontaran army (*The Poison Sky*) and Martha, who asks 'Mum, you know I love you don't you?' as she drifts slowly towards a burning sun (*42*). Indeed, it is Martha's mother who later verbalises the fundamental importance of family for the Doctor's companions when she tells her daughter: 'You came home. At the end of the world, you came back to me' (*The Stolen Earth* 2008). Moments such as these are key to the success of the show, ensuring that the characters and the storylines move beyond the constraints of pure science fiction into the real world and demonstrate that fantastical narratives do not have to sacrifice believable characterisation and emotional content to monsters, aliens and special effects. In this sense, the pairing of the Doctor and his companions symbolises *Doctor Who*'s combination of the science-fiction and contemporary drama genres.

The role of the companion is also important in terms of gender. While science fiction has historically tended to be a male-dominated genre in terms of its fandom, characters and narratives, *Doctor Who* refuses to conform to this model. While it does, of course, revolve around the eponymous male hero, the Doctor's companion is an equally integral part of the show and its plots. Davies has ensured that in Rose, Martha and Donna, we are presented with brave, intelligent and well-written female characters who are as important to the Doctor as he is to them and who do not simply fulfil the role of romantic interest. This is signposted from Davies's very first episode, entitled *Rose*, where he boldly focalises the entire narrative through the companion's eyes and allows the Doctor to be a supporting character in Rose's story. This idea of equality is again expressed in a later episode where Rose exclaims: 'I'm not his assistant!' when she is described as such (*School Reunion*). This determination to subvert the traditional narrative gender roles of male as rescuer and female as passive victim is demonstrated further in the finales of all four series, where conventional expectations that the Doctor will save the day are defied. It is in fact Rose who saves the Doctor by destroying the Daleks in *The Parting of the Ways* and then bravely sacrifices herself to save the world in *Doomsday*; Martha who embarks on a year-long lone quest in order to rescue the captive Doctor in *Last of the Time Lords*; and Donna who, despite her protestations that she is 'just a temp', ultimately defeats Davros and the New Dalek Empire in *The Stolen Earth* and *Journey's End*.

A further demonstration of why the series is such an excellent example of its genre is its thematic and metaphorical content. As with all texts that possess a strong sense of genre, *Doctor Who* uses its science-fiction premise to explore and comment on very real issues. One of its recurrent concerns is the nature of difference and prejudice, explored not only through the multitude of alien races which the programme introduces but also through the fact that the Doctor himself is an alien. In an early adventure, an overwhelmed Rose comments on the fact that 'The aliens are so alien. You look at them and they're alien', to which the Doctor unfairly replies 'Good thing I didn't take you to the Deep South' (*The End of the World*). Here, the concept of alien life is sensitively used as a metaphor for race and, despite the fact that many of the extraterrestrials which the Doctor encounters are enemies, regular viewers soon recognise that the programme rejects the 'simplistic even reactionary notion' traditionally seen in science fiction 'that whatever or whomever dwells beyond our planet is radically different from us and wishes our extermination' (Sanjek 2000: 119). In this sense, the Doctor can be viewed as a liberal educator, opening his companions' (and our) minds to the variety, wonder and beauty of difference. The programme explores the irony of the fact that the alien Doctor is the character who consistently displays the greatest sense of humanity. He refuses to hurt the Adipose babies as they are beamed up to their spaceship, claiming 'They're just children. They can't help where they came from' (*Partners in Crime* 2008); his initial description of a ferocious werewolf is that it is 'Beautiful!' (*Tooth and Claw* 2006) and he tells Donna that 'It's a "he", not an "it"' when they encounter one of the peaceful Ood race (*Planet of the Ood* 2008). In fact, it is frequently the humans themselves who are militaristic and aggressive and the series often asks us to consider the attitudes of our own species and face some uncomfortable truths. When the Sycorax retreat in *The Christmas Invasion*, it is the prime minister, Harriet Jones, who orders their ship to be obliterated as it is passively departing, and as the Sontarans invade Earth in *The Poison Sky*, the Doctor finds himself having to convince the human army that engaging in combat is not the answer.

Therefore the show, like the Doctor himself, has a strong moral core. It is rich with ideas, combining the thrills and excitement of the best science fiction with the kind of thought-provoking social commentary more usually seen in contemporary drama. It stands as an excellent example of a text which is proud to be a science-fiction narrative, but which also expands beyond the boundaries of its particular genre to become something which is relevant to the real world. For all its alien creatures and distant planets, the show is ultimately about what it is to be human, arguing for compassion, acceptance and understanding in our attitudes towards others. Just as Wilf (Bernard Cribbins) acknowledges the effect that the Doctor has had on his granddaughter Donna when he states that 'She was better with you' (*Journey's End* 2008), we too are better for having shared the Doctor's adventures.

5.2

Genre
Teaching Ideas

The following sessions aim to help pupils explore the concept of genre through visual media. They can be taught individually or as part of a longer programme of study. The activities are aimed at Year 6, but can be adapted for any age group. For further extension ideas and resources, see Chapter 5.3.

Film and genre

Learning objectives
- To consolidate existing knowledge of the idea of genre by identifying the visual markers of genre
- To explore the range of narrative genres
- To watch a film sequence, observe and assess it while taking notes and then discuss observations.

Resources
- DVDs: *Labyrinth* (The Jim Henson Company 1986)
- Star Wars: *Return of the Jedi* (Twentieth Century Fox 1983)
- *High School Musical* (Walt Disney Pictures 2006)
- *Spider-Man 2* (Columbia Pictures 2004)
- *Emma* (Miramax Films 1996)
- *Shrek 2* (DreamWorks Animation 2004)
- Interactive whiteboard.

- Ask the children to list the different types of story there are (horror, romance, science fiction). Write them on the board. Introduce (or reiterate) the term 'genre' as a word for narrative classification. You may also wish to discuss the idea of genre expectations here, explaining that we expect certain features and elements from a book if it is part of a specific genre. List some of these expectations on the board next to each genre.

- Explain that films, like books, have genres too. This is also a good opportunity to show children that film genres are slightly different – for example, there can be action films but not action books (we would be more likely to describe them as thrillers or adventure stories). Similarly, film has a drama genre but the novel does not.

- Show the children a clip from *Labyrinth*. A good section to use is the sequence which details Jareth (David Bowie)'s explanation of Sarah (Jennifer Connelly)'s challenge and her entry into the labyrinth, beginning at 13:22 and running until 15:24 where Sarah introduces herself to Hoggle. Ask the children, in pairs, to discuss the clip and then decide on the genre. When the children share their answers with the class, place the emphasis on them using evidence from the film to support the genre they have chosen. Ideally, the children will classify *Labyrinth* as a fantasy film, a magical adventure or even a quest story. Encourage them to use the following features to identify the genre:
  - Jareth's hair, make-up and costume
  - Jareth's setting of the challenge and use of magic
  - The setting: unearthly, magical, ancient
  - Hoggle the goblin and the fairies.

- Ask the children to think about similar elements in fantasy books or films that they have read or seen previously, in order to show them how we use other texts to help us when categorising.

- Next, show the children a series of clips from other films. Ask the children, who can work in pairs or individually, to write down three headings for each clip: the title of the film, the genre they think it belongs to and the reasons for this. Many of the following titles are popular children's films and therefore it is worth asking the children to bring in a copy of the DVD if they have it. If you do not have copies of these DVDs, then you can search online for the trailers to these films. Showing the trailers will in most cases give the children enough visual evidence to help them identify the genre. The following clips are from films certified U or PG. While there is nothing unsuitable in the clips, you will need to obtain parental or guardian permission to show the children PG material.

- Films which are strong examples of their genres are:

High School Musical

Genre: Musical/high school movie/romance

Clip: 13:00–15:07: Troy leads his basketball team in a musical number

Evidence: Young cast, high school hall setting, characters talk and then begin singing and performing choreographed moves when, in the 'real world' of the film, they are not actually singing or dancing.

Star Wars: Return of the Jedi

Genre: Science fiction

Clip: 01:52–02:48: Imperial spaceships enter the new Death Star

Evidence: Space setting, planets, spaceships, technical dialogue, computer screens display alien readout.

Shrek 2

Genre: Comedy/fantasy/adventure/fairy tale

Clip: 1:15:31–1:17:44: Shrek and Princess Fiona refuse to complete the magic spell and then change back into ogres

Evidence: Puss in Boots and Donkey provide comic relief, talking in modern voices and singing with microphones, a magic spell which must be completed by midnight, medieval setting, fantastical characters.

Spider-Man 2

Genre: Action/superhero/comic book movie

Clip: 48:14–49:16: Spider-Man and Doctor Octopus fight on the side of a building while Aunt May hangs nearby

Evidence: Fighting, a costumed villain and a hero with powers, destruction, people in peril.

Emma

Genre: Drama/period drama/romantic comedy

Clip: 1:14:35–1:15:39: Emma dances at a ball and tries to find a partner for Harriet

Evidence: Period costumes and mannered dialogue, men and women dancing and trying to pair one another up.

- Use as many or as few clips as necessary. When the children share their responses, use the opportunity to discuss how genre is represented visually, what our expectations are and also how we link each film to others in the same genre. It is also a good opportunity to clarify the difference between medium and genre; for example, animation is often cited as a genre when really it is a medium. In addition to this, the activity should encourage a discussion of sub-genres, if the children are capable of doing so. A film such as *Shrek 2* resists easy categorisation because it straddles several genres and sub-genres. It is at once a comedy, an adventure, a parody and a fairy tale and exploring how we categorise such a film with children will help them to develop their understanding of the concept of genre more effectively.

- As a conclusion to this activity, which can be done within this session or at a later stage, ask the children to select one of the film genres they have seen and write the opening of a screenplay for a film set within that genre. For example, a film script set in a fantasy world might begin with:

We see an old castle with flaming torches and heavy doors made from iron and wood. As the camera moves towards the doors, they burst open and a vast army of goblins clad in rusty black armour begins to troop towards us furiously.

The children can experiment with writing a few paragraphs, giving a brief description of the setting and opening events for a musical, an action film, a comedy or a fantasy. You may need to go over some of the basics of script writing (it is written in the present tense and set out with a description of setting and action first, followed by dialogue). The children do not need to think up complex plots or dialogue here and should focus instead on establishing a visual sense of genre through costume, set and props. If the children write these descriptions relatively rapidly, then encourage them to write a setting for more than one genre. These script settings can be shared at the end of the activity.

Genre: parody

Learning objectives
■ To introduce the idea of parody and how to identify it
■ To explore how texts use aspects of genre to create parody
■ To watch a film sequence, observe and assess it while taking notes and then discuss observations
■ To compare and contrast a text with its parody and discuss the reasons for these similarities and differences.

Resources
■ DVDs: *Enchanted* (Walt Disney Pictures 2007); *Snow White and the Seven Dwarves* (Walt Disney Pictures 1937)
■ Interactive whiteboard.

■ *Enchanted* is rated PG and you will therefore need to obtain parental permission before showing.
■ Discuss with the children the idea that every genre carries with it typical elements and that these elements can be mocked for humorous purposes in the form of a parody. Choose the fairy tale as a narrative genre and ask the children to list some of the features which we might reasonably expect to see in a fairy tale. Similarly, explain how different types of films have typical elements which we expect to see. Ask the children to think about Disney animated classic fairy tales such as *Cinderella*, *Snow White and the Seven Dwarves* and *Sleeping Beauty*. They may be unfamiliar with some of these, so explain some of the common elements to them such as the princess protagonist, the animals who befriend her and the songs.

- Show the sequence of 'Whistle While You Work' from *Snow White and the Seven Dwarves* (15:04–20:35) and allow the children to comment on any aspect they wish to, without shaping the discussion. It might be helpful, however, to repeat some of the elements listed earlier that are evident in the clip, such as the princess (Snow White), the animal friends who help her clean and the fact that she sings.

- Introduce *Enchanted*, a Disney film which blends live action and animated film to affectionately parody the early Disney fairy tales. In this story, a young woman, Giselle, has been transported from a fairy tale world to contemporary New York, where she must adjust to modern life. Show the sequence where Giselle enlists various animals and insects to help her clean the apartment. The clip starts at 23:40 and ends at 27:12. You will need to show the clip twice. Allow the children to simply watch it the first time and then, before the second viewing, remind the children that this is a parody of the *Snow White* clip and ask them to note down the ways in which it is similar to and different from 'Whistle While You Work'.

- After the second clip, ask the children to feed back their notes. These two sequences can be used to explore parody in as simple or as complex a manner as desired. On a basic level, you can ask the children the following questions:
  - What was the same and what was different about the two clips? (Similarities: female protagonist, animals helping to clear up the house, a musical number; differences: setting, period, animals in the first clip, vermin in the second, more 'realistic' elements in the second clip including the hair in the drain and cleaning the toilet)
  - Why were these things different in the second clip?

- For a more advanced response, ask the children to consider the following questions:
  - What is different in the two clips?
  - Why do you think *Enchanted* makes changes to the *Snow White* sequence?
  - Why is the *Enchanted* clip so funny?
  - The animals are different in the two clips. Why do you think there are animals such as rats and pigeons and insects such as flies in *Enchanted*?
  - *Enchanted* tries to show a more realistic cleaning sequence (scrubbing the toilet and unblocking the plughole). Why do you think this is?

- The children may well find these questions challenging but the objective of this activity is to get the children to really think about parody and how it works as humour. It is important to point out that *Enchanted* and *Snow White and the Seven Dwarves* are both made by Disney. This will help children to see that parody is not necessarily a critical or cruel use of humour, but can often be affectionate or simply a different way of looking at a genre or a text.

- Ask the children to note down the ways in which *Enchanted* functions as a parody of *Snow White* and then ask the children to write a short definition of parody.

- To end the session, show a short clip from *Snow White* – the sequence where she sings to the bluebirds (11:11–12:00). Compare this with the similar sequence in *Shrek*, where the bluebird explodes (47:15–48:04). This will hopefully reinforce the children's understanding of parody in a memorable way.

Writing science-fiction programmes and scripts

Learning objectives

- To explore how science fiction is represented visually as a genre
- To study a television programme in both its script and finished form and understand how a writer creates it
- To write a script in the science-fiction genre, combining images, dialogue, camera angles and sound effects effectively
- Experiment with different forms of writing for different audiences.

Resources

- DVD: *Doctor Who*, Series 3, Volume 1: episode entitled *Smith and Jones*
- Copies of selected pages from Russell T. Davies's script for *Smith and Jones* (available from BBC Writers' Room website, www.bbc.co.uk/writersroom/insight/downloads/scripts/doctor_who_3_ep_1.pdf).

■ Introduce the session by discussing genre and, in particular, science fiction as a genre. Make a list of science-fiction films and books and then get the children to discuss with one another the expectations they might have when reading or watching a science-fiction text. List the potential features of a science-fiction text on the board.

■ Show the children a clip from the *Doctor Who* episode *Smith and Jones* by Russell T. Davies. There are two clips which are particularly good examples. You can show both or just one. Clip A (09:08–10:54) shows the first meeting of the Doctor and Martha Jones when the hospital they are in gets transported to the moon, and Clip B (15:50–17:42) shows the invasion of the alien law force, the Judoon. While any clip from the show would be a good example of science fiction, it needs to be a clip for which the script is available. The script for *Smith and Jones* can be downloaded from the BBC Writers' Room online (web address above). However, you can find scripts for other episodes of *Doctor Who* in the book *The Writer's Tale* by Russell T. Davies and Benjamin Cook (2008) and on the site for the book (www.thewriterstale.com).

■ Show the chosen clip(s) and ask the children which of the features on the list on the board appears in the clip (for example, aliens, technology, spaceships and far-off planets). Ask the children to note down the specific elements on screen which indicate that *Doctor Who* is a science-fiction programme. This may be harder than it seems because it requires the children to imagine that they have not seen the programme before. For example, the Doctor himself appears to be a normal, if knowledgeable, human in these clips and the Tardis is not visible so it is really only the hospital on the Moon, the Judoon and their technology which indicate the science-fiction genre.

- Explain to the children that all television programmes begin with a written script and hand out the selected pages from the *Smith and Jones* script for the clip you are using. Clip A requires pp. 13–15 of the script and Clip B requires pp. 20–2. Take some time to discuss the format of the script. While older children will be familiar with the layout of playscripts, it is worth reading the scene through with the children, allowing them to take the parts. In this way, you can stop at the parts which they will be unfamiliar with. Some of these may include:
  - 'FX' – tells the director of the episode that a visual effect is required
  - 'CONT'D' – the character is continuing their previous dialogue
  - 'INT.'/'EXT.' – abbreviations for interior/exterior to show whether the scene is set inside or outside
  - 'b/g' – background
  - 'PRAC' – tells the director that a practical effect, one which is real and not added in later, is required
  - 'POV' – the camera represents a character's point of view.
- After you have discussed the script, watch the clip again and allow the children to read the scripts while they watch the scene. When they have done this, they can comment on any differences between the script and the finished programme or note any observations aloud.
- Ask the children to write a script for a science-fiction programme. It should be a script which clearly shows that it fits the science-fiction genre through its setting and dialogue. If you tell children that they do not need initially to think too much about where the story is heading but should just experiment with dialogue and camera instructions, they will be free to explore the medium and the style of writing. The script should conform to a simple layout of scene description, camera moves and dialogue; it does not need to include instructions such as FX and PRAC. In terms of content, ask the children to write something original, not an episode of *Doctor Who*. The children can work in pairs or individually.
- For children whose writing skills are not as developed (or who find it too difficult to come up with an original idea) use Figure 5.1 as a beginning from which they can then continue writing the script.
- While the children are writing their scripts, remind them to include features such as close-ups and wide shots (provide Figure 5.2 as a handout if the children need guidance on this) and to describe what is shown onscreen effectively so that if someone were to read their script, they would understand how the aliens, spaceships and costumes should look.
- The children may well require some more time in future sessions to finish their scenes, after which they can be read aloud in class, performed as part of a Drama session or even filmed with a video camera so that the filmmaking process is completed.

SCENE 1: A SPACE STATION.
WE CAN SEE A SMALL BUILDING IN THE MIDDLE OF A RED PLANET. THE
PLANET HAS NO LIFE ON IT — IT IS A BARREN, DUSTY DESERT.

SCENE 2: INTERIOR OF ONE OF THE ROOMS INSIDE THE SPACE STATION.
A SMALL, METAL ROOM WHICH IS SLIGHTLY DIRTY. ONE WALL HAS LOTS
OF COMPUTER SCREENS WHICH ARE COVERED WITH NUMBERS. BENEATH
THEM IS A DESK WITH LOTS OF FLASHING LIGHTS AND BUTTONS,
WHICH LOOK VERY COMPLICATED.

THERE IS A CORRIDOR WHICH LEADS TO THE REST OF THE SPACE STATION
AND, OPPOSITE, A BIG HEAVY DOOR.

CLOSE-UP ON A YOUNG MAN, JACK, SITTING AT THE DESK IN AN
UNCOMFORTABLE CHAIR. HE IS ABOUT 30 YEARS OLD, WITH MESSY BROWN
HAIR. HE IS LOOKING AT THE COMPUTER SCREENS — HE LOOKS TIRED AND
CAN HARDLY STOP HIMSELF FROM FALLING ASLEEP.

SARAH, A YOUNG WOMAN, ENTERS THE ROOM. SHE HAS LONG BLONDE HAIR
AND SHE TOO LOOKS TIRED. SHE CARRIES A CUP OF TEA WHICH SHE PUTS
DOWN ON THE DESK. CLOSE-UP ON THE CUP OF TEA BEING PUT DOWN
NEAR JACK.

SARAH (LOUDLY): OI! WAKE UP, JACK! I KNOW THIS IS
                BORING, BUT WE'RE GOING HOME TOMORROW.

JACK (JUMPING): YOU SCARED ME!

SARAH: ANYTHING ON THE SCANNERS?

AS SHE ASKS THIS, WE SEE A SHOT OF THE SCANNERS, ALL LOOKING
BLANK AND UNEXCITING.

JACK: NO, NOTHING. THIS PLANET DEFINITELY HAS NO
      LIFE ON IT!
SARAH: WELL, I'VE MADE TEA....

AT THAT MOMENT, WE HEAR A LOUD BANGING.
CLOSE-UP ON JACK AND SARAH AS THEY JUMP AND LOOK AT EACH
OTHER IN TERROR.

SARAH: WHERE'S THAT NOISE COMING FROM?

CAMERA PANS WITH JACK. HE WALKS SLOWLY OVER TO THE LARGE DOOR.
HE LISTENS CAREFULLY. SILENCE. THEN ANOTHER LOUD BANG! HE LEAPS
BACK AND RUNS BEHIND SARAH.

JACK (SHAKING): IT...IT'S COMING FR-FROM OUTSIDE. FROM THE PLANET.
                SOMETHING'S OUT THERE!

THE BANGING STARTS UP AGAIN. CLOSE-UP ON THE DOOR, THEN ON THE
TERRIFIED TWO.

SARAH: WE HAVE TO OPEN IT — IT MIGHT BE SOMEONE
       WHO NEEDS HELP.

BEFORE JACK CAN STOP HER, SHE HITS A LARGE RED BUTTON ON THE DESK
AND THE DOOR SLOWLY BEGINS TO OPEN.

JACK: NO! DON'T....

WE SEE THE DOOR SLOWLY PULL OPEN AND SMOKE POURS IN.

CLOSE-UP ON THE DOOR. CLOSE-UP ON JACK AND SARAH WHO ARE
CROUCHING UNDER THE DESK, LOOKING AT THE DOOR. THE SMOKE
SLOWLY CLEARS TO REVEAL A STRANGE CREATURE.

Figure 5.1 Sample script

Camera shots
Try to include a range of shots in your screenplay.
You might want to use:

Close-ups
To show how a character is feeling or to make sure the audience
notices something important.

Long shots
A far-away shot – used to show the setting of the scene or to
show lots of action

Tracking
The camera moves to follow the action – used to add movement
and excitement to a scene.

Figure 5.2 Camera shots

Hiding behind the table.

Jack: (whispering) I wonder who it is.

Sarah: Well. Let's have a look.

Sarah and Jack look around at the door
and then suddenly the creature comes
stalking in. It has two eyes and a
long nose, a short mouth, half rhino
half human. He comes onto the
space station and moves the table out
the way!   (crashes into wall)

The monster: (low voice) Oh hello, I'm a clomschome.
I'm half human half rhino.
(close up on clomschome)

Jack: (shaking) H- How's that.

Sarah: (confidently) Oh stop it Jack it was just
how he was born.

The monster: Where are we?

Jack: We're on a space station.

The monster: A what?!

Figure 5.3 Work by Jack

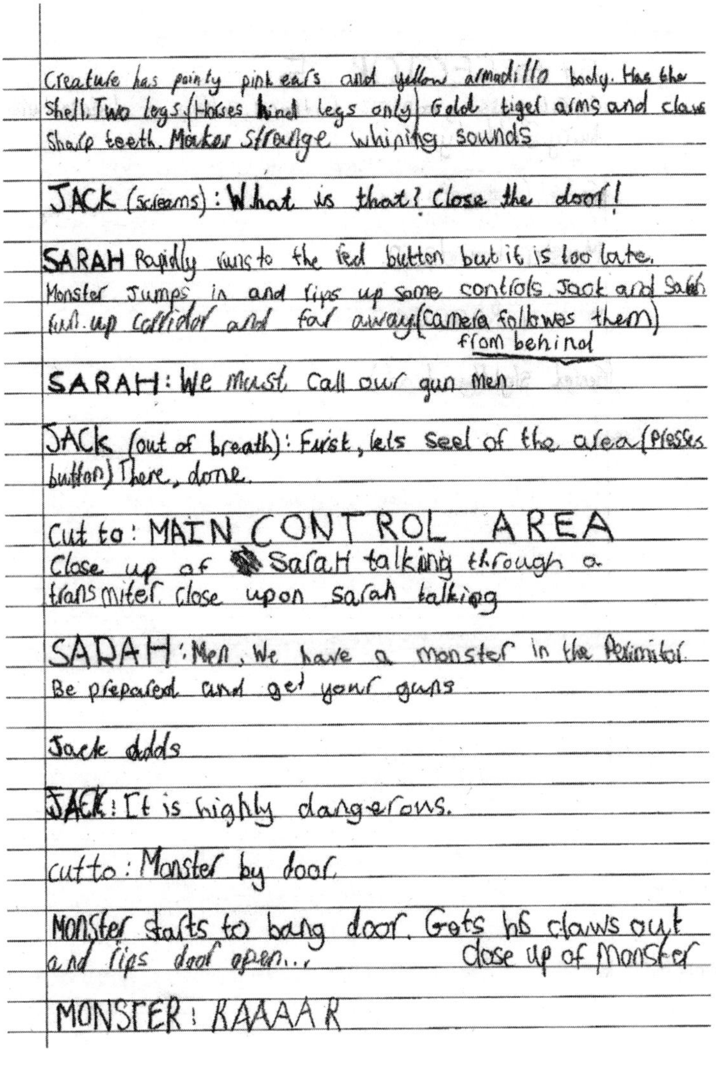

Creature has pointy pink ears and yellow armadillo body. Has the shell. Two legs (Horses hind legs only) Gold tiger arms and claws sharp teeth. Makes strange whining sounds

JACK (screams): What is that? Close the door!

SARAH rapidly runs to the red button but it is too late. Monster jumps in and rips up some controls. Jack and Sarah run up corridor and far away (camera followes them)
from behind

SARAH: We must call our gun men

JACK (out of breath): First, lets seel of the area (presses button) There, done.

Cut to: MAIN CONTROL AREA
Close up of Sarah talking through a transmiter. close upon sarah talking

SARAH: Men, We have a monster in the perimitor Be prepared and get your guns

Jack adds

JACK: It is highly dangerous.

cut to: Monster by door

MONSTER starts to bang door. Gets his claws out and rips door open...   close up of monster

MONSTER: KAAAAR

Figure 5.4 Work by Josh

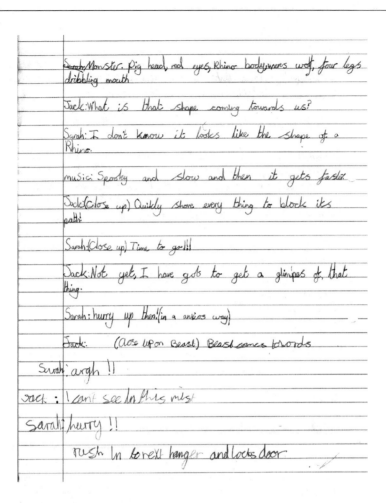

Sarah/Monster: Pig head, red eyes, Rhino body, wears wolf, four legs dribbling mouth

Jack: What is that shape coming towards us?

Sarah: I don't know it looks like the shape of a Rhino.

music: Spooky and slow and then it gets faster

Jack (Close up) Quickly shove every thing to block its path!

Sarah (Close up) Time to go!!!

Jack: Not yet, I have got to get a glimpes of that thing.

Sarah: hurry up then! (in a ansios way)

Jack: (Close up on Beast) Beast comes towards

Sarah: argh !!

Jack : I cant see In this mist

Sarah: hurry !!

rush In to next hanger and locks door

Figure 5.5 Work by Jack

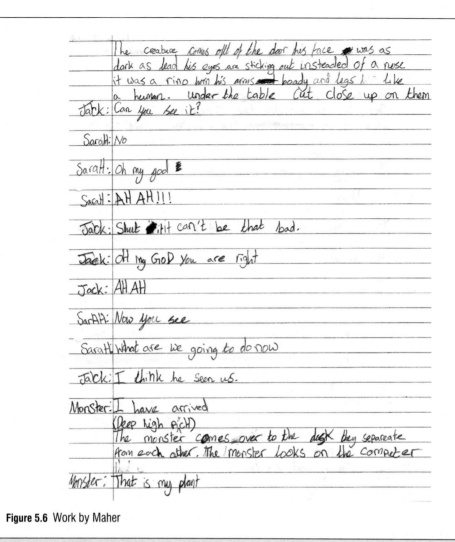

The creature comes out of the door his face was as dark as lead his eyes are sticking out insteaded of a nose it was a rino horn his arms boady and legs like a human. under the table Cut close up on them

Jack: Can you see it?

Sarah: No

Sarah: Oh my god

Sarah: AH AH!!!

Jack: Shut it it can't be that bad.

Jack: OH my GoD you are right

Jack: AH AH

SarAH: Now you see

Sarah: What are we going to do now

Jack: I think he seen us.

Monster: I have arrived
(Deep high pich)
The monster comes over to the desk they separeate from each other. The monster looks on the computer

Monster: That is my plant

Figure 5.6 Work by Maher

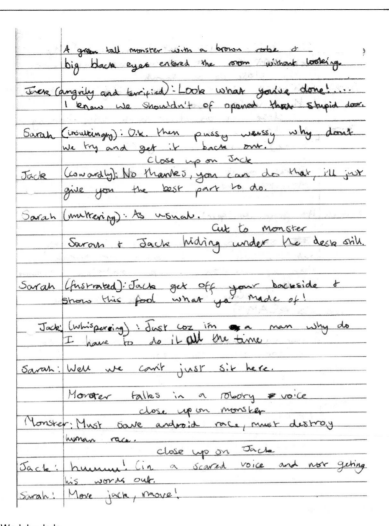

A green tall monster with a brown robe & big black eyes entered the room without looking.

Trek (angrily and terrified): Look what you've done!..... I knew we shouldn't of opened that stupid door.

Sarah (insultingly): O.k. then pussy wussy why don't we try and get it back out.

Close up on Jack

Jack (cowardly): No thanks, you can do that, i'll just give you the best part to do.

Sarah (muttering): As usual.

Cut to monster

Sarah & Jack hiding under the desk still.

Sarah (frustrated): Jack get off your backside & show this fool what ya' made of!

Jack (whispering): Just coz i'm a man why do I have to do it all the time.

Sarah: Well we can't just sit here.

Monster talks in a robotry voice

close up on monster

Monster: Must save android race, must destroy human race.

close up on Jack

Jack: hmmm! (in a scared voice and not getting his words out.

Sarah: Move jack, move!

Figure 5.7 Work by Jade

5.3

Genre

Further Ideas and Resources

These lists of resources and ideas for activities supplement the teaching ideas in Chapter 5.2 and offer suggestions for teaching activities based around visual markers of genre with other age groups.

Year 4

> **Resources**
> - A selection of picture books and novels
> - Genre sheet (see Figure 5.8).

- This activity can be used with children as a way of reinforcing genre knowledge and concepts. It can be taught after children have already been introduced to the idea of literary genre and have begun to understand the main types such as horror, comedy, action, adventure and science fiction.
- Arrange a selection of picture books and novels (you can also use reading-scheme books) on some of the tables. You may wish to arrange them randomly or, to make it more straightforward, you can display titles of a similar genre on each table.
- Revise ideas of genre with the children and discuss a few examples of picture books and novels. Using only the front and back covers, ask the children to list the clues which suggest a particular genre. These might include the title, the illustrations of people, places or objects and the blurb (for example, the stars on the front of *Harry Potter and the Philosopher's Stone* suggest magic, as do the robes). The children are not allowed to use the stories' content.
- Hand out the genre sheet (Figure 5.8) and ask the children to move between the tables, selecting two books. For each book, they need to complete a square of the sheet and draw or write down the aspects of the cover which suggest the type of story. Try to encourage the children to find two different types.
- Show some good examples of the sheets while the children are working. When the children have finished, bring the class back together and share the results, asking children

Book title:

What type of story is it?

Draw the clues:

Book title:

What type of story is it?

Draw the clues:

Figure 5.8 Genre worksheet

to come up and show one of their choices and discuss with the class why the book fits a particular genre based on its cover and title.

Year 5–6

> **Resources**
> - A DVD
> - Interactive whiteboard.

- Should you wish to focus on one particular genre in depth, then the following activity can be used to reinforce knowledge. It is best taught after having studied the genre in written text form as a way to consolidate the learning.
- Ask the children to list the main features of the particular genre (this will, of course, vary depending on the chosen genre). Make a class list of these features (the broader your genre features are, the better for this activity). If, for example, you are studying fantasy, you might list the following:
  - Magic and magicians
  - Fictional creatures such as dragons and monsters
  - Objects which have strange powers
  - Old-fashioned or medieval settings such as castles
  - Warriors and monarchs
  - Talking animals.
- When you have compiled a list of ten to fifteen things, ask the children to copy down the list as a series of headings, leaving space underneath each to add writing later.
- Show the children an extended clip from a film which is a clear example of the genre. It will be useful to use approximately a ten-minute clip, which you know will contain as many different features of the genre as possible. Ask the children to note down any evidence of each of the features on the list under the appropriate headings as they watch. For example, if they are watching an early sequence from *The Lion, the Witch and the Wardrobe*, they might write:

  Fictional creatures:

  A fawn (Mr Tumnus)

  Objects which have strange powers:

  The wardrobe, Mr Tumnus's fire

  Magic:

  The White Witch
- When the clip is finished, ask the children to discuss their examples and add each example under the appropriate heading on the board.

- This activity can also be done with a comic book. Again, ensure that you have chosen a title which displays features of the genre clearly and then read the comic book through on the whiteboard with the children instead of playing a clip. Ask the children to note down examples of the genre as they read it with you.

Genre film resources

The following list of films and television programmes, which are rated either U or PG, is divided into genre (remember to obtain parents' permission for PG films). They can be used with children as texts which have a strong sense of genre:

Fantasy

Labyrinth (Jim Henson Productions 1986)
The Lord of the Rings: The Fellowship of the Ring (New Line 2001)
The Tale of Despereaux (Universal 2008)
The Chronicles of Narnia: The Lion, the Witch and the Wardrobe (Walt Disney 2005)
The Chronicles of Narnia: Prince Caspian (Walt Disney 2008)

Action/adventure/quest narrative

Spider-Man 2 (Columbia 2004)
Up (Disney/Pixar 2009)
The Spiderwick Chronicles (Nickelodeon 2008)
Toy Story (Disney/Pixar 1995)
Jumanji (TriStar 1995)
Flushed Away (DreamWorks 2006)
Indiana Jones and the Temple of Doom (Paramount 1984)

Comedy

Monsters, Inc. (Disney/Pixar 2001)
Scooby-Doo (Warner Bros. 2002)

Science fiction

Doctor Who (BBC 2005)
The Sarah-Jane Adventures (BBC 2007)
Wall-E (Disney/Pixar 2008)
Fantastic Four (Twentieth Century Fox 2005)
Star Wars Episode 1: The Phantom Menace (Lucasfilm 1999)

Note

1 BARB (The Broadcaster's Audience Research Board) states that *Doctor Who*'s 2008 series (series four of 'New Who') scored an average audience of 8.41 million viewers per episode and that the most recent Christmas special, *The Next Doctor*, drew an audience of 13.1 million. In 2008, *Doctor Who* was the tenth most popular television series in the United Kingdom (Spilsbury 2009).

6.1

Adaptation

The process of adaptation, where a piece of work originally created in one medium is re-presented in a different medium, is highly appropriate as a conclusion to this study. Examining how and why artistic material is altered and remoulded into new forms provides children with a unique opportunity to develop their critical understanding of narrative elements across a range of media and reinforce what they have learned about each individual medium. Adaptation is by no means a recent phenomenon – some of the most famous pieces of literature and drama are in fact adaptations. Many of Shakespeare's most famous works are dramatisations of earlier poems or stories, including *Romeo and Juliet* (an adaptation of Arthur Brooke's 'The Tragical History of Romeus and Juliet') and *Twelfth Night* (based on a tale in Barnabe Riche's *Farewell to Military Profession*) (Wells 1998). The tradition is also evident in other media: Mozart's famous operas *The Marriage of Figaro* and *Don Giovanni* are based on existing plays and some of the most famous paintings in history are illustrations or 'adaptations' of other media, such as John Everett Millais's *Ophelia* (1851–2) and *Mariana* (1851), both of which depict incidents and characters from Shakespeare's plays. Therefore, some of the greatest artists, writers, composers and dramatists of all time have actively engaged in the process of adapting material with incredibly successful results.

Novel to film: an adaptive relationship

One of the most common forms of adaptation is the transformation of a novel into film, a process which is as old as cinema itself. Almost since the inception of film in the late nineteenth century, cinema has turned to the printed page for source material. The first narrative film, *The Great Train Robbery*, made in 1903, was in fact an adaptation of a play, and motion-picture history is of course littered with famous adaptations of novels including *Nosferatu* (1922), *The Wizard of Oz* (1939) and *Gone With The Wind* (1939). If we peruse the list of the biggest box-office hits of all time, we can see that eleven of the top thirty films are based on books and this number rises to seventeen if we include films which are based on comic books (Imdb 2009). In a business as costly and high-risk as the film industry, the decision to adapt books into films is a sensible one. When a book becomes a bestseller its film adaptation brings with it, in theory, a huge audience of fans, eager to see how the work has been presented on the big screen. Although of course there is no guarantee that a bestselling book will automatically translate into a blockbuster film, the evidence suggests that there is a positive correlation between the two media. Take, for example, Dan Brown's *The Da Vinci Code*, which has sold over forty million copies worldwide (Times Online 2006). The film of the novel, released in 2006, took over $757 million in cinemas upon its release. Similarly, the first five *Harry Potter* films have a combined gross of over $4.5 billion and *The Lord of the Rings* trilogy took nearly $3 billion. For the film companies who adapt successful books, the rewards are potentially huge because the stories and the characters who feature in them, such as Harry Potter and Gandalf, are already part of the cultural consciousness and have proven to be popular with millions of people before the film has even been made. From the reader's point of view, the opportunity to see how a favourite book's plot, characters and settings have been interpreted visually is often too good to pass up. Logically speaking, if we know the entire story and are familiar with the characters to the extent where we know everything about them, a film should hold little allure for us as cinemagoers, but the attraction of an adaptation is more intricate than this. It taps into the highly personal way in which we experience books and acknowledges the fact that many of us are constantly 'adapting' what we read mentally, visualising a novel's settings and characters in our minds. Adaptation is this interior process made real and it attempts to reflect how we read and engage with narratives. At its most basic level, an adaptation offers a reader the chance to compare 'their own mental images of the world of a novel … with those created by the film-maker' (McFarlane 1996: 7). However, when the vision the film presents of the book tallies with the reader's own, it also has the potential to foster a powerful sense of identification in the reader, which vindicates and gives official approval to their own imagined version of the story.

It is important when teaching this area that we move children away at an early stage from the idea that adaptations are only successful or 'good' if they are devoutly faithful to the book upon which they are based. When a film differs from a novel by making alterations to plot, character or setting for example, it often becomes a contentious issue for the section of the audience who are fans of the book. Erica Sheen states that, whether we like it or not, 'the central critical category of adaptation studies [is] the notion of "fidelity", or "faithfulness to the text"' (2000: 2), and it certainly seems that many adaptations, critically if not commercially, live or die depending on the extent to which the film mimics the book. Ginette Vincendeau puts it even more strongly, suggesting that '"fidelity" becomes a negative yardstick with which to beat film' (2001: xii). Indeed, 'fidelity' seems a highly appropriate term to apply to this relationship. Readers often have intense and passionate attachments to favourite novels (as, of course, we may do with films and music); the private, internalised and often drawn-out process of reading a book encourages us to form loyal and indeed loving bonds with the characters and their stories. When a film version is made, readers often feel betrayed over casting decisions, characters which are omitted and storylines which are altered. Brian McFarlane questions this 'unilluminating' method of judging film adaptations, rightly arguing that 'the critic who quibbles at failures of fidelity is really saying no more than: "This reading of the original does not tally with mine in these and these ways"' (1996: 9). To criticise an adaptation simply because it differs from its original source seems churlish, and yet, when we view the film of a book we have read, it is almost inevitable that both during and after watching it, we will be ceaselessly drawing comparisons between the two. Understandably, the similarities and differences between the book and the film are our first port of call in criticism, but we should be aware that, for both ourselves and our students, this is not the only way to analyse the film. When studying adaptations, we should bear in mind that the word 'adapt' does in fact mean to change something, to make it fit a different context or situation. On a rational level we must surely understand that, given the radically different nature of the two media, a film has to differ from a book and that it is fundamentally impossible to bring across every aspect of even a very short written narrative on screen. As with the proverbial quart and pint pot, it is a given that most novels can never be squeezed fully into a film with an average two-hour running time. One example of this is J.K. Rowling's *Harry Potter and the Goblet of Fire*, which at over 600 pages is one of the longer titles in the series. The film is approximately 160 minutes long, meaning that the filmmakers would have needed to cover approximately four pages a minute to film the entire novel. This being impossible, some storylines and characters were therefore cut, one notable example being Hermione's creation of S.P.E.W. (Society for the Promotion of Elfish Welfare). While it is admittedly disappointing for fans to have this excised from the film, it was clearly necessary to do so. The S.P.E.W. storyline is, after all, a *sub*plot – it adds humour and charm to the novel and reveals more about Hermione's compassionate and determined character, but the central narrative does not need this in order to function successfully. In fact, in terms of the viewing experience, the S.P.E.W. storyline may even have detracted from the film and made an already complex plot overly complicated. This need to fillet a narrative before its transition to the screen is something which Michael Goldenberg, the screenwriter of *Harry Potter and the Order of the Phoenix*, understands. He identifies the questions which the adapter must ask him or herself when considering which parts of the novel should be retained for the film version: ' "Do you absolutely need it? Does it make sense for the context? Can you use that information without spelling it out?" ' (cited in Murray 2007).

It is not therefore the case that any change made to a book as it undergoes the process of adaptation is necessarily a change for the worse. Put simply, what works on the page does not necessarily work on the screen. On a purely visual level this is proven by Bryan Singer's film of Marvel's *X-Men* comics. One of the central characters, Wolverine, is only five feet, three inches tall, and much is made of his relatively short stature in the original comics. Yet on screen, brilliantly played by Hugh Jackman (who at six feet, three inches is a foot taller), the decision to change a major feature of Wolverine in order to cast the right actor is clearly the right one. Similarly, the X-Men's costumes were famously altered for the film purely because the brightly coloured outfits which the superheroes sported in the pages of the comic book would look somewhat ridiculous on real people. As Singer says: 'Imagine them wearing suits of any other colour in a live-action movie … Just picture that in your head … It had to be black leather' (cited in Hughes 2003). It is, therefore, often in the best interests of the finished film to alter the source material in minor or major ways, visually as well as structurally. This is ably demonstrated by Andrew Adamson's recent film of the fourth in

C.S. Lewis's *Chronicles of Narnia* series, *Prince Caspian*. The film tells of an epic battle for the land of Narnia between the murderous King Miraz and his Telmarine army and the heroic Prince Caspian and his Narnian supporters (aided by the human children Peter, Edmund, Susan and Lucy). Lewis's strength as an author lies in his range of characters and ability to realise the world of Narnia, yet his plots and descriptive passages are relatively sparse. For much of the novel, Caspian and his followers are on the run from Miraz, resulting in a dearth of action which would potentially make a film version problematic (especially when we consider that it needs to appeal to its target audience of children and teenagers). At one point, Lewis tells us that 'Reepicheep and his Mice ... proposed storming Miraz in his own castle that very night' (1980b: 77). In the book this comment is ignored by the other characters, yet in Adamson's film this plan does come to fruition, Lewis's brief sentence forming the basis for a thrilling, violent and lengthy action set piece. The sequence is one of the highlights of the film, incorporating an aerial attack from gryphons, centaurs nimbly leaping over balconies and battlements and a delightful scene in which Reepicheep and his Mice tie up a cat. The point here is that the inclusion of this attack on the villain's stronghold is not a crass attempt to dumb down the story in any way but rather adds excitement to the film. It also undoubtedly resolves the structural problems by providing the audience with an extra action scene in the middle of the movie as opposed to making them wait until the very end. Similarly, Lewis's brief description of the book's climactic battle is little more than a page or two, where we are told through diegesis that the battle between Aslan's Tree Army and the Telmarines is over 'in a few minutes' (1980b: 168). This sequence is one of the most spectacular in the film, wherein impressive effects help to evoke the feeling of a dangerous and thrilling battle between the Trees and the men. Here at the film's conclusion, Adamson understands that the audience will not be satisfied with anything less than a substantial action scene and that the structure of the film demands that this must not be the brief scene which Lewis describes, but should instead be the longest and most epic sequence of the two-and-a-half-hour running time. Again, the film unarguably improves upon the book in this sense. Ultimately, however, the point to note here is that by examining the differences and similarities between the original source material and the film or television adaptation, we are giving children the chance to consider not only questions of visual imagery but also narrative issues such as structure, plot, subplot and the ways in which information can be implied to an audience subtly rather than stated explicitly.

Look closer: Tim Burton's *Charlie and the Chocolate Factory*

I have chosen the recent film adaptation of *Charlie and the Chocolate Factory* (2005) for closer analysis for a number of reasons. First and foremost, its director Tim Burton is unquestionably a unique talent; his beautifully stylised visuals, unconventional perspective on character and palpable sense of compassion make all of his films a joy to behold. He is, in every sense, an auteur, not only directing but also infusing every aspect of his films, from character to set and costume design, with his distinctive style. Second, in terms of this chapter's discussion of adaptation, *Charlie and the Chocolate Factory* is a perfect illustration of some of the aforementioned issues. It is undeniably a faithful adaptation of Roald Dahl's 1964 novel, accurately transferring its plot, themes and tone to the screen. However, it is also very much a Tim Burton film, in that he presents, or rather re-presents, the source material in his own particular way, resulting in a fusion of the director and the novelist's personal visions, which is ideally what an adaptation should be. In addition, Burton and his screenwriter John August are unafraid to alter the novel by adding new material where necessary so that, in places, the film offers some different ideas from the book and allows Burton to further explore some of the themes which recur throughout his body of work.

On paper, the idea of Tim Burton filming a Roald Dahl novel seems like the ideal marriage of director and author and, indeed, this proves to be the case. Much of Burton and Dahl's work shares a broadly similar outlook in that both often employ jet-black humour in their offbeat narratives and both celebrate the macabre and the weird. Indeed, as Joshua David Bellin states, 'Burton has been devoted throughout his career to making films that challenge the definition and stability of the norm' (2005: 183), and, like Dahl, this aversion to, and even mistrust of, normality is frequently reflected in the characters he presents to his audience. Both Burton and Dahl tell stories which constitute attempts to understand and frequently champion misunderstood outsiders who do not conform to what society considers 'normal'. Willy Wonka is just one in a long line of Burtonian protagonists who are set apart, either through choice or circumstance, from mainstream society. From Pee-wee Herman, the man-child hero of *Pee-wee's Big Adventure*, through Edward Scissorhands, Ed Wood, Batman, Sweeney Todd, *Sleepy Hollow*'s Ichabod Crane, to Jack Skellington in the Burton-produced *The Nightmare Before Christmas*, the director has shown a consistent desire to sympathetically explore characters who exist on the margins and are unable or unwilling to integrate easily with others. It is, however, important to note that, with the exception of Sweeney Todd, these outsiders are people who are only abnormal in the eyes of other people; they are in reality decent, honest and kindly characters. As Mark Salisbury puts it, they are 'misunderstood and misperceived ... misfits' (Burton and Salisbury 1995: xiv). His films, therefore, are often a defence of difference and diversity and constitute a celebration of those brave enough to resist the anaesthetising and deindividualising effects of normal society, represented visually in *Edward Scissorhands* by the depressingly identical houses of a pastel-hued suburbia. Burton himself has attributed this consistent focus on the misunderstood outsider to the beloved B-movies of his youth:

> That goes back to the monster movies I liked as a kid. They were perceived as frightening and bad, but they weren't ... I always liked characters who were passionate and felt certain ways, but weren't what they were perceived to be.
>
> (Burton and Salisbury 1995: 116)

Willy Wonka, the mysterious, child-like but ultimately good-hearted chocolate magnate, fits perfectly into this glorious collection of non-conformists, and Burton brings the character even further into line with his own thematic interests by providing him with a back story.

Through a series of flashbacks, we see Willy's troubled relationship with his candy-hating dentist father (played with authoritarian relish by Christopher Lee), culminating in their estrangement. In many of Burton's movies, the father–son relationship is bittersweet and often fraught with difficulty and emotionally distant, dangerous or tragically absent fathers abound. Edward Scissorhands's elderly creator dies leaving him alone, *Batman Returns* begins with the attempted infanticide of the Penguin by his parents, Ichabod Crane's father in *Sleepy Hollow* is revealed (again via flashback) to have persecuted and murdered Ichabod's mother and *Big Fish* movingly focuses on the relationship between a man and his father.

In terms of character, the film ably captures Wonka's complexity and magnifies his inherent contradictions. Burton regular Johnny Depp's masterful and darkly funny interpretation constructs Wonka as a troubled, bizarre and frequently sinister individual, capable of naivety, cruelty, warmth and indifference in equal measure. If his performance differs somewhat from the initial impression Dahl gives of Wonka, then it is certainly justified by later events. In the novel, the first proper appearance of Wonka encourages the reader to view him as flamboyant yet hospitable, warmly introducing himself to the families of the lucky Golden Ticket winners: 'He smiled at the five children who were clustered near the gates, and he called out, "Welcome, my little friends! Welcome to the factory!"' (Dahl 2007a: 80). It is not until later in the story, when the spoilt children start to become victims of their own greed, that Wonka's true personality is revealed through his indifference to their fates: '"The children are disappearing like rabbits! But you mustn't worry about it! They'll *all* come out in the wash!"' (Dahl 2007a: 149). Depp, however, from his first appearance leaves us in no doubt that Wonka is a dark and complex individual, hinted at by the large sunglasses which obscure his features, the gloves (which here are not merely fashion accessories but barriers that enable him to avoid having to touch anyone) and his nervous and forced introductory speech delivered through a stilted reading of cue cards. Depp's Wonka doesn't even *pretend* to like children, responding to Violet Beauregarde's introduction of herself with the immortal line: 'I don't care.' Burton in fact offers us the intriguing view that Wonka is in fact 'every bit as damaged as the wee terrors who have won a day in his company' (Gilbey 2005).

Depp's performance also offers a masterclass in interpreting character through facial expression, his mask of confused naivety slipping at key moments. As Augustus Gloop nearly drowns in the chocolate river, Depp's face registers flickers of disgust, irritation and then curious delight as the suction pipe moves ominously closer to the floundering lad, betraying Wonka's true attitude to his guests. Similarly, when Veruca Salt has been set upon by enraged squirrels and tossed into a rubbish chute, Wonka advises her father to go and get her. As he unlocks the gate to the room, his light-hearted verbal tone and dialogue ('Just reach in and pull her out') are immediately contradicted by his sinister and humourless expression as he sends the doomed Mr Salt on his way – Wonka knows exactly what he is doing. In fact Depp's performance, while darker than the Wonka which Dahl presents, is far more fitting to the story as a whole, as is Burton's direction. The idea of a bizarre genius who invites people into his factory where they are punished for their sins in inventive but horrific ways is certainly, at its core, extremely dark and Burton understands that the story 'is basically a slasher film for kids' (Odell and Le Blanc 2005: 132). Just as Depp's performance shows the occasional slippage of Wonka's public face, revealing the more sinister one underneath, Burton allows us to catch brief but macabre glimpses of the less enchanting side of the factory which is ever-present beneath the explosion of officially sanctioned colour and sweetness that the visitors are supposed to see. This is foreshadowed in the aforementioned scene in which the children arrive at the factory. Before we are allowed to see the mysterious owner, we are treated to a hilariously saccharine parody of Disney's 'It's a Small World' ride, where stereotypically cute dolls of children chirrup a song introducing Willy Wonka. Of course, Burton cannot resist subverting this received notion of charm and sweetness and has the display catch fire, the dolls' voices becoming distorted and their eyeballs dripping down their cheeks as their faces melt horrifically. Later, as the remaining children speed through the factory in the Great Glass Elevator, they travel over a vast retro-style hospital where these same dolls are being wheeled around on beds as patients. Wonka announces cheerily: 'This is the Puppet Hospital and Burns Center ... It's relatively new.' They also pass through a room wherein pink sheep are being sheared (presumably for some warped strain of candy floss) prompting a guilty Wonka to state 'I'd rather not talk about this one.' Therefore, tonally, the film accurately bottles the essence of Dahl's twisted humour. Wonka, the factory and the events that occur within it all display a strong undercurrent of darkness and threat and would provoke fear and uncertainty, were the viewer allowed to dwell on them. Yet the things we see are so wonderful and Depp's Wonka so likeable that we tend to laugh at the more disturbing aspects of the story, encouraged by the fact that the factory's victims are so fully deserving of their fates.

Similarly, the elements which Burton and August have seamlessly woven into the original story are consistent with Dahl's work in terms of tone and narrative. In a series of flashbacks spaced evenly throughout Charlie's visit to the factory, we see Wonka's disturbing childhood and difficult relationship with his dentist father. Here, Burton's Gothic aesthetic emerges clearly, depicting Wonka at Halloween contained within a black wiry brace reminiscent of a torture device, forced to watch as his father burns his haul of candy from trick or treating. In true Dahlian style, Burton balances these darker scenes with some nice gags. In one strong example of visual humour, Willy threatens to run away to 'the candy capitals of the world' and we see a montage of him striding happily along as a series of flags of different countries swirl around his head, only to discover that he is in fact walking through an exhibit entitled 'Flags of the World' at his local museum. This is followed by a second striking image as Willy returns home from his abortive attempt to run away only to find that his father has carried out his earlier threat that 'I won't be here when you come back' in a literal sense: there is a gaping hole in the terraced street where Willy's house should stand. Towards the end of the film, when Charlie convinces the reluctant Wonka to visit his estranged father, we learn that the house still stands exactly as it was when torn from its surroundings, but now relocated, unchanged, in a snowy wasteland on the outskirts of town. The images of the empty hole in the street where Willy's house should be and the solitary domicile in its new lonely location are pure Dahl, acting not only as a powerful visual representation of

Willy's cold and dysfunctional relationship with his father but also echoing the warped childhoods of the author's other protagonists such as Matilda and James Trotter. Additionally, the flashbacks add a rich layer of symbolism to the film. The irony of Wonka's father being a dentist who is so paranoid about cavities that he will not let his son even taste candy infuses the story of the adult Willy Wonka, whose life is dedicated to the production of sweets, with hitherto unforeseen significance and pathos. Set in the context of the flashbacks, candy becomes more than just candy; it represents Wonka's spirit of rebellion, creativity and independence and shows us that we are all ultimately able to triumph over cruel and oppressive forms of authority. Therefore, the changes made to the story fulfil the necessary criteria of alterations in the adaptation process. First, they match the tone of the existing material by using humour to present often harsh and disturbing events. Second, the changes enrich the overall storyline both in an emotional sense (revealing in a way which is both funny and tragic the explanations for Wonka's behaviour and helping us to empathise with him) and in a symbolic sense (adding a new depth to the film's central motif of candy). In this way, Burton has preserved the book's narrative while enriching it and making it work on screen.

Other forms of adaptation

We should be quick to point out to children that there are other forms of adaptation than book to film. Examples of ways in which material is adapted across a range of media need to be discussed including stage, audio and comic book adaptations of novels, films which have been adapted into stage plays or musicals and even examples of how books and films have been turned into computer games. Emphasising this is important for two reasons. First, children can see that adaptation is not synonymous with the transition from novel to film and, second, it provides an excellent opportunity to explore the features and relative merits and weaknesses of each medium. For example, I recently saw a dance production of *Edward Scissorhands* at the theatre, directed and choreographed by Matthew Bourne. Based on Tim Burton's film, this version retold the story through music and dance, with no dialogue. Bourne's adaptation worked exceptionally well and was as engaging, moving and entertaining as Burton's film and watching it highlighted several interesting points. It emphasised how strong Burton and Caroline Thompson's original story is, its simplicity allowing it to be told only through music and movement and still retaining great emotional power. It also demonstrated clearly what the medium of theatre can offer (live music, three-dimensional settings and costumes, a focus on physical movement) and what it cannot (close-ups, cuts, multiple locations), and illustrated some of the ways in which the theatrical version has to modify the film version in order to play to the medium's strengths. Similarly, the recent stage musical *Wicked*, based on Gregory Maguire's 1995 novel (itself a retelling of *The Wizard of Oz*) radically altered its source material. The novel is aimed at an adult audience and uses the story of Elphaba, the 'Wicked Witch of the West', to explore ideas of politics, terrorism, gender and sexuality. Yet when it was re-presented as a blockbusting musical, the show was only loosely based on the novel and Maguire's storyline was substantially altered. As well as the addition of the requisite musical numbers, the darker, more violent and sexual elements of the story-line (including state-sanctioned murder and adultery) were toned down or removed and the focus of the narrative placed firmly on the friendship between Elphaba and Glinda (the 'Good Witch'). It is important to note here, however, that both the novel and the show work extremely well in their own right and have both enjoyed great success in their respective fields. In terms of the stage version, this is arguably because the creative team behind it understand that the audience for a musical will not, for the most part, be the same as the audience Maguire is writing for. In other words, the theatregoer who pays to see a two-hour musical will surely have different expectations from the reader who sits down to read a 300-page book. It was therefore necessary to *adapt* the material (in the truest sense of the word) to make it more suitable for its intended audience. Crucially, however, the alterations do not disrespect the source material, the feminist and political themes of which remain intact, but are simply presented in a different way. In this case, the changes between book and show are in fact measures of how intelligently and how sensitively the novel has been adapted to fit a new medium and its audience and are not in any way a betrayal of Maguire's work.

Therefore, if we widen our study of adaptation to consider how material is re-presented across a wide range of media, children will inevitably be prompted to explore ideas of medium, genre and audience in detail. For example, if we were to ask pupils to adapt a book into a radio play, they would need to consider what we can and cannot do within this purely aural medium, how we can compensate for losing the novel's interior monologues and also the importance of considering the audience it is aimed at (which age ranges and which demographic listen to radio and what might they expect?). Children are often expected to show an understanding of audience in their writing, which is no small requirement for primary-age pupils who may not have substantial life experience. Through the study of adaptation, they will be able to see how material is repackaged and reshaped to fit specific audiences and to apply this to their own work.

6.2

Adaptation

Teaching Ideas

The following sessions aim to help pupils explore the process of adaptation between different media. They can be taught individually or as part of a longer programme of study. The activities are aimed at Years 5 and 6, but can be adapted for any age group. For further extension ideas and resources, see Chapter 6.3.

Novel to film: *Charlie and the Chocolate Factory*

Learning objectives

- To examine how a novel is presented onscreen
- To explore how the adaptation process can affect our understanding of character
- To compare and contrast the different ways in which a story can be presented
- To watch a film sequence, assess it and take notes and then discuss their observations in a whole-class situation.

Resources

- Book: *Charlie and the Chocolate Factory* by Roald Dahl
- DVD: *Charlie and the Chocolate Factory* (Warner Bros. 2005)
- Two sections of the *Charlie and the Chocolate Factory* novel scanned or retyped and saved as a word-processed document
- Interactive whiteboard.

- Ask the children to think about the process of adaptation. Explain the term, which means to change something to fit different circumstances or a different environment. Remind the children that, in textual terms, adaptation does not mean simply making a book into a film but is a way of changing any text into another medium. We can, for example, present a film as a ballet, change a poem into a prose story or a book into a comic. The children will, however, be most likely to understand the term in relation to books and films, so ask them to write a list of the books they know which have been turned into films.

- When the children have done this, ask them to comment on specific examples and give their opinions on whether they preferred the book or the film and why. It is important at this point to state that, just because a film version may change or omit details from the book, it does not necessarily mean that this makes it a bad adaptation. Ask the children to consider why filmmakers often change the plot or characters in a book (for timing reasons, from a desire to simplify the plot or to reduce the number of characters).

- Place the first extract from *Charlie and the Chocolate Factory* on the whiteboard. This is the scene where Willy Wonka greets the Golden Ticket winners for the first time, beginning at the start of Chapter 14 where 'Mr Wonka was standing all alone just inside the open gates of the factory' and ending with 'It was quite a large party of people when you came to think of it. There were nine grown-ups and five children, fourteen in all' (Dahl 2007a: 80–4). Please note, the film *Charlie and the Chocolate Factory* is rated PG, so you will need to obtain parents'/guardians' permission before using the clips with the class.

- Read the extract through with the children and allow them to study it for a few minutes. Next show the corresponding clip from the film, beginning at 35:01 and ending at 38:19. Watch the clip twice and then put the extract back up on the board so the children can see it. Ask the children, with their partners, to make a list of the similarities and differences between the book and the film for this scene.

- Allow some time to discuss the children's observations. The conversation will naturally evolve based on what the children have noticed but it is worth directing the children's attention to certain points:
  - The character of Willy Wonka (Johnny Depp's sinister performance shows Wonka as a man who actively dislikes children and their families, as opposed to Dahl's more genial presentation)
  - The reduced number of characters (one parent for each child in the film, two in the book)
  - Changed/additional dialogue (Wonka's rejection of the children in the film, as well as his disgust at the word parent)
  - Wonka's costume (big glasses hide his eyes in the film while Dahl describes his 'twinkling eyes' (Dahl 2007a: 80)).

- For every difference they notice, ask the children to consider why this change has been made. It is also a good opportunity to discuss the character of Wonka here. Ask the children which they prefer: Johnny Depp's portrayal or the book's portrayal and why. This will hopefully encourage a sustained discussion of character.

- Put the second extract on the board and read it through. This is the section of the factory tour where Augustus Gloop falls into the river, contaminates it and then becomes stuck in a pipe. The extract starts with the last paragraph of Chapter 16: ' "Augustus!" shouted Mrs Gloop.' It finishes with: 'The pressure was terrific' in Chapter 17 (Dahl 2007a: 96–9).

■ Watch the corresponding section on film, beginning at 46:17 and ending at 47:40. Watch the clip twice and allow the children to see the novel extract again afterwards as they discuss the differences between the book and the film versions of this scene. Again, allow the children to make their own observations but try to make this task different from the previous activity by asking them specific questions which encourage them to focus on the filmmaking techniques:

● What do Johnny Depp's facial expressions suggest about what Willy Wonka is thinking as he watches Augustus in the river? (Depp's facial expression at 46:32 suggests Wonka is almost indifferent to Augustus's plight initially and that he feels the boy has deserved his punishment but then, as the suction pipes come across (46:46), his face subtly registers fascinated excitement at what will happen)

● Why are there close-ups of Wonka, Mrs Gloop and the other characters? What does this let us see?

● How is Mrs Gloop presented differently in the two versions? (Significantly, Mrs Gloop shows some thoughtfulness in the novel when she worries that Augustus's cold will infect other children who eat the chocolate.)

■ When the children have finished the discussion, ask them to write two or three paragraphs individually, summarising the differences between the novel and the film and also the differences in the presentation of Wonka.

Film to novel

Learning objectives
■ To adapt film into a written narrative
■ To explore how pace and tone can be created through writing
■ To develop descriptive writing from visual stimulus
■ To integrate dialogue, description and action in a piece of writing.

Resources
■ DVD: *Casper* (Universal 1995)
■ Interactive whiteboard.

■ You can use any film or television programme for this activity. I have selected *Casper* because it is a well-written film with a good mix of action scenes and more character-based, emotional scenes. This activity will be more effective if taught after the above session.

- Remind the children of the process of adaptation and the way in which it seeks to capture the feel of the original text but turns it into another form. Explain that the children are going to do the reverse of turning a novel into a film and turn a film into written prose.

- Introduce the film *Casper* as a comedy ghost story. *Casper*'s plot concerns a young girl Kat (Christina Ricci) and her father James (Bill Pullman) who move into Whipstaff Manor, a haunted mansion where Kat befriends a young ghost named Casper. Show the first clip, explaining that it has been chosen because it is an action scene. The clip begins at 1:00:01 and finishes at 1:02:17 and follows Kat as she discovers a secret underground laboratory in the manor. Explain to the children that they are going to try to capture the feel of the sequence as a written story. Show the clip again and allow the children to take notes if necessary. There is not much dialogue in the scene but it will help the children if you have the dialogue written on the board so that they do not have to remember it:

KAT: Don't you know a short cut?

CASPER: You got it!

KAT: Casper! No! Wall! Human!

CASPER: Hey! Over here!... Go ahead, sit down.... I would hold on!

KAT: Why?.... Casper!

CASPER: Well?

KAT: What was that?

- The children will certainly need guidance on how to present the film as a written extract, so some modelling will be necessary. It will help if you can show children that a simple summary of events will not be suitable; for example: 'Kat sat in the chair and it took her along a track. She went down into a laboratory.' A better version might begin: 'Casper flew at full speed while Kat pelted down the corridor behind him. She didn't know where he was taking her, but she could see that they were heading for a brick wall!' Encourage the children to really think about how to describe what they see on screen and how best to bring across the pace and speed of the sequence. Working from the film will mean that the children do not have to create a plot or characters and can instead focus solely on their descriptive skills.

- If necessary, show the clip again when the children are halfway through their writing, this will help them to remember what they need to include in the latter part of their work.

- When the children have finished, share some of the best examples of the children's work and discuss with the class how they have captured an action scene in writing (using short sentences, a range of interesting verbs and adverbs, appropriate use of punctuation).

- The activity will most likely take an entire session so as a follow-up session, you can show a second clip from *Casper* which is slower in pace and more moving. The scene is a conversation between Kat and Casper, where the ghost tells her that he cannot remember what his life was like when he was alive. The clip begins at 48:17 and ends at 49:22. This scene forms a nice contrast to the previous one, featuring the same characters but requiring a very different style of writing to express the sad tone. Again, it is useful to have the dialogue prepared for the children on the board so that they can concentrate on describing the characters and their emotions.

■ Compare examples of the two extracts when the class have adapted both clips and ask the children to consider how slower, more emotional scenes are presented in written form.

Novel to film: storyboards

Learning objectives

■ To adapt a written text into visual form
■ To use storyboarding features to tell a story
■ To compare the same story in different forms
■ To tell a story combining words, pictures and sounds.

Resources

■ DVD: *Charlie and the Chocolate Factory* (Warner Bros. 2005)
■ Book: *Charlie and the Chocolate Factory* by Roald Dahl
■ Typed extract from the *Charlie and the Chocolate Factory* novel
■ A3 storyboard sheet (use Figure 6.1 doubled)
■ Sample storyboards (available at www.storyboards-east.com/storybrd.htm).

■ This session can easily be taught individually but will work best after the earlier session in which children were asked to compare the film and novel versions of *Charlie and the Chocolate Factory*. If you have not taught the previous session, then you may find it helpful to show the children the two clips featured in the activity (Clip A: 35:01–38:19 and Clip B: 46:17–47:40). This will give children an idea of the tone of the film. As you watch these clips, draw the children's attention to camera techniques:

■ Wide shots (used to show a group of people or to show a landscape and set the scene)

■ Close-ups (for emotion on the actor's faces or to draw our attention to something)

■ Movement shots (where the camera pans or tracks to follow the action).

■ Explain to the children that films start off as screenplays (like scripts) and are then turned into storyboards. Show the children an example of a storyboarded film sequence on the board (there are numerous excellent examples at the Animatics and Storyboards website www.storyboards-east.com/storybrd.htm). The purpose of the storyboard is to break the main shots of the sequence down and show the camera operator what will be seen on screen and what the camera will film. Many DVDs have storyboard examples as part of the extra features on the disc and it may be helpful to the children if you can show them some of these as well.

- Hand out a storyboard sheet (see Figure 6.1) to each pupil or one to each pair if you wish them to work with a partner. You can use four frames (as shown) if you wish to simplify the activity, but eight frames will be more useful, so simply double up Figure 6.1 to make one A3 sheet. Explain to the children that the boxes represent what the camera will show and the lines underneath each box are for notes and any dialogue.

- Explain to the children that they are going to storyboard a section of the *Charlie and the Chocolate Factory* novel which was not included in the film. In this short extract, the remaining children are shown a room that contains square sweets which Mr Wonka claims 'look round' (Dahl 2007a: 135). It begins at the start of Chapter 23 ('Everybody stopped and crowded to the door') and ends with ' "By golly, he's right!" said Grandpa Joe'. This section is suitable for use because it contains characters with whom the children will already be familiar but does not appear in the finished film version, so their adaptation of it will not simply repeat an existing sequence. Give each child a typed copy of the extract and read through it as a class.

- Turning this extract into a storyboard is not a simple process so the children will need guidance through each stage. The first step is to edit the extract. The children need to take on the role of adapters and decide which parts of the extract can be cut. They may decide, for example, that some of the dialogue can be cut, or that Mrs Salt's dialogue can be spoken by Veruca Salt in order to simplify the scene. Give the children examples of how they can edit but leave the final decisions up to them; ideally, each pair or individual will adapt the scene in a slightly different way.

- When the children have decided the parts they want to keep, ask them to divide the extract up into the eight camera shots that will be shown on the storyboard. Children may wish to use different coloured pens and actually divide up the photocopied extract into eight sections which will represent the eight shots on the storyboard.

- Once this is done, remind the children that they need to draw a rough sketch of what the camera will show in each of the eight boxes and write any notes (for example 'close-up' or 'camera zoom') and dialogue on the lines underneath each box. Explain to the children that they will need to show a range of different camera shots in their sequence, such as wide shots and close-ups. It will help if you have prepared the first two or three boxes of your own storyboard so that the children know what they are expected to do.

- Give the children enough time to work on their storyboards and then ask them to present their work to the class when finished. Explain that their final storyboards should be clear enough for a director and camera operator to be able to use it to film the sequence.

Figure 6.1 Storyboard sheet

Figure 6.2 Work by Lewis and Amy

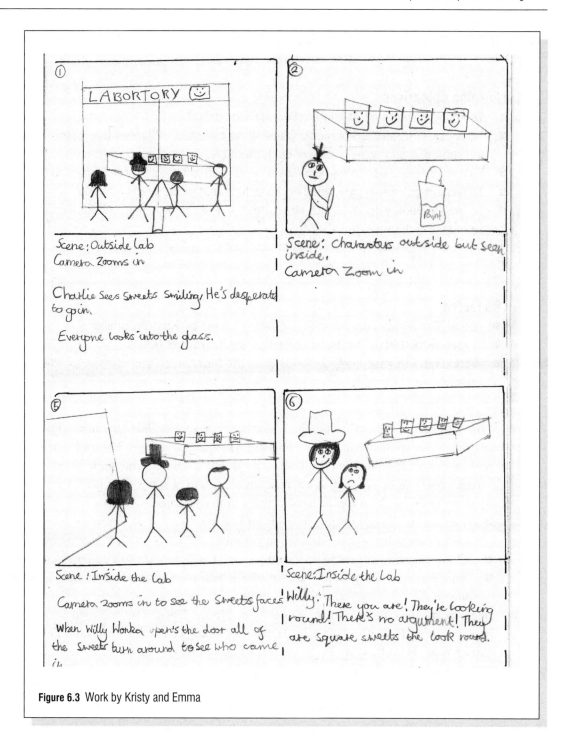

Figure 6.3 Work by Kristy and Emma

Adapting novels: *The Miraculous Journey of Edward Tulane*

Learning objectives

- To change a written text into a different medium
- To consider how different media transmit narratives in different ways, discussing the strengths and weaknesses of each medium
- To compare and contrast the different ways in which the same story can be told
- To work in groups to plan, write and create an extended piece of work
- To experiment with different structures of texts, combining words, images, sounds and drama to tell a story.

Resources

- Book: *The Miraculous Journey of Edward Tulane* by Kate DiCamillo
- Typed extract from *The Miraculous Journey of Edward Tulane*
- Various media resources depending on the form which you choose to adapt the extract into.

- This activity can be carried out in a number of ways, in order to show children that adaptation does not mean simply changing a book into a film. The children will start with an extract from a novel and later adapt it into a different medium. There are many ways a novel can be adapted: as a screenplay for a film, a script for a play, a comic book or an audio drama. You can plan the activity in one of three ways:
  - The whole class (working individually) adapts the extract from the novel into a medium which you have decided in advance
  - The whole class adapts the extract into a medium of their choice after discussion
  - Split the class into groups, each of which has to adapt the extract into a different medium.
- Begin by introducing the extract. Give the children a typed copy and then read through it. Kate DiCamillo's *The Miraculous Journey of Edward Tulane* has been used here but an extract from almost any piece of children's literature will do. The novel follows the adventures of Edward Tulane, a selfish and vain china rabbit who is passed across America via different owners and learns what is to lose and what it is to love along the way. The extract chosen tells the story of how Edward is separated from his owner Abilene when he falls into the ocean from a ship. It begins in Chapter 5 with 'Two young boys, brothers named Martin and Amos, took a particular interest in Edward', and finishes at the end of the chapter with 'Instead, Edward Tulane went overboard' (DiCamillo 2006: 41–4).

- As stated earlier, you may wish to read the extract with the class and let them decide the medium to adapt the text into or you may wish to simplify the task by deciding before-hand yourself. Begin by asking the children to list some of the features of the medium they are going to adapt the novel into. For example, if you have decided to turn the extract into an audio drama, list the elements it will require such as clear dialogue to inform the listener of events, sound effects, music and possibly a narrator. If they are adapting it into a comic book, they will need clear drawings, a variety of panels and speech bubbles.

- When the children have given some thought to how they will need to change the extract, allow them to annotate their copies of the extract. Encourage them to edit dialogue where necessary, note where they might require close-ups or long shots (if they are writing a screenplay) or sound effects (if they are creating an audio drama). The children should have free reign with the extract as long as their adaptation still retains the essential narrative, tone and characterisation of the novel.

- Allow the children to begin adapting the extract into whichever medium has been agreed. This process of adaptation may take longer than one session and would ideally be carried out over two or more sessions. You will need to reiterate certain points to the children depending on which form they are adapting the extract into. Table 6.1 shows some of the main considerations for each medium.

Table 6.1 Points to consider when adapting material into different forms

FORM OF ADAPTATION	ELEMENTS TO CONSIDER
Comic book	Shape, size and number of panels Amount of dialogue and size of speech bubbles Use of narrative boxes and onomatopoeia A mix of close-ups, long shots and a variety of panel layouts
Screenplay for film	Variety of close-ups, long shots and instructions as to how the camera should move Change dialogue to compensate for lack of interior monologue Use of special effects Use of sound effects Use of music Set and props
Playscript for drama	Change dialogue to compensate for lack of interior monologue Consider if narrator is necessary Use of music/sound effects Set and props
Script for an audio recording	Change dialogue to compensate for lack of visuals Sound effects Consider if narrator is necessary or not Use of music

- By the end of the adaptation process, the children do not have to have finished the final product but should have their adaptation ready to be made. For example, if they are adapting the text into a film, they do not have to have filmed it, but should have the screenplay written. This can be a satisfactory end in itself and it is worth discussing the adaptations with the class to find out how the extract was edited, what was added and how they managed to tell the story in another form. If you have time, the activity can be extended over the following weeks to allow the children the opportunity to complete the adaptation process by creating the finished product. They could perform it in Drama if they have written playscripts, film it if they have written a screenplay and record it if they have adapted it into an audio recording. If the children have worked in groups on different media, a good way to conclude the work is to compare how each medium tells the story in a different way and to discuss the strengths of each format with the children.

6.3

Adaptation

Further Ideas and Resources

These lists of resources and ideas for activities supplement the teaching ideas in Chapter 6.2 and offer suggestions for teaching activities based around adaptation with other age groups.

Teaching adaptation to younger children

While the study of adaptation requires an understanding of how different types of text operate in order to explore it at higher levels, this is not to say that younger children are not able to study it too. It is important to choose the correct material here; showing children how a story which is familiar to them has been re-presented in another form can be an excellent way to introduce film and comics into the Literacy curriculum. The fact that the children will be familiar with the story already will allow them to watch a film version, for example, and think about *how* the story is told rather than having to work out what is going on. The following three outlines for sessions are intended for Key Stage One and lower Key Stage Two but can easily be used with other age groups if required:

Lost and Found

Age group: Key Stage One

Learning objectives
- To introduce the idea of adaptation
- To compare and contrast a film with a picture book.

Resources
- Book: *Lost and Found* by Oliver Jeffers
- DVD: *Lost and Found* (E1 Entertainment 2008).

■ In the weeks leading up to the activity, read *Lost and Found* at least two or three times with the class so that they are familiar with the story and the characters.

■ Explain that you are going to show the class the animated film that has been made of the book. The children might like to see the cover of the DVD and look at the information on the back of it too. Watch the film with the children, explaining that you want them to think about how the film is different from, and the same as, the picture book.

■ When you have watched the film, ask some of the children to describe their favourite parts and maybe watch some of these clips back. Discuss the adaptation, asking the children what they thought about it. If necessary, reread the book quickly with the children. Ask them some simple comparison questions:

● What was the same about the film and the book?

● What was different?

● Did the characters look and act the same? (Show selected pages from the book to demonstrate how closely the film resembles the illustrations)

● What things have been added to the film?

● Why do you think the filmmakers added extra things?

● Which did you prefer and why? (Children discuss in pairs and then report back)

● Ask children to suggest other picture books that they would like to see a film of.

Meet the Robinsons

Age group: Key Stage One/Two

Learning objectives
■ To compare a book with a film
■ To consider the features of a film and the features of a book and how they differ.

Resources
■ Book: *A Day with Wilbur Robinson* by William Joyce
■ DVD: *Meet the Robinsons* (Walt Disney Pictures 2007).

■ Read *A Day with Wilbur Robinson* to the class (perhaps twice) a few days before the activity. Ask one of the children to retell the story in their own words. Tell the children that there has been an animated film made of this. Ask the children why this book might be difficult to turn into a ninety-minute film (lack of any real eventful plot, a short story is difficult to stretch into a long film).

■ Watch the film with the children (the film is around ninety minutes so this might be done over two sessions or in an afternoon session).

- Ask the children to think about what is the same and what is different in the film and the book as they watch. Afterwards, allow the children to discuss in pairs what they thought were the main differences between the two media.
- Write a list of the differences on the board (for example, extra characters added into the film including a villain, a time-travelling storyline added into the film and different settings).
- Ask the class to think about why these changes were made for the film. You can either write up these reasons on the board as a whole class or get the children to do this individually as a written task, depending on the age and ability of the children. If the children are doing the activity individually, ask them to make a table with two headings on their paper:
  What was different? Why do you think it was different?
- Encourage the children to really consider why the film required a villain and an extended storyline.
- Ask the children to discuss their answers after they have had time to think about it. As a conclusion, ask the children to discuss with each other (or write) which they preferred (the book or the film) and why. If appropriate, summarise some of the features that a film needs to have (especially a children's film) such as a hero, a villain, a range of characters we can identify with and a story which will hold a viewer's interest for over an hour and a half.

The Snowman

Age group: Key Stage Two

Learning objectives
- To explore how a graphic novel can be turned into a film
- To consider how a story can be told without words

Resources
- Book: *The Snowman* by Raymond Briggs
- DVD: *The Snowman* (Snowman Enterprises 1982).

- Before you show the film, the children will need to have read the book of *The Snowman*. As the book is told in comic strip form with no words, it is difficult to read with a whole class as the children need to see the pictures up close. It might be better for the children to read it in pairs or threes in the weeks leading up to the viewing of the film.

- Tell the children that they are going to watch the film of *The Snowman*. Ask them to make a note of what is the same and what is different from the book.
- When the film is finished, ask the children to work with a partner and discuss, then write down, all the similarities and differences between the film and the book version. Ask them to think about the lack of dialogue in both.
- After discussing their answers, ask the children why they think the film was made as an animated feature and not a live-action film. Then ask the children why they think the filmmakers decided not to add any speech to the film. Try to encourage the children to think how the film might have deviated too far from the vision of the book if they had had real actors or dialogue.
- Examine one particular sequence closely (this can be done in a separate session if you are short of time). Look at the moving closing moments from the film, where James runs downstairs and into the garden to discover that the Snowman has melted away. This is on pp. 28–30 in the book and 24:08–25:05 in the film. Look at the sequence in the book on the visualiser or as a scanned image on the computer and then watch the sequence from the film. Ask the children how the mood, or tone, is established in the film version. Discuss the use of music and how it conveys emotion.
- Ask the children which sequence they find more moving and why. Try to get at least one child to argue their reasons for each of the formats.
- Compare the sequence in the book and the film where the Snowman first comes alive and meets James. This is pp. 4–6 in the book and 04:28–06:38 in the film. Again, ask the children to consider the strengths of each version of the story. Conclude the session by asking the children to write down what the strengths are of each medium.

Adaptation resources

There are a number of excellent book-to-film adaptations which can be used with children.

Key Stage One

Book	*Film*
How The Grinch Stole Christmas!	*The Grinch*
By Dr Seuss	(Universal Pictures 2000)
Horton Hears a Who	*Horton Hears a Who*
by Dr Seuss	(Twentieth Century Fox 2008)
Where the Wild Things Are	*Where the Wild Things Are*
by Maurice Sendak	(Warner Bros. 2009)
The Cat in the Hat	*The Cat in the Hat*
by Dr Seuss	(Universal Pictures 2003)

Key Stage Two

Book	*Film*
The Witches by Roald Dahl	*The Witches* (Jim Henson Pictures 1990)
The Spiderwick Chronicles by Tony DiTerlizzi and Holly Black	*The Spiderwick Chronicles* (Nickleodeon Movies 2008)
The City of Ember by Jeanne DuPrau	*City of Ember* (Walden Media 2008)
Jumanji by Chris Van Allsburg	*Jumanji* (TriStar Pictures 1995)
James and the Giant Peach by Roald Dahl	*James and the Giant Peach* (Walt Disney Pictures 1996)
Matilda by Roald Dahl	*Matilda* (TriStar Pictures 1996)
The Tale of Despereaux by Kate DiCamillo	*The Tale of Despereaux* (Universal Pictures 2008)
Fantastic Mr Fox by Roald Dahl	*Fantastic Mr. Fox* (Twentieth Century Fox 2009)
Harry Potter and the Philosopher's Stone by J.K. Rowling	*Harry Potter and the Philosopher's Stone* (Warner Bros. 2001)
Harry Potter and the Chamber of Secrets by J.K. Rowling	*Harry Potter and the Chamber of Secrets* (Warner Bros. 2002)
Harry Potter and the Prisoner of Azkaban by J.K. Rowling	*Harry Potter and the Prisoner of Azkaban* (Warner Bros. 2004)
Northern Lights (His Dark Materials, vol. 1) by Philip Pullman	*The Golden Compass* (New Line Cinema 2007)
The Chronicles of Narnia: The Lion, the Witch and the Wardrobe by C.S. Lewis	*The Chronicles of Narnia: The Lion, the Witch and the Wardrobe* (Walt Disney Pictures 2005)
Prince Caspian by C.S. Lewis	*Prince Caspian* (Walt Disney Pictures 2008)
The Sheep-Pig by Dick King–Smith	*Babe* (Universal 1995)
Coraline by Neil Gaiman	*Coraline* (Universal 2009)
A Christmas Carol by Charles Dickens	*A Christmas Carol* (Walt Disney 2009)
Alice's Adventures in Wonderland and Through the Looking Glass by Lewis Carroll	*Alice in Wonderland* (Walt Disney 2010)

Comic adaptations

Many books have been adapted into comic book format. Studying a novel as prose and then as a comic book provides an interesting opportunity to develop visual literacy skills. When comparing the original novels with their comic book adaptations, there are several basic activities that can be taught:

- Compare a page of the novel with its comic book counterpart, looking for the ways in which the comic book author and artist have used panel structure, angle and close-ups/long shots to tell the story.
- Explore what has been cut from the original novel in the second version and consider why these cuts have been made.
- Ask the children to create their own comic book adaptation of a section of the novel which they have not studied beforehand, or from a novel of their choice.

The following titles are good examples of comic books that have been adapted from novels which are suitable for use with children:

The Wonderful Wizard of Oz by Eric Shanower (writer) and Skottie Young (artist)
Treasure Island by Roy Thomas (writer) and Mario Gully (artist)
Artemis Fowl: The Graphic Novel by Eoin Colfer and Andrew Donkin (writers) and Giovanni Rigano and Paola Lamanna (artists)
Artemis Fowl – The Arctic Incident: The Graphic Novel by Eoin Colfer and Andrew Donkin (writers) and Giovanni Rigano and Paola Lamanna (artists)
Stormbreaker: The Graphic Novel by Anthony Horowitz and Antony Johnston (writers) and Kanako and Yuzuru (artists)
Point Blanc: The Graphic Novel by Anthony Horowitz and Antony Johnston (writers) and Kanako and Yuzuru (artists)
The Tale of Despereaux: The Graphic Novel by Matt Smith and David Tilton

Glossary

auteur
a director is termed an auteur when their style or personality is evident in many aspects of their films, for example the characters, the screenplay, the costumes, the design and the soundtrack. Alongside Tim Burton, whose distinctive visual style and subject matter make his films clearly identifiable as his work, other filmmakers who are auteurs include Quentin Tarantino, Spike Jonze, Sofia Coppola and Martin Scorsese.

diegesis
when a writer tells, or summarises, events in a novel. For example, 'the group fought bitterly for hours and then gave up'. Here a battle has been transmitted to the reader in one sentence without going into detail. The opposite technique is mimesis where events or speech would be shown or reported by the author directly.

focalisation
the way in which a narrative is told, relating specifically to the character or characters from whose perspective the story is viewed. The *Harry Potter* series, for example, is focalised through Harry as we only see, hear and understand that which Harry sees, hears and understands.

genre
the type of narrative which a text may be classified as, such as fantasy.

graphic novel
there is much debate over the precise definition of a graphic novel and how it is different from a comic book, but the general consensus is that a graphic novel is a longer, complete story in one volume whereas a comic book is a single issue (approximately twenty-four pages) which tells part of a longer story spread across a number of issues.

gutter
the space between panels in a comic book.

icon
a drawn, painted or printed representation of any object, idea or living thing.

iconography
the visual aspects of a genre such as costume, props and locations which are shown on screen in film, as discussed by Colin McArthur.

image
any piece of visual material which we observe, inevitably bounded by a frame or an edge where the material stops. An image can be as small as one single mark on a piece of paper or as large as a cinema screen.

narrative boxes
the rectangular boxes filled with text and placed inside panels in a comic book, which usually denote narrative information such as the passing of time or location.

panel
the individual blocks which make up a comic book page. They can be any shape but are usually square or rectangular.

postmodernism
a movement or period in the arts, the texts of which are characterised by their fragmented and seemingly chaotic representation of elements such as time and character and by the way in which they draw attention to their own form. For example, a postmodern narrative might be one which explores the act of writing or reminds the reader that they are reading a book.

speech balloons/ bubbles	the (usually white) shapes which are filled with text and placed by a character in a comic book to show their dialogue.
structuralism	a critical movement and way of analysing texts based on the work of Ferdinand de Saussure, who argued that we can only understand acts of speech when we relate them to the larger frameworks or contexts which they are a part of. This can be applied to texts. Saussure termed the individual speech act the *parole* and the wider framework the *langue*.
symbol	an icon which, due to the context it is situated in, may represent much more in terms of themes and ideas than simply the object which it depicts. For example, an icon of a book might also be interpreted as a symbol of knowledge or education.
trompe l'oeil	a style of decoration commonly seen on the interior walls of stately homes where two-dimensional images are painted to look as if they are three-dimensional objects; for example, the image of a pillar painted onto a flat wall to make it look as if it were really there. The French term translates as 'trick the eye'.

Bibliography

300 (2006) Film directed by Zack Snyder, screenplay by Zack Snyder, Kurt Johnstad and Michael Gordon, 117 minutes, released by Warner Bros. Pictures.

Alice in Wonderland (2010) Film directed by Tim Burton, screenplay by Linda Woolverton, 108 minutes, released by Walt Disney Pictures.

Alley, Z.B. (writer) and Alley, R.W. (artist) (2008) *There's a Wolf at the Door*, New York: Roaring Brook Press.

Arizpe, E. and Styles, M. (2003) *Children Reading Pictures: Interpreting Visual Texts*, London: RoutledgeFalmer.

Armstrong, E. (2007) *Riveting Reads: Boys into Books 11–14*, Wanborough: The School Library Association.

Babe (1995) Film directed by Chris Noonan, screenplay by George Miller and Chris Noonan, 89 minutes, released by Universal Pictures.

Baddeley, P. and Eddershaw, C. (1994) *Not So Simple Picture Books*, Stoke-on-Trent: Trentham Books.

Balász, B. (2004) 'The Close-Up', in L. Braudy and M. Cohen (eds) *Film Theory and Criticism*, 6th edn, New York: Oxford University Press.

Baltazar, A. and Franco (2009a) *Tiny Titans*, Book 1, *Welcome to the Treehouse*, New York: DC Comics.

Baltazar, A. and Franco (2009b) *Tiny Titans*, Book 2, *Adventures in Awesomeness*, New York: DC Comics.

Barry, P. (2002) *Beginning Theory*, 2nd edn, Manchester: Manchester University Press.

Batman (1989) Film directed by Tim Burton, screenplay by Sam Hamm and Warren Skaaren, 126 minutes, released by Warner Bros. Pictures.

Batman Begins (2005) Film directed by Christopher Nolan, screenplay by Christopher Nolan and David S. Goyer, 140 minutes, released by Warner Bros. Pictures.

Batman Returns (1992) Film directed by Tim Burton, screenplay by Daniel Waters, 126 minutes, released by Warner Bros. Pictures.

Battlestar Galactica (2004) British Sky Broadcasting, NBC and Universal Media Studios, created by Glen Larson, Ronald D. Moore and David Eick, first episode transmitted 18 October 2004.

Belleville Rendez-Vous (2003) Film directed by Sylvain Chomet, screenplay by Sylvain Chomet, 80 minutes, released by Metro Tartan.

Bellin, J.D. (2005) *Framing Monsters: Fantasy Film and Social Alienation*, Carbondale: Southern Illinois University Press.

Bester, A. (1956) *Tiger! Tiger!*, London: Penguin.

Big Fish (2003) Film directed by Tim Burton, screenplay by John August, 125 minutes, released by Columbia Pictures.

Black Books (2000) Assembly Film and Television and Channel 4, created by Dylan Moran, first episode transmitted 29 September 2000.

Boggs, J.M. and Petrie, D.W. (2008) *The Art of Watching Films*, 7th edn, New York: McGraw Hill.

Box Office Mojo (2009a) *2008 Worldwide Grosses*. Online: www.boxofficemojo.com/yearly/chart/?view2=worldwide &yr=2008&p=.htm (accessed 28 April 2009).

Box Office Mojo (2009b) *All Time Box-Office Worldwide Grosses*. Online: www.boxofficemojo.com/alltime/world (accessed 13 June 2009).

Briggs, R. (1978) *The Snowman*, London: Hamish Hamilton Children's Books.

Briggs, R. (1996) *The Bear*, London: Random House Children's Books.

Briggs, R. (2003) *Fungus the Bogeyman*, London: Puffin. Originally published 1977.

Brown, C. (2008) *Riveting Reads Plus: Boys into Books 5–11*, Wanborough: The School Library Association.

Brown, D. (2004) *The Da Vinci Code*, London: Corgi Books.

Brown, H. (2009) 'If We Have a Spare Dollar We Will Spend It on a Book', *Telegraph Review*, 10 January 2009: 10–11.

Browne, A. (2008) *Gorilla*, London: Walker Books. First published 1983.

Burningham, J. (2009) *It's A Secret!*, London: Walker Books.

Burton, T. and Salisbury, M. (ed.) (1995) *Burton on Burton*, London: Faber and Faber.

Butler, M.C. (writer) and Chapman, J. (artist) (2008) *The Dark, Dark Night*, London: Little Tiger Press.

Carroll, L. (2003) *Alice's Adventures in Wonderland and Through the Looking-Glass*, London: Penguin. First published 1865.

Casino Royale (2006) Film directed by Martin Campbell, screenplay by Neal Purvis, Robert Wade and Paul Haggis, 144 minutes, released by Metro-Goldwyn-Mayer.

Casper (1995) Film directed by Brad Silberling, screenplay by Sherri Stoner and Deanna Oliver, 96 minutes, released by Universal Pictures.

Cat in the Hat, The (2003) Film directed by Bo Welch, screenplay by Alec Berg, David Mandel and Jeff Schaffer, 82 minutes, released by Universal Pictures.

Charlie and the Chocolate Factory (2005) Film directed by Tim Burton, screenplay by John August, 115 minutes, released by Warner Bros. Pictures.

Chen, K. (2008) 'The Lovely Smallness of Doctor Who', *Film Int.*, 6 (2): 52–9.

Child, L. (2000) *Beware of the Storybook Wolves*, London: Hodder Children's Books.

Child, L. (2003) *Who's Afraid of the Big Bad Book?*, London: Hodder Children's Books.

Child, L. (2007) *I Am too Absolutely Small for School*, London: Orchard Books.

Christmas Carol, A (2009) Film directed by Robert Zemeckis, screenplay by Robert Zemeckis, 96 minutes, released by Walt Disney Pictures.

Chronicles of Narnia, The: The Lion, the Witch and the Wardrobe (2005) Film directed by Andrew Adamson, screenplay by Ann Peacock, Andrew Adamson, Christopher Markus and Stephen McFeely, 143 minutes, released by Walt Disney Pictures.

Chronicles of Narnia, The: Prince Caspian (2008) Film directed by Andrew Adamson, screenplay by Andrew Adamson, Christopher Markus and Stephen McFeely, 144 minutes, released by Walt Disney Pictures.

Cinderella (1950) Film directed by Clyde Geronimi, Wilfred Jackson and Hamilton Luske, screenplay by Bill Peet, Erdman Penner, Ted Sears, Winston Hibler, Homer Brightman, Harry Reeves, Ken Anderson and Joe Rinaldi, 74 minutes, released by Walt Disney Pictures.

City of Ember (2008) Film directed by Gil Kenan, screenplay by Caroline Thompson, 90 minutes, released by Walden Media.

Claremont, C. (writer) and Byrne, J. (writer and artist) (2000) *Essential X-Men Volume 2*, New York: Marvel Comics.

Colfer, E. and Donkin, A. (writers) and Rigano, G. and Lamanna, P. (artists) (2007) *Artemis Fowl: The Graphic Novel*, London: Puffin.

Colfer, E. and Donkin, A. (writers) and Rigano, G. and Lamanna, P. (artists) (2009) *Artemis Fowl – The Arctic Incident: The Graphic Novel*, London: Puffin.

Coraline (2009) Film directed by Henry Selick, screenplay by Henry Selick, 100 minutes, released by Universal Pictures.

Dahl, R. (1973) *James and the Giant Peach*, Harmondsworth: Puffin. Originally published 1961.

Dahl, R. (2007a) *Charlie and the Chocolate Factory*, London: Puffin. Originally published 1964.

Dahl, R. (2007b) *Fantastic Mr Fox*, London: Puffin. Originally published 1970.

Dahl, R. (2007c) *Matilda*, London: Puffin. Originally published 1988.

Dahl, R. (2007d) *The Witches*, London: Puffin. Originally published 1983.

Dark Knight, The (2008) Film directed by Christopher Nolan, screenplay by Jonathan Nolan and Christopher Nolan, 152 minutes, released by Warner Bros. Pictures.

Davies, R.T. (2007) *Doctor Who: Smith and Jones*. Online: www.bbc.co.uk/writersroom/insight/downloads/scripts/doctor_who_3_ep_1.pdf (accessed 19 August 2009).

Davies, R.T. and Cook, B. (2008) *Doctor Who: The Writer's Tale*, London: BBC Books.

Day, A., Dean, J., Graham, J., Leyland, M., Mottram, J., Mueller, M., Russell, J. and Salisbury, M. (2009) 'Comic Book Movie Preview', *Total Film*, 152, March 2009: 65–98.

Department for Children, Schools and Families (2008) *Primary Framework for Literacy*. Online. Reproduced under the terms of the Click-Use Licence: www.standards.dfes.gov.uk/primaryframework/literacy (accessed 4 November 2008).

Department for Education and Employment (1998) *The National Literacy Strategy*, London: DfEE.

Desperate Housewives (2004), Touchstone Television and ABC, created by Marc Cherry, first episode transmitted 3 October 2004.

DiCamillo, K. (2004) *The Tale of Despereaux*, London: Walker Books.

DiCamillo, K. (2006) *The Miraculous Journey of Edward Tulane*, Cambridge: Candlewick Press.

Dickens, C. (2006) *A Christmas Carol and other Christmas Books*, Oxford: Oxford University Press. Originally published 1843.

Dirks, T. (2009) *The Great Train Robbery (1903) Review*. Online: www.filmsite.org/grea.html (accessed 10 February 2009).

DiTerlizzi, T. and Black, H. (2003) *The Spiderwick Chronicles – Book 1: The Field Guide*, New York: Simon and Schuster.

Dix, A. (2008) *Beginning Film Studies*, Manchester: Manchester University Press.

Docherty, T. (2009) *Little Boat*, Dorking: Templar Publishing.

Doctor Who: 42 (2007) Episode directed by Graeme Harper, screenplay by Chris Chibnall, 45 minutes, released by BBC. First transmitted 19 May 2007.

Doctor Who: Doomsday (2006) Episode directed by Graeme Harper, screenplay by Russell T. Davies, 45 minutes, released by BBC. First transmitted 8 July 2006.

Doctor Who: Gridlock (2007) Episode directed by Richard Clark, screenplay by Russell T. Davies, 45 minutes, released by BBC. First transmitted 14 April 2007.

Doctor Who: Journey's End (2008) Episode directed by Graeme Harper, written by Russell T. Davies, 63 minutes, released by BBC. First transmitted 5 July 2008.

Doctor Who: Last of the Time Lords (2007) Episode directed by Colin Teague, screenplay by Russell T. Davies, 45 minutes, released by BBC. First transmitted 30 June 2007.

Doctor Who: Partners in Crime (2008) Episode directed by James Strong, screenplay by Russell T. Davies, 45 minutes, released by BBC. First transmitted 5 April 2008.

Doctor Who: Planet of the Ood (2008) Episode directed by Graeme Harper, screenplay by Keith Temple, 45 minutes, released by BBC. First transmitted 19 April 2008.

Doctor Who: Rose (2005) Episode directed by Keith Boak, screenplay by Russell T. Davies, 45 minutes, released by BBC. First transmitted 26 March 2005.

Doctor Who: School Reunion (2006) Episode directed by James Hawes, screenplay by Toby Whithouse, 45 minutes, released by BBC. First transmitted 29 April 2006.

Doctor Who: Smith and Jones (2007) Episode directed by Charles Palmer, screenplay by Russell T. Davies, 45 minutes, released by BBC. First transmitted 31 March 2007.

Doctor Who: The Christmas Invasion (2005) Directed by James Hawes, screenplay by Russell T. Davies, 60 minutes, released by BBC. First transmitted 25 December 2005.

Doctor Who: The End of the World (2006) Episode directed by Euros Lyn, screenplay by Russell T. Davies, 45 minutes, released by BBC. First transmitted 2 April 2005.

Doctor Who: The Next Doctor (2008) Episode directed by Andy Goddard, screenplay by Russell T. Davies, 60 minutes, released by BBC. First transmitted 25 December 2008.

Doctor Who: The Parting of the Ways (2005) Episode directed by Joe Ahearne, screenplay by Russell T. Davies, 45 minutes, released by BBC. First transmitted 18 June 2005.

Doctor Who: The Poison Sky (2008) Episode directed by Douglas Mackinnon, screenplay by Helen Raynor, 45 minutes, released by BBC. First transmitted 3 May 2008.

Doctor Who: The Stolen Earth (2008) Episode directed by Graeme Harper, screenplay by Russell T. Davies, 45 minutes, released by BBC. First transmitted 28 June 2008.

Doctor Who: Tooth and Claw (2006) Episode directed by Euros Lyn, screenplay by Russell T. Davies, 45 minutes, released by BBC. First transmitted 22 April 2006.

Doctor Who: World War Three (2005) Episode directed by Keith Boak, screenplay by Russell T. Davies, 45 minutes, released by BBC. First transmitted 23 April 2005.

Dondis, D.A. (1973) *A Primer of Visual Literacy*, Cambridge, MA: MIT Press.

Doonan, J. (1993) *Looking at Pictures in Picture Books*, Woodchester: Thimble Press.

Dougill, P. (1993) *The Primary Language Book*, 2nd edn, Buckingham: Open University Press.

Dr. Strangelove or How I Learned to Stop Worrying and Love the Bomb (1964) Film directed by Stanley Kubrick, screenplay by Stanley Kubrick, Terry Southern and Peter George, 93 minutes, released by Columbia Pictures.

DuPrau, J. (2003) *The City of Ember*, New York: Yearling.

Edward Scissorhands (1990) Film directed by Tim Burton, screenplay by Caroline Thompson, 105 minutes, released by Twentieth Century Fox.

Edward Scissorhands (2008) Stage production directed and choreographed by Matthew Bourne, story by Caroline Thompson, adapted by Caroline Thompson and Matthew Bourne, music by Terry Davis and Danny Elfman, produced by New Adventures. Originally performed 2005.

Ed Wood (1994) Film directed by Tim Burton, screenplay by Scott Alexander and Larry Karaszewski, 127 minutes, released by Touchstone Pictures.

Eisner, W. (2001) *Comics and Sequential Art*, Tamarac: Poorhouse Press. Originally published 1985.

Emma (1996) Film directed by Douglas McGrath, screenplay by Douglas McGrath, 116 minutes, released by Miramax Films.

Enchanted (2007) Film directed by Kevin Lima, screenplay by Bill Kelly, 107 minutes, released by Walt Disney Pictures.

English Patient, The (1996) Film directed by Anthony Minghella, screenplay by Anthony Minghella, 162 minutes, released by Miramax Films.

Fabe, M. (2004) *Closely Watched Films*, London: University of California Press.

Fantastic Four (2005) Film directed by Tim Story, screenplay by Mark Frost and Michael France, 106 minutes, released by Twentieth Century Fox

Fantastic Mr. Fox (2009) Film directed by Wes Anderson, screenplay by Wes Anderson and Noah Baumbach, 87 minutes, released by Twentieth Century Fox.

Fer, B. (2008) 'Seeing in the Dark', in A. Borchardt-Hume (ed.) *Rothko*, London: Tate Publishing.

Finding Nemo (2003) Film directed by Andrew Stanton and Lee Unkrich, screenplay by Andrew Stanton, Bob Peterson and David Reynolds, 100 minutes, released by Walt Disney Pictures.

Finding Neverland (2004) Film directed by Marc Forster, screenplay by Allan Knee and David Magee, 106 minutes, released by Miramax Films.

Foreman, M. (2006) *Seal Surfer*, London: Andersen Press Ltd.

French, J. (writer) and Whatley, B. (artist) (2005) *Diary of a Wombat*, London: HarperCollins Children's Books.

French, J. (writer) and Whatley, B. (artist) (2009) *Emily and the Big Bad Bunyip*, London: HarperCollins Children's Books.

Gaiman, N. (2002) *Coraline*, London: Bloomsbury.

Geri's Game (1997) Film directed by Jan Pinkava, screenplay by Jan Pinkava, 5 minutes, released by Pixar Animation Studios.

Gilbey, R. (2005) 'Charlie and the Chocolate Factory Review', *Sight and Sound*, September 2005. Online: www.bfi.org.uk/sightandsound/review/2502 (accessed 27 February 2008).

Gillatt, G. (2008) ' "The sheer brilliance of Doctor Who" ', *Doctor Who Magazine*, 400: 16–26.

Giorgis, C., Johnson, N.J., Bonomo, A., Colbert, C., Conner, A., Kauffman, G. and Kulesza, D. (1999) 'Children's Books: Visual Literacy', *The Reading Teacher*, 53 (2): 146–53.

Godfather, The (1972) Film directed by Francis Ford Coppola, screenplay by Mario Puzo and Francis Ford Coppola, 175 minutes, released by Paramount Pictures.

Godfather Part II, The (1974) Film directed by Francis Ford Coppola, screenplay by Francis Ford Coppola and Mario Puzo, 200 minutes, released by Paramount Pictures.

Godfather Part III, The (1990) Film directed by Francis Ford Coppola, screenplay by Mario Puzo and Francis Ford Coppola, 162 minutes, released by Paramount Pictures.

Gold, G.D. (2002) *Carter Beats the Devil*, London: Sceptre.

Gold, G.D. (2009) *Sunnyside*, London: Sceptre.

Golden Compass, The (2007) Film directed by Chris Weitz, screenplay by Chris Weitz, 113 minutes, released by New Line Cinema.

Gone with the Wind (1939) Film directed by Victor Fleming, screenplay by Sidney Howard, 226 minutes, released by Metro-Goldwyn-Mayer.

Goscinny, R. and Uderzo, A. (2007) *Asterix Omnibus Volume 1*, London: Orion.

Gravett, E. (2006) *Wolves*, London: PanMacmillan.

Gravett, E. (2007) *Little Mouse's Big Book of Fears*, London: Macmillan Children's Books.

Great Train Robbery, The (1903) Film directed by Edwin Porter, screenplay by Scott Marble and Edwin Porter, 11 minutes, released by Edison Manufacturing Company.

Grinch, The (2000) Film directed by Ron Howard, screenplay by Jeffrey Price and Peter S. Seaman, 104 minutes, released by Universal Pictures.

Gustines, G.G. (2008) 'Film Trailer Aids Sales of "Watchmen" Novel', *New York Times*, 13 August 2008. Online: www.nytimes.com/2008/08/14/arts/14arts-FILMTRAILERA_BRF.html?_r=3&ref=arts&oref=slogin (accessed 28 April 2009).

Harris, P. (writer) and Allwright, D. (illustrator) (2005) *The Night Pirates*, London: Egmont.

Harry Potter and the Chamber of Secrets (2002) Film directed by Chris Columbus, screenplay by Steve Kloves, 161 minutes, released by Warner Bros. Pictures.

Harry Potter and the Goblet of Fire (2005) Film directed by Mike Newell, screenplay by Steve Kloves, 157 minutes, released by Warner Bros. Pictures.

Harry Potter and the Order of the Phoenix (2007) Film directed by David Yates, screenplay by Michael Goldenberg, 132 minutes, released by Warner Bros. Pictures.

Harry Potter and the Philosopher's Stone (2001) Film directed by Chris Columbus, screenplay by Steve Kloves, 152 minutes, released by Warner Bros. Pictures.

Harry Potter and the Prisoner of Azkaban (2004) Film directed by Alfonso Cuaron, screenplay by Steve Kloves, 141 minutes, released by Warner Bros. Pictures.

Hazen, B. and Ungerer, T. (1984) *The Sorcerer's Apprentice*, London: Methuen.

Hergé (2007) *The Adventures of Tintin Volume 1*, London: Egmont Books Ltd.

High School Musical (2006) Film directed by Kenny Ortega, screenplay by Peter Barsocchini, 98 minutes, released by Walt Disney Pictures.

Horowitz, A. and Johnston, A. (writers) and Kanako and Yuzuru (artists) (2006) *Stormbreaker: The Graphic Novel*, London: Walker Books.

Horowitz, A. and Johnston, A. (writers) and Kanako and Yuzuru (artists) (2007) *Point Blanc: The Graphic Novel*, London: Walker Books.

Horton Hears a Who (2008) Film directed by Jimmy Hayward and Steve Martino, screenplay by Ken Daurio and Cinco Paul, 86 minutes, released by Twentieth Century Fox.

Hughes, D. (2003) *Comic Book Movies*, London: Virgin Books Ltd.

Hulk (2003) Film directed by Ang Lee, screenplay by John Turman, Michael France and James Schamus, 138 minutes, released by Universal Pictures.

Hutchins, P. (1970) *Rosie's Walk*, Harmondsworth: Penguin Books.

Incredible Hulk, The (2008) Film directed by Louis Leterrier, screenplay by Zak Penn, 112 minutes, released by Universal Pictures.

Incredibles, The (2004) Film directed by Brad Bird, screenplay by Brad Bird, 115 minutes, released by Walt Disney/Pixar Pictures.

Indiana Jones and the Temple of Doom (1984) Film directed by Steven Spielberg, screenplay by Willard Huyck and Gloria Katz, 118 minutes, released by Paramount Pictures.

Iron Man (2008) Film directed by Jon Favreau, screenplay by Mark Fergus, Hawk Ostby, Art Marcum and Matt Holloway, 126 minutes, released by Paramount Pictures.

James and the Giant Peach (1996) Film directed by Henry Selick, screenplay by Karey Kirkpatrick, Jonathan Roberts and Steve Bloom, 79 minutes, released by Walt Disney Pictures.

Jeeves and Wooster (1990) Granada, created by P.G. Wodehouse, first episode transmitted 22 April 1990.

Jeffers, O. (2006) *Lost and Found*, London: HarperCollins Children's Books.

Jeffers, O. (2007) *The Incredible Book Eating Boy*, London: HarperCollins Children's Books.

Jeffers, O. (2008) *The Great Paper Caper*, London: HarperCollins Children's Books.

Jennings, L. (writer) and Chapman, J. (artist) (1997) *Penny and Pup*, London: Little Tiger.

Joyce, W. (2007) *A Day with Wilbur Robinson*, London: HarperCollins Children's Books.

Jumanji (1995) Film directed by Joe Johnston, screenplay by Jonathan Hensleigh, Greg Taylor and Jim Strain, 104 minutes, released by TriStar Pictures.

Jurassic Park (1993) Film directed by Steven Spielberg, screenplay by Michael Crichton and David Koepp, 127 minutes, released by Universal Pictures.

Kaveney, R. (2005) *From Alien to the Matrix: Reading Science Fiction Film*, London: I.B. Tauris.

King-Smith, D. (2003) *The Sheep-Pig*, London: Puffin. Originally published 1983.

Knapman, T. (writer) and Cort, B. (artist) (2010) *Little Ogre's Surprise Supper*, London: Macmillan.

Knapman, T. (writer) and Millward, G. (artist) (2007) *Guess What I Found in Dragon Wood*, London: Puffin.

Knapman, T. (writer) and Stower, A. (artist) (2006) *Mungo and the Picture Book Pirates*, London: Puffin.

Knapman, T. (writer) and Stower, A. (artist) (2007) *Mungo and the Spiders from Space*, London: Puffin.

Knapman, T. (writer) and Stower, A. (artist) (2008) *Mungo and the Dinosaur Island*, London: Puffin.

Knick Knack (1989) Film directed by John Lasseter, screenplay by John Lasseter, 4 minutes, released by Pixar Animation Studios.

Kracauer, S. (1997) *Theory of Film*, Chichester: Princeton University Press.

Labyrinth (1986) Film directed by Jim Henson, screenplay by Terry Jones, 101 minutes, released by The Jim Henson Company.

Lee, S. (writer) and Kirby, J. (artist) (2001) *Essential Captain America Volume 1*, New York: Marvel Comics.

Lee, S. (writer) Kirby, J. (artist) *et al.* (2004) *Essential Uncanny X-Men Vol. 1*, Tunbridge Wells: Panini UK Ltd.

Lewis, C.S. (1980a) *The Lion, the Witch and the Wardrobe*, London: Fontana Lions. First published 1950.

Lewis, C.S. (1980b) *Prince Caspian*, London: Fontana Lions. First published 1951.

Lilo and Stitch (2002) Film directed by Chris Sanders and Dean DeBlois, screenplay by Chris Sanders and Dean DeBlois, 85 minutes, released by Walt Disney Pictures.

Little Mermaid, The (1989) Film directed by Ron Clements and John Musker, screenplay by John Musker and Ron Clements, 83 minutes, released by Walt Disney Pictures.

Lord of the Rings, The: The Fellowship of the Ring (2001) Film directed by Peter Jackson, screenplay by Fran Walsh, Philippa Boyens and Peter Jackson, 178 minutes, released by New Line Cinema.

Lord of the Rings, The: The Return of the King (2003) Film directed by Peter Jackson, screenplay by Fran Walsh, Philippa Boyens and Peter Jackson, 201 minutes, released by New Line Cinema.

Lord of the Rings, The: The Two Towers (2002) Film directed by Peter Jackson, screenplay by Fran Walsh, Philippa Boyens, Stephen Sinclair and Peter Jackson, 179 minutes, released by New Line Cinema.

Lost (2004) ABC, created by J.J. Abrams, Jeffrey Lieber and Damon Lindelof, first episode transmitted 22 September 2004.

Lost and Found (2008) Film directed by Philip Hunt, screenplay by Philip Hunt, 50 minutes, released by E1 Entertainment.

Ludden, J. (2005) 'A Conversation with Maurice Sendak'. Interview produced by Alice Winkler, 18 minutes. *NPR*. Online: www.npr.org/templates/story/story.php?storyId=4680590 (accessed 30 July 2009).

Luxo Jr. (1986) Film directed by John Lasseter, screenplay by John Lasseter, 2 minutes, released by Pixar Animation Studios.

Marvel (2005) 'The Marvel Rating System'. Online: www.marvel.com/catalog/ratings.htm (accessed 21 September 2009).

McAllister, M. (2006) 'Blockbuster meets Superhero Comic, or Art House Meets Graphic Novel?: The Contradictory Relationship Between Film and Comic Art', *Journal of Popular Film and Television*, 34 (3): 108–14.

McArthur, C. (1972) *Underworld U.S.A.*, London: Secker and Warburg.

McCay, W. (2000) *Little Nemo 1905–1914*, Cologne: Evergreen. Originally published 1905.

McCloud, S. (1994) *Understanding Comics*, New York: Kitchen Sink Press for Harper Perennial.

McFarlane, B. (1996) *Novel to Film*, Oxford: Oxford University Press.

McKee, D. (1990) *Elmer*, London: Random House Children's Books.

McNary, D. (2009) '"Wolverine" Bites into Foreign Box Office', *Variety*. Online: www.variety.com/article/VR1118003127.html?categoryid=19&cs=1 (accessed 4 May 2009).

Maguire, G. (2006) *Wicked*, London: Headline. First published 1995.

Makin, L. and Whitehead, M. (2004) *How to Develop Children's Early Literacy*, London: Paul Chapman Publishing.

Man Who Would Be King, The (1975) Film directed by John Huston, screenplay by John Huston and Gladys Hill, 129 minutes, released by Allied Artists Pictures.

Martin, T. (2009) 'How Comic Books Became Part of the Literary Establishment', *Telegraph*. Online: www.telegraph.co.uk/culture/books/bookreviews/5094231/How-Comic-Books-became-part-of-the-literary-establishment.html (accessed 20 April 2009).

Matilda (1996) Film directed by Danny DeVito, screenplay by Nicholas Kazan and Robin Swicord, 98 minutes, released by TriStar Pictures.

Meek, M. (1988) *How Texts Teach What Readers Learn*, Woodchester: Thimble Press.

Meek, M. (1991) *On Being Literate*, London: The Bodley Head.

Meet the Robinsons (2007) Film directed by Stephen J. Anderson, screenplay by Jon Bernstein, Michelle Bochner, Don Hall, Nathan Greno, Aurian Redson, Joe Mateo and Stephen Anderson, 95 minutes, released by Walt Disney Pictures.

Millar, M. (writer), Hitch, B. (penciller) and Currie, A. (inker) (2002) *The Ultimates Volume One Super-Human*, New York: Marvel Comics.

Millar, M. (writer), Hitch, B. (penciller), Currie, A. and Neary, P. (inkers) (2004) *The Ultimates Volume Two Homeland Security*, New York: Marvel Comics.

Miller, F. and Varley, L. (2000) *300*, Milwaukie: Dark Horse.

Moffat, S. (2009) 'Production Notes', *Doctor Who Magazine*, 405: 11.

Monaco, J. (2000) *How to Read a Film*, 3rd edn, New York: Oxford University Press.

Monsters, Inc. (2001) Film directed by Pete Docter, David Silverman and Lee Unkrich, screenplay by Andrew Stanton and Daniel Gerson, 92 minutes, released by Pixar and Walt Disney.

Monty Python's Flying Circus (1969) BBC, created by Eric Idle, John Cleese, Terry Gilliam, Terry Jones, Michael Palin and Graham Chapman, first episode transmitted 5 October 1969.

Moore, A. (writer) and Gibbons, D. (artist) (1987) *Watchmen*, New York: DC Comics.

Morpurgo, M. (2000) *Kensuke's Kingdom*, London: Mammoth.

Morpurgo, M. and Birmingham, C. (2000) *Wombat Goes Walkabout*, London: HarperCollins Publishers Ltd.

Murray, R. (2007) 'Director David Yates, Imelda Staunton and Michael Goldenberg Talk Harry Potter', *About.com*. Online: www.movies.about.com/od/harrypotter5/a/harrypot5071007.htm (accessed 16 February 2009).

Nightmare before Christmas, The (1993) Film directed by Henry Selick, screenplay by Caroline Thompson, 76 minutes, released by Touchstone Pictures.

Nodelman, P. (1988) *Words about Pictures*, Athens: University of Georgia Press.

Nosferatu, eine Symphonie des Grauens (1922) Film directed by F.W. Murnau, screenplay by Henrik Galeen, 94 minutes, released by Jofa-Atelier Berlin-Johannisthal.

Numbers, The (2009) *Glossary of Movie Business Terms*. Online: www.the-numbers.com/glossary.php (accessed 2 July 2009).

Odell, C. and Le Blanc, M. (2005) *The Pocket Essential Tim Burton*, Harpenden: Pocket Essentials.

Oxford Reference Dictionary (1986) Oxford: Oxford University Press.

Orwell, G. (2004) *Nineteen Eighty-Four*, London: Penguin. First published 1949.

Peake, M. (2009) *Captain Slaughterboard Drops Anchor*, London: Walker Books. Originally published 1939.

Peck, J. and Coyle, M. (2002) *Literary Terms and Criticism*, 3rd edn, Basingstoke: Palgrave Macmillan.

Pee-wee's Big Adventure (1985) Film directed by Tim Burton, screenplay by Paul Reubens, Michael Varhol and Phil Hartman, 90 minutes, released by Warner Bros. Pictures.

Peel, R. and Bell, M. (1994) *The Primary Language Leader's Book*, London: David Fulton.

Petersen, D. (2007) *Mouse Guard: Fall 1152*. Fort Lee: ASP Comics LLC.

Pirandello, L. (author) and Musa, M. (translator) (1995) *Six Characters in Search of an Author and Other Plays*, London: Penguin. First performed 1921.

Pirates of the Caribbean: At World's End (2007) Film directed by Gore Verbinski, screenplay by Ted Elliot and Terry Rossio, 169 minutes, released by Walt Disney Pictures.

Pirates of the Caribbean: Dead Man's Chest (2006) Film directed by Gore Verbinski, screenplay by Ted Elliot and Terry Rossio, 151 minutes, released by Walt Disney Pictures.

Pirates of the Caribbean: The Curse of the Black Pearl (2003) Film directed by Gore Verbinski, screenplay by Ted Elliot and Terry Rossio, 137 minutes, released by Walt Disney Pictures.

Pixar Short Films Collection (2008) Short films directed by John Lasseter *et al.*, screenplay by John Lasseter *et al.*, 52 minutes, released by Walt Disney Pictures.

Play It Again Sam (1972) Directed by Herbert Ross, screenplay by Woody Allen, 85 minutes, Paramount Pictures.

Portis, A. (2008) *Not a Box*, London: HarperCollins Children's Books.

Portis, A. (2009) *Not a Stick*, London: HarperCollins Children's Books.

Public Enemies (2009) Film directed by Michael Mann, screenplay by Ronan Bennett, Michael Mann and Ann Biderman, 140 minutes, released by Universal Pictures.

Pullman, P. (2007) *His Dark Materials Trilogy*, London: Scholastic.

Quantum of Solace (2008) Film directed by Marc Forster, screenplay by Paul Haggis, Neal Purvis and Robert Wade, 106 minutes, released by Metro-Goldwyn-Mayer.

Rose, G. (2001) *Visual Methodologies*, London: Sage.

Rowling, J.K. (1997) *Harry Potter and the Philosopher's Stone*, London: Bloomsbury.

Rowling, J.K. (1998) *Harry Potter and the Chamber of Secrets*, London: Bloomsbury.

Rowling, J.K. (1999) *Harry Potter and the Prisoner of Azkaban*, London: Bloomsbury.

Rowling, J.K. (2000) *Harry Potter and the Goblet of Fire*, London: Bloomsbury.

Runton, A. (2004) *Owly Volume 1: The Way Home and the Bittersweet Summer*, Marietta: Top Shelf.

Runton, A. (2005a) *Owly Volume 2: Just a Little Blue*, Marietta: Top Shelf.

Runton, A. (2005b) *Owly Volume 3: Flying Lessons*, Marietta: Top Shelf.

Runton, A. (2007) *Owly Volume 4: A Time to Be Brave*, Marietta: Top Shelf.

Runton, A. (2008) *Owly Volume 5: Tiny Tales*, Marietta: Top Shelf.

Sanjek, D. (2000) 'Same as It Ever Was: Innovation and Exhaustion in the Horror and Science Fiction Films of the 1990s', in W.W. Dixon (ed.) *Film Genre 2000*, Albany: State University of New York Press.

Sarah-Jane Adventures, The (2007) BBC, created by Russell T. Davies, first episode transmitted 1 January 2007.

Sassoon, R. and Gaur, A. (1997) *Signs, Symbols and Icons*, Exeter: Intellect Books.

Satrapi, M. (2007) *The Complete Persepolis*, New York: Pantheon.

Schelde, P. (1993) *Androids, Humanoids, and Other Science Fiction Monsters: Science and Soul in Science Fiction Films*, New York: New York University Press.

Scooby-Doo (2002) Film directed by Raja Gosnell, screenplay by James Gunn, 86 minutes, released by Warner Bros. Pictures.

Scream (1996) Film directed by Wes Craven, screenplay by Kevin Williamson, 111 minutes, released by Dimension Films.

Sendak, M. (2000) *Where the Wild Things Are*, London: Red Fox. Originally published 1963.

Sendak, M. (2001) *In the Night Kitchen*, London: Red Fox. Originally published 1970.

Seuss, Dr (2003) *How the Grinch Stole Christmas!*, London: Picture Lions. Originally published 1957.

Seuss, Dr (2003) *The Cat in the Hat*, London: Collins. Originally published 1957.

Seuss, Dr (2004) *Horton Hears a Who!*, London: HarperCollins Children's Books. Originally published 1954.

Shakespeare, W. (2005a) *Romeo and Juliet*, London: Penguin. First performed *c*.1595.

Shakespeare, W. (2005b) *Twelfth Night*, London: Penguin. First performed *c*.1602.

Shanower, E. (writer) and Young, S. (artist) (2009) *The Wonderful Wizard of Oz*, New York: Marvel.

Sheen, E. (2000) 'Introduction', in R. Giddings and E. Sheen (eds) *The Classic Novel: From Page to Screen*, Manchester: Manchester University Press.

Shrek (2001) Film directed by Andrew Adamson and Vicky Jenson, screenplay by Ted Elliot, Terry Rossio, Joe Stillman and Roger S.H. Schulman, 90 minutes, released by DreamWorks Animation.

Shrek 2 (2004) Film directed by Andrew Adamson, Kelly Asbury and Conrad Vernon, screenplay by Andrew Adamson, Joe Stillman, J. David Stem and David N. Weiss, 93 minutes, released by DreamWorks Animation.

Six Feet Under (2001) HBO, created by Alan Ball, first episode transmitted 3 June 2001.

Slade, C. (2007) *Korgi Book 1: Sprouting Wings!*, Marietta: Top Shelf.

Slade, C. (2008) *Korgi Book 2: The Cosmic Collector*, Marietta: Top Shelf.

Sleeping Beauty (1959) Film directed by Clyde Geronimi, screenplay by Erdman Penner, Joe Rinaldi, Winston Hibler, Bill Peet, Ted Sears, Ralph Wright and Milt Banta, 75 minutes, released by Walt Disney Pictures.

Sleepy Hollow (1999) Film directed by Tim Burton, screenplay by Andrew Kevin Walker, 105 minutes, released by Paramount Pictures.

Smith, J. (2009) *Little Mouse Gets Ready*, New York: RAW Junior, LLC.

Smith, M. and Tilton, D. (2008) *The Tale of Despereaux: The Graphic Novel*, Somerville: Candlewick Press.

Snowman, The (1982) Film directed by Dianne Jackson, screenplay by Dianne Jackson, Hilary Audus and Joanna Fryer, 26 minutes, released by Channel 4 Television Corporation.

Snow White and the Seven Dwarves (1937) Film directed by David Hand, screenplay by Ted Sears, Richard Creedon, Otto Englander, Dick Rickard, Earl Hurd, Merill de Maris, Dorothy Ann Blank and Webb Smith, 83 minutes, released by Walt Disney Pictures.

Sopranos, The (1999) HBO, created by David Chase, first episode transmitted 10 January 1999.

Spider-Man (2002) Film directed by Sam Raimi, screenplay by David Koepp, 121 minutes, released by Columbia Pictures.

Spider-Man 2 (2004) Film directed by Sam Raimi, screenplay by Alfred Gough, Miles Millar and Michael Chabon, 127 minutes, released by Columbia Pictures.

Spiderwick Chronicles, The (2008) Film directed by Mark Waters, screenplay by Karey Kirkpatrick, David Berenbaum and John Sayles, 96 minutes, released by Nickelodeon Movies.

Spilsbury, T. (2009) 'Over 13 Million Viewers Watch *The Next Doctor*!', *Doctor Who Magazine*, 405: 15–16.

Spitz, E.H. (2009) 'Ethos in Steig's and Sendak's Picture Books: The Connected and the Lonely Child', *Journal of Aesthetic Education*, 43 (2): 64–76.

Stafford, T. (2009) 'Powers and Responsibilities', in D. Duncan *Teaching Children's Literature*, Abingdon: Routledge.

Star Wars (1977) Film directed by George Lucas, screenplay by George Lucas, 121 minutes, released by Lucasfilm and Twentieth Century Fox.

Star Wars: Episode 1 The Phantom Menace (1999) Film directed by George Lucas, screenplay by George Lucas, 136 minutes, released by Lucasfilm.

Star Wars: Return of the Jedi (1983) Film directed by Richard Marquand, screenplay by Lawrence Kasdan and George Lucas, 134 minutes, released by Lucasfilm and Twentieth Century Fox.

Stott, J.C. And Francis, C.D. (1993) '"Home" and "Not Home" in Children's Stories: Getting There and Being Worth It', *Children's Literature in Education*, 24 (3): 223–33.

Stower, A. (2005a) *Slam!*, Dorking: Templar.

Stower, A. (2005b) *Two Left Feet*, London: Bloomsbury.

Superman (1978) Film directed by Richard Donner, screenplay by Mario Puzo, David Newman, Leslie Newman and Robert Benton, 143 minutes, released by Warner Bros. Pictures.

Superman II (1980) Film directed by Richard Lester, screenplay by Mario Puzo, David Newman and Leslie Newman, 127 minutes, released by Warner Bros.

Sweeney Todd: The Demon Barber of Fleet Street (2007) Film directed by Tim Burton, screenplay by John Logan, 116 minutes, released by DreamWorks Pictures.

Tale of Despereaux, The (2008) Directed by Sam Fell and Robert Stevenhagen, screenplay by Gary Ross, 93 minutes, released by Universal Pictures.

Tan, S. (2007) *The Arrival*, London: Hodder Children's Books.

Tan, S. (2008) *The Lost Thing*, Sydney: Hachette Livre.

Thomas, R. (writer) and Gully, M. (artist) (2008) *Treasure Island*, New York: Marvel.

Times Online (2006) *Authors Enjoying 'Enormous' Sales Boost from* Da Vinci Code *Case*. Online: www.entertainment.timesonline.co.uk/tol/arts_and_entertainment/books/article739299.ece (accessed 11 February 2009).

Torchwood (2006) BBC, created by Russell T. Davies, first episode transmitted 22 October 2006.

Toy Story (1995) Film directed by John Lasseter, screenplay by Joss Whedon, Andrew Stanton, Joel Cohen and Alek Sokolow, 81 minutes, released by Pixar and Walt Disney Pictures.

Travis, M. (2008) *The Bigger Picture*. Online: www.booktrustchildrensbooks.org.uk/show/feature/Features%20Interviews/The-Bigger-Picture (accessed 17 March 2009).

Ungerer, T. (1985) *Zeralda's Ogre*, London: Methuen Publishing Ltd.

Up (2009) Film directed by Pete Docter and Bob Peterson, screenplay by Bob Peterson and Pete Docter, 96 minutes, released by Pixar and Walt Disney Pictures.

Van Allsburg, C. (1984) *Jumanji*, Boston: Houghton Mifflin.

Vincendeau, G. (2001) 'Introduction', in G. Vincendeau (ed.) *Film/Literature/Heritage*, London: British Film Institute.

Wall-E (2008) Film directed by Andrew Stanton, screenplay by Andrew Stanton and Jim Reardon, 98 minutes, released by Pixar and Walt Disney.

Wallis, M. and Shepherd, S. (2002) *Studying Plays*, 2nd edn, London: Hodder Arnold.

Watchmen (2009) Film directed by Zack Snyder, screenplay by David Hayter and Alex Tse, 162 minutes, released by Warner Bros. Pictures and Paramount Pictures.

Watson, V. and Styles, M. (1996) *Talking Pictures*, London: Hodder and Stoughton.

Watson, D. and Wallis, K. (2004) *Wonderland*, Orange: Image.

Wells, S. (1998) *A Dictionary of Shakespeare*, Oxford: Oxford University Press. Online: www.oxfordreference.com/views/BOOK_SEARCH.html?book=t57 (accessed 6 February 2009).

Whedon, J. (writer) and Cassaday, J. (artist) (2004) *Astonishing X-Men Volume 1: Gifted*, New York: Marvel Comics.

Where the Wild Things Are (2009) Film directed by Spike Jonze, screenplay by Spike Jonze and Dave Eggers, 101 minutes, released by Warner Bros. Pictures.

Wicked (2003) Stage production directed by Joe Mantello, story by Gregory Maguire, book by Winnie Holzman, music and lyrics by Stephen Schwartz, produced by Marc Platt, Universal Pictures, The Araca Group, Jon B. Platt and David Stone.

Wicked – The Musical Website (2008) *The Hit Musical* Wicked *Reaches £50 Million Gross and Continues to Break Records.* Online: www.wickedthemusical.co.uk/readnews.asp?id=14wkd (accessed 21 February 2009).

Wire, The (2002) HBO, created by David Simon, first episode transmitted 2 June 2002.

Witches, The (1990) Film directed by Nic Roeg, screenplay by Allan Scott, 91 minutes, released by Jim Henson Pictures.

Wizard of Oz, The (1939) Film directed by Victor Fleming, screenplay by Noel Langley, Florence Ryerson and Edgar Allan Woolf, 101 minutes, released by Metro-Goldwyn-Mayer.

Wodehouse, P.G. (2008) *The Code of the Woosters*, London: Arrow. Originally published 1938.

Wright, M. (2009) 'Death Knell for Drama?', *The Stage*. Online: blogs.thestage.co.uk/tvtoday/2009/04/death-knell-for-drama (accessed 3 July 2009).

X-Men (2000) Film directed by Bryan Singer, screenplay by David Hayter, 104 minutes, released by Twentieth Century Fox.

X-Men Origins: Wolverine (2009) Film directed by Gavin Hood, screenplay by David Benioff and Skip Woods, 107 minutes, released by Twentieth Century Fox.

X-Men: The Last Stand (2006) Film directed by Brett Ratner, screenplay by Simon Kinberg and Zak Penn, 104 minutes, released by Twentieth Century Fox.

X2 (2003) Film directed by Bryan Singer, screenplay by Michael Dougherty, Dan Harris and David Hayter, 133 minutes, released by Twentieth Century Fox.

Websites

Arena (2009) Online: www.arenaworks.com (accessed 7 November 2009).

BBC Writers Room (2009) BBC. Online: www.bbc.co.uk/writersroom (accessed 19 August 2009).

Big Picture, The (2008) Booktrust. Online: www.bigpicture.org.uk (accessed 23 March 2009).

DC Kids (2009) DC Comics. Online: www.dccomics.com/dckids (accessed 21 September 2009).

Doctor Who Comic Maker (2009) BBC. Online: www.bbc.co.uk/doctorwho/comicmaker (accessed 21 September 2009).

Empire – *Alice In Wonderland* Images (2009) Images property of Walt Disney. Online: www.empireonline.com/futurefilms/gallery.asp?id=2365&fid=135686 (accessed 14 August 2009).

Harry Potter (2009) Warner Bros. Entertainment, Inc. Online: www.harrypotter.com (accessed 14 August 2009).

Imdb (2009) *All-Time Worldwide Box Office*. Online: www.imdb.com/boxoffice/alltimegross?region=world-wide (accessed 11 February 2009).

Marvel Digital Comics Unlimited (2009) Marvel Comics. Online: www.marvelcomics.com/digitalcomics (accessed 21 September 2009).

Mitra Tabrizian (2009) Online: www.mitratabrizian.com (accessed 7 November 2009).

Musée d'Orsay (2006) Online: www.musee-orsay.fr (accessed 7 November 2009).

National Gallery, The (2009) Online: www.nationalgallery.org.uk (accessed 7 November 2009).

Tate, The (2009) Online: www.tate.org.uk (accessed 7 November 2009).

Writer's Tale, The (2008) BBC Books. Online: www.thewriterstale.com (accessed 19 August 2009).

Index

Locators in **bold** type indicate figures, those in *italics* indicate tables.